Materials & skills for historic building conservation

This book is part of a series on historic building conservation:

Understanding Historic Building Conservation
Edited by Michael Forsyth
9781405111720

Structures & Construction in Historic Building Conservation
Edited by Michael Forsyth
9781405111713

Materials & Skills for Historic Building Conservation
Edited by Michael Forsyth
9781405111706

Interior Finishes & Fittings for Historic Building Conservation
Edited by Michael Forsyth and Lisa White
9781405190220

Other books of interest:

Managing Built Heritage: the role of cultural significance
Derek Worthing & Stephen Bond
9781405119788

Conservation and Sustainability in Historic Cities
Dennis Rodwell
9781405126564

Building Pathology
Second Edition
David Watt
9781405161039

Architectural Conservation
Aylin Orbaşlı
9780632040254

Urban Heritage Management: best practice from UNESCO sites worldwide
Francesco Bandarin & Ron van Oers
9780470655740

Materials & skills for historic building conservation

Edited by

Michael Forsyth

**Department of Architecture and Civil Engineering
University of Bath**

A John Wiley & Sons, Ltd., Publication

Blackwell Publishing was acquired by John Wiley & Sons in February 2007. Blackwell's publishing program has been merged with Wiley's global Scientific, Technical and Medical business to form Wiley-Blackwell.

Registered office:
John Wiley & Sons, Ltd, The Atrium, Southern Gate, Chichester, West Sussex, PO19 8SQ, UK

Editorial offices:
9600 Garsington Road, Oxford, OX4 2DQ, UK
The Atrium, Southern Gate, Chichester, West Sussex, PO19 8SQ, UK
2121 State Avenue, Ames, Iowa 50014-8300, USA

For details of our global editorial offices, for customer services and for information about how to apply for permission to reuse the copyright material in this book please see our website at www.wiley.com/wiley-blackwell.

First published 2008 by Blackwell Publishing Ltd

ISBN: 9781405111706 Hardback
ISBN: 9781118440575 Paperback

Library of Congress Cataloging-in-Publication Data
Materials & skills for historic building conservation / edited by Michael Forsyth.
p. cm. – (Historic building conservation)
Includes bibliographical references and index.
ISBN-13: 978-1-4051-1170-6 (hardback : alk. paper)
ISBN-10: 1-4051-1170-4 (hardback : alk. paper)   1. Building materials.   2. Historic buildings–Conservation and restoration–Materials. I. Forsyth, Michael, 1951–   II. Title: Materials and skills for historic building conservation.

TA403.8.M376 2007
690′.24–dc22
2007021649

A catalogue record for this title is available from the British Library

Set in 10 on 12.5 pt Avenir by Toppan Best-set Premedia Limited
Printed and bound in Malaysia by Vivar Printing Sdn Bhd
2   2013

Contents

Preface

This is one of a series of volumes on Historic Building Conservation that combine conservation philosophy in the built environment with knowledge of traditional materials and structural and constructional conservation techniques and technology. The chapters are written by leading architects, structural engineers and related professionals, who together reflect the interdisciplinary nature of conservation work.

While substantial publications exist on each of the subject areas – some by the authors of Historic Building Conservation – few individuals and practices have ready access to all of these or the time to read them in detail. The aim of the Historic Building Conservation series is to introduce each aspect of conservation and to provide concise, basic and up-to-date knowledge within three volumes, sufficient for the professional to appreciate the subject better and to know where to seek further help.

Of direct practical application in the field, the books are structured to take the reader through the process of historic building conservation, presenting a total sequence of the integrative teamwork involved. *Understanding historic building conservation* provides understanding of the planning, legislative and philosophical background, followed by the process of researching the history of a building and the formulation of a conservation policy and plan. *Structures & construction in historic building conservation* traces the history of structures in various materials and contains much guidance on the survey, assessment and diagnosis of structures, the integration of building code requirements within the historic fabric and much else besides.

The present volume, *Materials & skills for historic building conservation*, which will be complemented by *Interior finishes for historic building conservation*, provides within a single volume essential information on the properties of the principal traditional external building materials. Subjects covered include their availability and sourcing, the causes of erosion and decay, the skills required for their application on conservation projects and the impact the materials have on the environment. A note is due on the volume's limits. It does not attempt to address areas of material conservation that are highly specialist and where the professional would be guided by the expertise of the conservator – stained glass, for instance – while rather less common materials such as faience and Code stone are omitted. Some vernacular materials are also omitted – notably thatch – because there is a great deal of information on the internet, such as guidance notes by county authorities which are region-specific. Wood sash windows are included, being 'standard' in 'polite' houses throughout the Georgian and Victorian period, whereas vernacular casement window detailing, where again there is regional variation, is best advised on by the local authority.

The series is particularly aimed at construction professionals – architects, surveyors, engineers – as well as postgraduate building conservation students and undergraduate architects and surveyors as specialist or optional course reading. The series is also of value to other professional groups such as commissioning client bodies, managers and advisers, and interested individuals involved in house refurbishment or setting up a building preservation trust. While there is a focus on UK practice, most of the content is of relevance overseas (just as UK conservation courses attract many overseas students, for example from India, China, Australia and the USA).

Acknowledgements

I am grateful to the following for permission to reproduce illustrations: David McLaughlin (2.1, 2.4, 2.5); Bath and North Somerset Council (2.2, 2.3); English Heritage (2.6–2.9, 4.1–4.9, 6.3); Mike Stock (3.1–3.3); Michael Bussell (5.1–5.8, 7.2, 7.3); Christopher Harris (6.1–6.5); Geoff Wallis (7.1, 7.4–7.7); Charley Brentnall (9.1–9.9); the late Gus Astley (11.2) and Patrick Baty (13.1–13.5).

Contributors

Gus Astley

Before sadly passing away in 2003, highly respected conservation architect with Bath and North East Somerset Council, active in the Institute of Historic Building Conservation (IHBC) and, before that, the Association of Conservation Officers (ACO). After graduating, held the Society for the Protection of Ancient Buildings (SPAB) Scholarship. Lectured at the University of Bath.

Patrick Baty

Joined family business, Papers and Paints, after leaving the Army. For many years has run a consultancy that advises on the use of paint and colour in historic buildings. Projects have ranged from private houses to palaces, museums to London housing estates. Recent restoration projects include Kew Palace and the Royal Festival Hall. Lectures widely and has published numerous articles. Trustee of the Georgian Group. In 2007 the firm was granted a Royal Warrant of Appointment to Her Majesty The Queen.

Charley Brentnall

Technical Director, Carpenter Oak & Woodland. Started a timber framing and vernacular buildings business in 1979 and the present company in 1987. Also runs a freelance consultancy. Studied at St Albans School of Arts and Bath Academy of Arts. Visiting lecturer at Universities of Bath, York and elsewhere; member of Timber Framers Guild, Carpenters' Fellowship, ICOMOS-UK and SPAB; formerly on BWF British Standards committee. Works with intuition and creativity, and knowledge of and fascination for wood, and strives for high standards of design, craftsmanship and service. Uses home-grown timbers, respecting the spirit of the materials in their natural form. Believes in challenging precepts on how we live and work in the environment. Notable conservation projects include Charlton Court Barn, Sussex; Windsor Castle Royal Kitchen Roof; Stirling Castle, Great Hall Roof; Shackleton and Scott's Huts, Antarctica; Botley Manor Farm Museum; and Bursledon Windmill.

Michael Bussell

Structural engineer specialising in the appraisal and reuse of existing buildings of the nineteenth and twentieth centuries. Has written and lectured widely on the historical development of structural iron, steel and reinforced concrete. His *Appraisal of Existing Iron and Steel Structures* (Steel Construction Institute, 1997) is the first full-length study of its subject. Currently deeply involved in the various railway and regeneration projects in the King's Cross and St Pancras area of London.

Robert Cotta

Licensed Structural Engineer in the United States, with registration in six Northeastern and Midwest states. Thirty years of consulting design experience in existing building assessments and design of structural systems for a broad range of building types. Holds a Bachelor of Science degree from the Massachusetts Institute of Technology in Cambridge, Massachusetts, and a Master of Science degree in the Conservation of Historic Buildings of the University of Bath. Member of the Structural Engineers' Institute of the American Society of Civil Engineers (ASCE) and the Structural Engineers' Association of Illinois.

Michael Forsyth

Architect and director of the postgraduate degree course in the Conservation of Historic Buildings, University of Bath. Studied at the University of Liverpool, held the Rome Scholarship in Architecture and, after residence in Italy, moved to Canada, working on the design of the new concert hall for the Toronto Symphony Orchestra with the architect Arthur Erickson. Lectured at the University of Bristol, 1979–89 and has lived and practised in Bath since 1987. Books include *Pevsner Architectural Guides: Bath* (Yale University Press, 2003) and *Buildings for Music: The architect, the musician, and the listener from the seventeenth century to the present day* (MIT Press and Cambridge University Press, 1985), which won the 19th Annual ASCAP-Deems Taylor Award; translations in French, German, Italian and Japanese. Holds a Doctor of Philosophy degree of the University of Bristol.

Tony Graham

Tony Graham is an engineering graduate from the University of Nottingham and completed a postgraduate degree in the conservation of historic buildings at the University of Bath in 2004. Building upon many years of hands-on experience, he set up his own conservation business in Wiltshire, working on both vernacular buildings and classical architecture. Areas of expertise include structural diagnostics and repairs, lime plasters and wattle and daub.

Christopher Harris

From an engineering background, branched out into the supply of new stone slates as a consequence of having to re-roof his own stone-roofed property. Began importing stone from the Jurassic limestone belt that crosses France and manufactured slates in the UK, as British planning policies dictated against opening new quarries. Subsequently invited to join English Heritage committees to revise the guidance and encourage the opening of small quarries ('delves') to supply the conservation market. Formed companies to develop 'campaign quarrying', opening delves for a very short time to supply stone for the conservation of specific important buildings, with reinstatement within a few months. Currently a director of The Listed Building Consultancy Ltd.

David McLaughlin

Conservation Architect with Bath and North East Somerset Council and its predecessor, Bath City Council, from 1975 until 2005. Established McLaughlin Ross LLP in partnership with Kay Ross in 2005, combining expertise and skills in the understanding, conservation and development of historic buildings and areas, and of new building in historic contexts, for both private and public clients. Has served on the Bath and Wells Diocesan Advisory Committee for the Care of Churches in a voluntary capacity since 1983.

Brian Ridout

Biologist and expert on the treatment of dry rot and timber infection. Director of Ridout Associates since 1987, specialising in the scientific assessment of timber decay and other damp-related problems in buildings; philosophy is to avoid the expensive damage caused by unnecessary or incautious remedial treatments. Projects have included royal palaces, urban regeneration of large industrial buildings, the Golden Temple of Amritsar, India, and heritage buildings in Bahrain, Vietnam, Greece, Turkey and Morocco, together with numerous small privately owned vernacular buildings. Publications include *Timber Decay in Buildings: The conservation approach to treatment* (1999). Elected Honorary Research Fellow of Birkbeck College, University of London (1996); Scientific Coordinator for the international Woodcare Research Project (1994–97).

Mike Stock

Architect and historic buildings consultant. Following an early career as a design engineer, worked for both the highly respected Historic Buildings Division of the Greater London Council and the London Region of English Heritage. Currently director of Upsilon, a London-based consultancy that specialises in the investigation and analysis of historic building material failures.

Geoff Wallis

Founder and Director of Dorothea Restorations Ltd, with over thirty years' practical experience. Consultant on architectural and structural metalwork conservation to English Heritage, the Heritage Lottery Fund and many other preservation bodies. Lectures widely on the conservation of historic metalwork and machinery, and is course leader of the Architectural Metalwork Conservation Masterclass at West Dean College.

Ian Williams

Chartered Surveyor and member of the Institute of Historic Buildings Conservation. After graduating with a Bachelor of Science degree in Urban Estate Surveying, worked as a general practice surveyor for seventeen years. Graduated with a Master of Science degree in the Conservation of Historic Buildings at the University of Bath in 1999 and has since worked in local government in Edinburgh.

Rory Young

Designer, craftsman, conservator of buildings. Gained a BA(hons) in Fine Art at Camberwell School of Arts & Crafts, then toured the north of England studying architecture and building methods and materials. Self-trained in masonry and carving, he designs and makes statuary, memorials and architectural components in stone and marble. Since 1980 he has used non-hydraulic limes for mortars, plasters and colour washes in building repairs and stone conservation. He gives advice and education on the aesthetics, techniques and materials involved in the traditional building crafts and is asked to guide building professionals on site.

1 The philosophy of repair

Michael Forsyth

Traditional or vernacular building is concerned with utilising indigenous materials and with local knowledge of climate and topography. The geology and topography of a region determine the character of its buildings, as was first consciously articulated by William Smith, the 'father of geology', whose pioneering geological map in the early nineteenth century 'changed the world'.[1] Nearer to our own time, the essential and distinctive character of the English counties was captured by Sir Nikolaus Pevsner's introductions to his county architectural guides. These always start with landscape and the earth – granite, sand, slate, chalk, clay – and the first illustrations are of hills and fields, because it is these features that give each county, and its buildings, their character. In *Herefordshire* 'there is not a mile that is unrewarding or painful'. In *Northumberland* it is 'rough the winds, rough the miners, rough the castles'. Gentle *Hertfordshire* is 'uneventful but lovable'. Regional character is quickly eroded by unsympathetic repair and alteration using materials imported into the region and by renewal rather than repair, consolidation and effective ongoing maintenance.

The key to appropriate historic building repair is awareness of the fundamental difference between modern construction and traditional building. Modern construction is based around impermeability and relative 'thinness', as with cavity wall construction, known in North America as using the 'rain screen principle'. If, through capillary action, moisture should penetrate the outer masonry leaf or the cladding, the air cavity (which may be partially filled with insulation) is wide enough to break the capillary action and surface tension of the water, which then descends by gravity and drains through weep holes. The further function of the cavity is to eliminate thermal bridging. Steel and glass may be thought of as the ultimate 'thin' impermeable building construction.

Traditional building by contrast is based around very different principles: thermal mass; breathability; flexibility; and, depending on the construction, the use of a protective, sacrificial skin. Thick walls provide thermal mass, sustaining warmth in winter and coolness in summer. The walls (and traditionally the floor) are breathable and admit moisture, which then evaporates freely. For masonry construction, lime mortar separating the stones or bricks is softer than the structural material and allows the building to move and settle differentially without cracking. Lime mortar is also more breathable than these materials, so the majority of evaporation is through the joints. When hard, impermeable Portland cement pointing was introduced a century or so ago, the brick or stone became the principal conduit for evaporation, causing leaching of salts and consequent chemical corrosion in the material, and water collecting at the joints caused mechanical deterioration due to freeze–thaw action.

In limestone areas rubble construction also traditionally relies on a protective skin of lime render which is sacrificial to the structural material. The render is then coated with limewash, which may be coloured with earth-based pigments and, if the finish is smooth as opposed to roughcast, sometimes scored for 'joints' to produce poor man's ashlar. The twentieth-century taste for hacking off render and plaster and revealing the stone-work beneath – think of the worst pub interiors, historic plaster removed and the rubble wall beneath pointed with grey cement – began with the Victorians, and opposition to the practice by the Society for the Protection of Ancient Buildings (SPAB), founded by William Morris and others in 1877, launched the bitter war of 'scrape versus anti-scrape'.

It is essential that traditional buildings are repaired sympathetically, and it is the stark fact that the majority of historic building repair today is required less as a result of the natural degradation of the building fabric from its original state, than of damage resulting from inappropriate repair over the last century, whether from incorrect pointing and mortar repairs, expanding rusted iron in old stone repairs causing spalling or delaminating Portland cement render.

Historic building repair embraces a spectrum of interventions from routine maintenance and the 'do nothing' option, through a comprehensive repair programme, to restoration, the replacing of lost features or entire rebuilding (as with the National Trust's Uppark, West Sussex, almost destroyed by fire in 1989 and rebuilt), provided there is precise evidence of what was there. Replacement is never acceptable when it is conjectural. Sir Bernard Feilden lists this spectrum as consisting of seven degrees of intervention: (1) prevention of deterioration; (2) preservation of the existing state; (3) consolidation of the fabric; (4) restoration; (5) rehabilitation; (6) reproduction; (7) reconstruction.[2]

The preferred option is always minimal intervention, and the general principle is to use traditional materials and techniques wherever possible. In the case of ruined monuments, minimal intervention may extend to retaining ivy on the basis that it may actually protect the structure that it covers – a kind of managed 'picturesque decay'. However, the basic well-known golden rules of conservation – minimal intervention, conserve as found, 'like for like' repairs, and reversibility – are not always compatible with these principles, or with each other. For example, when repairing a timber roof structure, discrete insertion of steelwork – far from a 'like for like' repair – may result in minimal or no loss of historic fabric compared with cutting back to sound material for a 'like for like' repair with a scarfed joint using new, similar timber; indeed, iron has been used for strengthening timber structures for centuries. The 'conserve as found' principle, meanwhile, may fly in the face of a philosophical decision to wind the clock back to the original architect's intention, while some repairs, such as grouting a rubble stone wall, are intrinsically non-reversible.[3]

These are but imperfect guidelines and each situation must be assessed. A philosophy or policy for the building fabric and its repair must be adopted, not only for major projects where this might form part of a conservation plan, but also for localised repairs, such as a small repair to a lime render (Chapter 4) or to wattle and daub (Chapter 10). Once conservation work is under way, recording at all stages is essential. It has always been a tenet of SPAB that repairs should be identifiable, and in the early days masonry repairs would be carried out with tiles, though today more subtle means would usually be used such as writing a date on new timber in a roof space.

The manifesto which William Morris and the other SPAB founder members issued in 1877 was written in reaction to the over-zealous, over-confident church and cathedral restoration work of the eighteenth and nineteenth centuries where the aim was to return the buildings to a uniform style and to make them look smooth and crisp:[4]

> It is for all these buildings . . . of all times and styles, that we plead, and call upon those who have to deal with them, to put Protection in the place of Restoration, to stave off decay by daily care, to prop a perilous wall or mend a leaky roof by such means as are obviously meant for support or covering, and show no pretence of other art, and otherwise to resist all tampering with either the fabric or ornament of the building as it stands; if it has become inconvenient for its present use, to raise another building rather than alter or enlarge the old one; in fine to treat our ancient buildings as monuments of a bygone art, created by bygone manners, that modern art cannot meddle with without destroying.

The manifesto may predate the concept of adaptive reuse, but it laid the ground rules of modern building conservation practice and still forms the basis of the SPAB's philosophy. Another influential publication that is still available was *Repair of Ancient Buildings* by the architect A.R. Powys, Secretary of the SPAB before and after World War I.[5]

An interesting monitor of the continuing evolution of conservation philosophy today is the presentation of country houses by the National Trust and English Heritage. The sanitising of country houses in the early days of the National Trust, involving the rather lifeless restoration of their interiors to a given, original period, was advanced at Kingston Lacy, Dorset, from 1982, towards an approach of retaining the history of the building with its nineteenth-century alterations. The 'conserve as found' option had more radical expression at Brodsworth Hall, South Yorkshire. Here, English Heritage carried out a full conservation programme for the building fabric from 1988, but carefully retaining – and, where necessary, removing then later reinstating – water-stained wallpaper, faded fittings and everyday objects that had been left in the house, as if the owners had simply gone out for the day. Newhailes House, near Edinburgh, was perhaps the extreme swing of the conservation pendulum – more 'conserve as left' than 'conserve as found'. After conservation had taken place, the furniture was carefully heaped back into the corner of the library as it was when the property was acquired by the National Trust for Scotland. The last occupant's sitting room was reinstated with television and electric fire, and the ironwork to the steps up to the front door consolidated but left rusty.

Endnotes

1. Simon Winchester, *The Map that Changed the World: A tale of rocks, ruin and redemption* (Penguin Books Ltd, London, 2002).
2. Bernard M. Feilden, *Conservation of Historic Buildings* (Butterworth Heinemann, London, 2003), p. 8.
3. See also *Understanding historic building conservation*, Chapter 1, and *Structures & construction in historic building conservation*, Chapters 1 and 2.
4. The best account of this era is Gerald Cobb, *English Cathedrals: The forgotten centuries: restoration and change from 1530 to the present day* (Thames and Hudson, London, 1980).
5. A.R. Powys, *Repair of Ancient Buildings* (J.M. Dent & Sons Ltd, London, 1929; Society for the Protection of Ancient Buildings, 1996).

2 Stone

TYPES OF WALL CONSTRUCTION
Ian Williams

Stone construction in traditional building can be initially divided into two types: rubble and ashlar. These two methods of construction are subject to further division. In the last century or so stone has also been used as cladding. Repairs must follow carefully previous methods of preparation and setting.

Rubble

Rubble walls are either **random**, the stones being used more or less as they come to hand, or **squared**, with straightened edges. These two types further subdivide. Random rubble is either **coursed**, the stones roughly levelled up to form layers of varying thicknesses, or **uncoursed**, the larger stones being wedged by smaller stones, known as pinnings or spalls, with no attempt to form accurate vertical or horizontal joints. Broken residual rubble from dressed-down blocks and more thinly bedded stone was used as the infill between the inner and outer leaves of rubble walls. This infill was either consolidated by a semi-liquid sand : lime mortar to form a largely solid core, or left ungrouted.

Squared rubble may be laid uncoursed, coursed or regularly coursed. Uncoursed walls are usually formed of four stone sizes: large bonding stones (risers), two thinner stones (levellers) and small stones (snecks). Coursed walling is formed of larger stones of the same height, levelled off by thinner stones to form the courses. Regular coursed walls are formed of rows or courses of identical height stones, although the height of the courses can vary up the wall.

Caution must be exercised when cheaper means of repair are considered. 'Pitched-face' stones sawn to bed heights are a convenient way to use offcuts from high-speed saws; it is considerably cheaper to install these for repair purposes than produce a traditional squared rubble block, but they bear little resemblance and are totally inappropriate when a proper match to the original stonework is required. Random rubble stone can be produced through extraction by means of a dragline or a JCB, when it will either be broken into manageable pieces as it is lifted or broken further by a blow from the JCB's bucket. Any further reduction can be achieved with a heavy hammer. Dressing off will be carried out with either a walling hammer or, more usually, a hydraulic guillotine.

Ashlar

Ashlar masonry is formed of smooth squared stones with very thin mortar joints, usually laid in horizontal courses with stones of identical height, but each course may vary in height. 'Random' ashlar, often associated with later Victorian machine-cut stone, may be laid to a repeated pattern.

Ashlar can have various surface finishes. A **polished** finish to sandstone, achieved by rubbing the stone with a mixture of carborundum, sand and water, was advocated in 1883 by the quarry master and builder James Gowans, because 'polishing removes the bruised material, and presents to wasting agents a surface more likely to prevent decay than any other kind of work'. Masonry may have **rustication**, usually to form a basement (that is, a ground floor storey) in a Palladian situation or quoins. The edges of the blocks are either rebated or chamfered (V-jointed ashlar), to all sides or to the top and bottom edges, to form **channelled rustication**. Other finishes include **droved** or **boasted** work, where a 2-inch chisel was worked over the surface to create parallel horizontal, vertical or diagonal lines (a technique also used on pennant stone paving to prevent slipping). A 'tooled' finish was similar to droved work except that it was carried out using a 4-inch chisel. A pointed chisel forms holes in the surface for a 'stugged' or 'punched' finish – 'jabbed' or 'picked' if using finer-pointed chisels. Often a droved margin was worked around both these punched finishes and around a 'broached' finish – horizontal or vertical lines formed with a gouge or toothed chisel. A **rock-faced** finish, as the name suggests, has a raised rough surface, sometimes set within a margin. Finally, **vermiculation** is a pattern of irregular grooves suggestive of worm-eaten material.

OOLITIC LIMESTONE

David McLaughlin

Even in the present Age Bath is as happily situated for beautiful works of Architecture as a City can be; and, from the remotest Times, her Free Stone Quarries have been famous.

John Wood, *Essay Towards a Description of Bath* (1765)

History and application of oolitic limestone

Oolitic limestones sweep up England in a belt running from Portland, off the Dorset coast, through Beer in Devon, Ham Hill in Somerset, Bath, the Cotswolds in Gloucestershire, Taynton in Oxfordshire and Clipsham in Rutland.[1] Bath stone is the generic term for a range of oolitic limestones that are quarried and mined in and around the Bath area and of which Bath's historic buildings are built. The architect John Wood (1704–54) extolled the merits of Bath stone: 'a most excellent Building Material, as being Durable, Beautiful and Cheap;[2] . . . which in Truth, is fit for the Walls of a Palace for the Greatest Prince in Europe'.[3]

Oolitic limestone is a sedimentary stone formed about 170 million years ago when this area was covered in a warm shallow sea. Spherical grains of calcium carbonate formed around marine skeletal fragments on the sea floor. Transported by tides, these grains, or ooliths, were deposited in layers. Their accumulation and compaction led to the formation of beds of oolitic limestone. This naturally occurring stratification of oolitic limestone leads to the stone being quarried or mined in its natural bed.

Traditionally, different beds or quarries were used to supply the most appropriate stone for each specific element of the building. Different beds have different characteristics, whereby some are better for building stone than others, or for different parts of the building; other beds may be more suitable for burning to form lime for slaking as lime putty. The subsequent correct bedding of the stone in differing building applications is crucial to its longevity.

Oolitic limestone is a 'freestone', which means that it can be freely worked: that is, it can be cut and worked in any plane. However, it is important to ensure that oolitic limestone is correctly bedded both in new building and in repairs. The external front elevation of a typical eighteenth-century house built entirely of Bath stone illustrates the correct bedding (Figure 2.1):

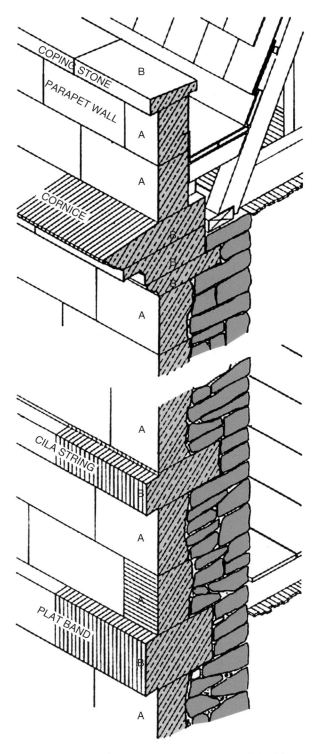

COPING STONE
B
PARAPET WALL
A
A
CORNICE
B
B
B
A
A
CILA STRING
B
A
A
PLAT BAND
B
A

Figure 2.1 Typical construction of an eighteenth-century Bath building.

- The principal elevation is laid as ashlar in its natural bed (A).
- Band courses, sills and sill courses, cornices and other projecting elements are laid edge-bedded (B).
- The parapet is laid as ashlar in its natural bed.
- Coping stones are laid edge-bedded.
- Window and door lintels are laid edge-bedded.
- Voussoirs are laid with their natural bed perpendicular to the thrust of the load they transmit.
- Railing bases and their drip courses are laid edge-bedded.

Exposed elements of the building such as cornices and other projecting stonework are more vulnerable to decay than areas of plain ashlar. This is because moulded and deeply undercut forms have a greater surface area in relation to their volume than do areas of plain ashlar. This is also why corners of ashlar, window and door surrounds and rusticated ashlar are more prone to decay. Ledges and sheltered or recessed areas of stonework are also at risk because acid-laden soots and particles can collect, and when activated by moisture can leach harmful acids into the stonework.

Oolitic limestone should be bedded and pointed in lime mortar. This enables the mortar joints to be sacrificial to the stonework, allowing moisture absorbed by the stonework to evaporate through the mortar joints as well as the stonework itself.

Chemical agents that degrade oolitic limestone

Soiling, sulphur dioxide and the impact of **weather** all take their toll on oolitic limestone. Chemically, oolitic limestone is a form of calcium carbonate. Like other natural building materials, oolitic limestone needs to 'breathe', absorbing moisture in and being able to evaporate it out in a natural cycle of wetting and drying. But the heavy soiling of buildings inhibits this natural cycle as the pores of the stone get clogged up and it cannot breathe; it is not simply an aesthetic problem but a major cause of decay, as the surface of the stone begins to break up.

A 1971 'before' photograph of 14 Circus, Bath (Figure 2.2), illustrates extensive damage resulting from the effect of acid rain. While the metopes and triglyphs have survived practically unscathed, the mutules of the Doric cornice are decayed almost beyond recognition. The volutes of the Ionic capitals have disintegrated and both the upper and lower beds of the Ionic cornice are severely eroded. The Corinthian order is similarly affected. The 1975 photograph of 14 Circus (Figure 2.3) after the repairs of 1973–74 emphasises the extent of decay that was caused by the effects of acid rain. By the 1990s the building was re-soiling from water run-off from poorly detailed lead cover flashings to the Ionic and Corinthian cornices.

'Acid rain' is the generic term for air pollution which increases the acidity of the environment, either through wet forms like rainwater or snow, dry forms like dust, or mists like fog or low cloud. While the term 'acid rain' has only recently come into use, the problem of acid rain is not a new

Figure 2.2 'Before' photograph of 14 Circus in 1971 emphasising the amount of decay caused by the effects of acid rain.

Figure 2.3 After repairs to 14 Circus during 1973/74.

Figure 2.4 Damage caused by calcium sulphate crystals.

phenomenon.[4] Oolitic limestone is susceptible to decay caused by sulphur dioxide in the atmosphere. The reaction of sulphur dioxide with calcium carbonate forms calcium sulphate, a form of gypsum. As gypsum crystals are larger than calcium carbonate crystals, the formation of gypsum can cause oolitic limestone to rupture or spall (Figure 2.4). Damaging calcium sulphate forms when moisture evaporates. The drying effect of wind around projecting elements such as cornices draws moisture and salts towards the surface. This is even more accentuated if the architectural ornament faces west to south and therefore receives the full brunt of the prevailing weather. Sudden bursts of rain followed by intense sun can lead to thermal shock in the stonework, accelerating its decay. Black deposits on the stone cause it to act as a black body radiator, leading to higher thermal stresses.[5]

While recent reports indicate a decrease in the emission of sulphur dioxide, they worryingly show an increase in the emission of oxides of nitrogen, including nitrogen dioxide. Although it may at first appear to be good news that sulphur dioxide levels are falling, nitrogen dioxide acts as a catalyst with sulphur dioxide, causing stone to decay faster than when exposed to only one of these pollutants. Limestone exposed in an atmosphere containing both sulphur dioxide and nitrogen dioxide at high relative humidity and in the presence of ozone (another by-product of the pollution process) will corrode significantly faster, at 43 times the rate of decay caused by the presence of sulphur dioxide on its own.[6]

Pollutants generated by road traffic are the primary cause of this further damage.[7,8] The 'memory effect'[9] of 'historic pollution' within previously cleaned stone can also compound this. The re-soiling and subsequent cleaning and conservation of major historic buildings in Bath, including houses in the Circus and Bath Abbey, confirm the impact of this further damage.[10]

Architectural elements such as cornices or swags have a large surface area in relation to their volume, which causes increased evaporation of moisture from these parts and therefore a greater build-up of solid and dissolved pollutants. Windborne soots and solids are blown into inaccessible corners where they can be activated by moisture, causing sulphates to leach into the stone.

Four major **black encrustations** can form on oolitic limestone in polluted atmospheres:

- **Thin surface parallel laminar black crusts** are the most common.
- **Thick surface parallel black encrustation that partly incorporates the substrate** exclusively develops on porous and softer oolitic limestone.
- **Globular black crusts** are found where moisture is available for long periods of the year and there is a continuous source of particulates. These have the highest gypsum content.
- On protected and temporarily dry surfaces, **dust crusts** can cover globular crusts or surface parallel black crusts. Particulates mostly accumulate in dust crusts. These have the lowest gypsum content.

The most important factors controlling the development of crusts on limestone substrates are the size, distribution and effective porosity of the pores in the stone, its texture, especially of the carbonate cement type, and the surface strength. The main environmental control factors are pollution levels, moisture availability and the exposure to wind and rain.[11]

Water-shedding elements such as cornices and sill courses protect the main facade by sacrificing themselves.[12] Correctly detailed lead cover flashings can protect the stone and help promote water run-off evenly along the length of the cornices. This is done by welting the front edge of a code 7 lead cover flashing, having it turned down and angled slightly out from the cornice and diagonally nipping the bottom edge of the welt at 50 mm centres, and finishing the lead with patination oil.

Earlier lead cover flashings focused the run-off of water in two extremely damaging ways: bays of lead were not correctly welted at their junctions but simply overlapped, causing focused water run-off at the junction of the bays; and window cleaners' ladders were leant against the lead cover flashings, causing further focused water run-off. Focused run-off of water leads to localised accelerated stone decay both through the leaching out of calcium carbonate and the saturation of vulnerable ornately carved work which is then prone to frost damage.

Rising damp causes the breakdown of oolitic limestone's pore structure by capillary action, finding its natural level in a wall's stonework. This process alters the stone's pore structure irrevocably. As rising damp evaporates it leaves behind a residue of **salts** that combine with the calcium carbonate of the stone to form calcium sulphate. This leads to the breakdown of the stone surface.

Fluctuating water tables and weather conditions can both cause further episodes of rising damp. Because of the alteration of the stone's pore structure by the first occurrence of rising damp, subsequent incidences of rising damp allow moisture to shoot through the previously affected stonework. The result is an ever higher level of damaged stonework, which rises up the building like a tide mark.

The footprint of a wall on the ground has a direct relationship to the height that rising damp will rise to. For example, if a 1 metre length of wall has a footprint of $0.5\,m^2$ followed by a 1 metre length of wall with an engaged column with a total footprint of $1\,m^2$, the damage will be higher at the engaged column. This effect is also noticeable at door surrounds and wall returns.

Salt damage can be aggravated by the inappropriate storage of road salts against stone walls as well as by salt spray from adjacent roads.

Assessment techniques

Of the **non-destructive surveying techniques**, the most basic is **visual inspection**. Walking 10–15 metres away from a building in most cases enables the stonework to be viewed stone by stone using binoculars. With good weather and careful timing to optimise natural lighting conditions, a great deal of information about the detailed condition of the stone can be recorded from ground level without the use of scaffolding.

For complex facades it may be helpful to erect an **inspection scaffold** to allow a detailed stone-by-stone, joint-by-joint inspection and analysis to take place. This was done in 1989 on the West Front of Bath Abbey, enabling Nimbus Conservation to make their detailed assessment of the condition of the stonework and for its archaeological recording to be undertaken by Jerry Sampson (Figure 2.5).

Figure 2.5 Archaeological recording of the West Front, Bath Abbey.

Sonic testing is the simplest but most accurate way to assess the soundness or consistency of a block of oolitic limestone built into a building. The simplicity of the stone tapper, a hollow 300 mm length of 12.5 mm diameter steel pipe, belies the consistent results it will give. Held loosely in the hand and tapped against a stone, the length of pipe will cause the stone to 'ring' if it is sound or to produce a dull 'thud' if there is a fault within the stone, giving consistent results. This is a particularly thorough way to assess individual stones in situ when a building is fully scaffolded. Equally, this technique can be used when only limited access to suspect stones is possible by hydraulic platforms, for example when inspecting suspect parapets or capitals.

Infrared **temperature guns** can be used to detect temperature differences of otherwise inaccessible materials. Inappropriate dense cement-based mortars can be pinpointed for comparison to surrounding stonework as the temperature of the denser cement-based mortar will be approximately half a degree centigrade cooler than the adjacent stonework in ambient conditions. Temperature guns can also be helpful in locating areas of water ingress at high level in gloomily lit interiors, damp areas again registering a slightly cooler temperature than surrounding comparatively dry areas.[13]

Comparative recording and mapping of building condition surveys is a valuable means of monitoring the cleaning, re-soiling and re-cleaning of listed buildings. The re-soiling of cleaned stonework of listed buildings in Bath is a significant problem. In 2004 the soiling condition of the stonework of 355 listed buildings along the London Road, Bath, was assessed following earlier condition surveys in 1996, 1992 and 1975. The soiling condition of each listed building was classified as clean, re-soiling, grimy or black. These latter two categories refer to buildings that have never been cleaned whereas buildings that have been classified as re-soiling are buildings that were previously cleaned one or more times. The 1996 survey, undertaken as part of a public inquiry on a proposed superstore development, revealed that 50 of the 105 listed buildings classified as 'clean' in the 1992 survey were then re-soiling. The council argued that the new development would lead to further unacceptable air pollution as a result of vehicle emissions. The 2004 survey revealed that a total of 121 listed buildings along the London Road were then re-soiling.

The University of Bristol Interface Analysis Centre was commissioned to undertake tests on 32 mm diameter cored oolitic limestone samples from a series of buildings at levels varying from 23 to 220 metres above sea level. These tests confirmed that topography was an important factor in the soiling and decay of the oolitic limestone of the city's historic buildings. Oxides of nitrogen were confirmed as a catalyst to sulphur dioxide in the decay of oolitic limestone.

The rate and extent of re-soiling appears to be related to the distance of the building facade from the highway. Front gardens, trees, bushes and walls appears to delay the re-soiling process, but properties screened in this way are showing signs of discoloration. The stonework on properties elevated above the highway is also re-soiling.

Unlisted buildings have also been affected by the re-soiling of their stonework. The appearance of re-soiled stonework differs from that of stonework that has never been cleaned and is 'black'. The re-soiling deposits are grey rather than black and sooty. Re-soiled stonework appears at first 'dusty', then the deposits darken in patches on the surface of the stone. There is considerable evidence of re-soiling on the stonework of buildings alongside major roads and where traffic regularly accumulates at traffic junctions. The effects of pollution created by vehicle emissions are a major contributing factor in the re-soiling process.

A detailed comparative **photographic record** should be made of the stonework of all listed buildings which are re-soiling and whose conservation histories are already well documented. Dr David Searle of the University of Wolverhampton developed a computer program to count pixels of varying shades of soiling recorded on black-and-white photographs. His program counts the number of pixels of all shades of grey, enabling a comparison to be made with a future photograph from the same viewpoint to accurately record any changes in the degree of weathering and soiling.

A very interesting by-product of Searle's program is that the cursor line follows the exact pattern of a specific pixel shade. As the cursor line is pulled down the image, the pixel shades change and the cursor line changes to follow in turn the varying pixel shades which are themselves the record of past weathering and soiling. The cursor line can therefore be seen to echo the soiling and weathering pattern flowing down the building just as though it were water running down the face of the building in a storm.

As calcium sulphate is the product of stone decay caused by sulphur in the atmosphere, a series of 32 mm diameter × 30 mm deep **core samples** – an **intrusive technique** – were taken from a number of sites to determine the amount and depth of sulphur present in the stone. This was assessed by X-ray diffraction analysis and spectrometer analysis at the University of Bristol Interface Analysis Centre in 1996. This revealed that historic stone samples taken from along the London Road, Bath, at 23–27 metres above sea level had sulphur present at up to 1 mm deep. Samples taken higher up the slopes of Bath at the east end of Lansdown Place East at 108.41 metres above sea level had only a minimal level of sulphur present and the Lansdown Cemetery gateway at 229.57 metres above sea level had no detectable level of sulphur present.[14]

Techniques to restore, consolidate or improve condition

An old building's greatest value lies in the actual fabric of which it is made. Every attempt should be made to retain the original stones and their existing surfaces. William Morris emphasised his concern for the care of original surfaces with their honourable scars of age in his 1877 Manifesto for the foundation of the Society for the Protection of Ancient Buildings:

> In the course of this . . . process of destruction and addition the whole surface of the building is necessarily tampered with; so that the appearance of antiquity is taken away from such old parts of the fabric as are left . . .

Any specification for the cleaning and repair of masonry should be prepared with the intention of arresting as far as possible the decay of the existing fabric and leaving it in a sound state of repair. It is not the intention to make the building appear new.

Careful **stone cleaning** is a subtle process. Successful cleaning is where the cleaning process is taken to a point where surface deposits – sulphate-bearing particles – and deposits within the stone – calcium sulphate crystals – which are both harmful to the stone are removed without damaging the structure of the stone.

The 1956 model guide for stone repairs and stone cleaning in the Circus, Bath, states that

> Spray nozzles should be of a type to give a fine, misty spray, each nozzle emitting not more than 2 gallons of water per hour. Each spray nozzle should have a control tap immediately behind it and main control valves should be incorporated in the hose pipe system to enable groups of sprays to be cut off as and when necessary. In addition there should be a main control valve at the T connection on the main supply pipe . . . each spray should be capable of being clamped with an easily adjustable clamp to the scaffold. The direction of the jets should be altered from time to time to avoid over-washing of any particular part of the work to obviate (i) the possibility of water penetration and (ii) the reduction to a minimum of the brown staining resulting from prolonged washing.

This remains the basis for **nebulous spray water cleaning**.

Over-washing of stonework, colloquially known as burning the stone, causes iron compounds within oolitic limestone to go into solution and migrate to the surface where they appear as indelible deep rusty-brown stains. This extremely unsightly damage can be avoided simply by carefully specifying and controlling the amount of water used in stone cleaning. All too often water sprays are seriously over-used, either being left on overnight or used at far too high a volume or, even worse, both. As in all masonry conservation works, it is critical to clean stonework in frost-free weather.

The overriding principle in all works of intervention to historic buildings is to keep all replacement of original fabric to an absolute minimum. **Stone replacement** involves repairing seriously decayed stonework and earlier bad repairs where the intention is to keep as much as possible of the original stonework, only replacing stones that are completely decayed or decaying without the possibility of arresting their decay. Renewal in ashlar work should always use suitable new stone, and a lime-based mortar must be used that is softer than the stone. New work should not be faked to look like old and it is important to ensure that where new moulded stonework has to be inserted it is kept to the original section.

Lime-based conservation techniques were pioneered by Professor Robert Baker at Wells Cathedral in the 1970s. The use of these techniques continues to evolve and respond to site-specific conditions. This brief review of techniques is based on work carried out to 3, 12, 15, 21, 22 and 23 Circus, Bath, by Nimbus Conservation during 1989.

Carefully directed, low-volume, low-pressure fine mists of water were used to **clean** the stonework. The water was regulated by a simple water balance which turned the water supplies on and off. Minimal amounts of water were used, the amounts being continuously assessed by observing

- the rate of clean
- the amount of run-off
- the friability of the stone
- the amount of 'burning'

At least thirty applications of **lime water** (calcium hydroxide) were applied to consolidate all carved surfaces. The lime water was flooded on, not sprayed on, with any excess lime water carefully mopped up to avoid lime staining.

Mortar repairs were designed to be more porous than the surrounding stone and so attract the passage of moisture preferentially. Increased evaporation in the repair enables the greater crystallisation of calcium sulphate in the repair and so protects the surrounding stone. It is critical to press back the repairs while keeping them damp with wet cotton wool.

Shelter coats form a breathable barrier to sulphur-laden airborne solids that collect on the recesses of carvings and mouldings as well as on the weathered surfaces of ashlar and that are activated by damp weather. Shelter coats even out roughened weathered surfaces and so reduce the surface area of the stone. Making shelter coats is extremely skilled and very dependent on the experience and eye of the craftsperson. Mixes need to vary to match variations in the colour of the building, and the relationship of the wet shelter coat mix to its dry colour must be understood. The colour of the shelter coat can also be affected if damp conditions persist too long.

Conclusion

The 1990s cleaning and conservation work in the Circus and on the West Front of Bath Abbey both highlight the importance of regular careful cleaning of stonework by washing down with low-volume, low-pressure mists of water as the first stage of a carefully prepared campaign of conservation. In certain cases it has been necessary to make a major intervention – the conservation process itself – and then get the maintenance cycle back onto a proper footing. Part of the present problem has been that interventions have been too far apart and the need for the maintenance of stone has not been fully appreciated.

Further reading

Arkell, W.J., *Oxford Stone* (1947; republished S.R. Publishers, Wakefield, 1970).
Ashurst, J. and Ashurst, N., *Practical Building Conservation: Volume 1: Stone masonry*, English Heritage Technical Handbook (Gower Technical Press, Aldershot, 1988).
Ashurst, Nicola, *Cleaning Historic Buildings* (Donhead, London, 1994), vols 1 and 2.
Ayres, James, *Building the Georgian City* (Yale University Press, London, 1998).

Building Effects Review Group, *The Effects of Acid Deposition on Buildings and Building Materials in the United Kingdom*, (HMSO, London, 1989).

Clifton-Taylor, Alec, *The Pattern of English Building* (Faber and Faber, London, 1972).

Cooke, R.U. and Gibbs, G.B., *Crumbling Heritage? Studies of stone weathering in polluted atmospheres* (National Power plc, Swindon, 1993).

Devon, E., Parkins, J. and Workman, D., *Bath in Stone: A guide to the city's building stones* (Thematic Trails, Kingston Bagpuize, 2001).

Fidler, John (ed.), *Stone: Stone building materials, construction and associated component systems: their decay and treatment*, English Heritage Research Transactions (London, 2002), vol. 2.

Gauri, K. Lal, and Bandyopadhyay, Jayanta K., *Carbonate Stone: Chemical behavior, durability and conservation* (Wiley, Chichester, 1999).

Mansfield, Trudie, 'Sources of building soiling and a review of the stone cleaning industry 1991', in R.G.M. Webster (ed.), *Stone Cleaning and the Nature, Soiling and Decay Mechanisms of Stone* (Donhead, London, 1992).

Schaffer, R.J., *The Weathering of Natural Building Stones*, Department of Scientific and Industrial Research, Building Research Special Report No.18 (London, 1932).

Schofield, Jane, *Lime in Building: A practical guide* (Black Dog Press, Crediton, 1994; 2003).

Sutherland, D.S., *Northamptonshire Stone* (Dovecote Press, Wimborne, 2003).

Wood, John, *Essay Towards a Description of Bath* (1765; Kingsmead Reprints, Bath, 1969).

Woodward, Christopher, Kelly, Francis and McLaughlin, David, *Stone*, Building of Bath Museum (Bath, 1994).

Endnotes

1. Alec Clifton-Taylor, *The Pattern of English Building* (Faber and Faber, London, 1972), p. 67.
2. John Wood, *Essay Towards a Description of Bath* (1765; Kingsmead Reprints, Bath, 1969) p. 338.
3. Wood, *Essay Towards a Description of Bath*, p. 425.
4. David McLaughlin, 'Acid rain and the cleaning and conservation of stonework in Bath' (Bath City Council Department of Environmental Services, Bath, 1993), p. 4.
5. Nimbus Conservation Group, 'The Cleaning and Conservation of Nos 3, 12, 15, 21, 22 and 23 The Circus, Bath', unpublished report (1989; copy held at Bath Record Office).
6. G.C. Allen, A. El-Turki, K.R. Hallam, D. McLaughlin and M. Stacey, 'Role of NO_2 and SO_2 in degradation of limestone', *British Corrosion Journal*, **35**, 1 (2000), 35–38.
7. Bath & North East Somerset Council, Air Quality Report 2001/2002, Executive Summary.

    This report presents the results of air quality monitoring networks within the boundaries of Bath & North East Somerset. These are then compared with current regulatory standards and previous years' results to build a picture of air quality in the district.

    Pollution monitoring is carried out for nitrogen dioxide, carbon monoxide, sulphur dioxide, particulate matter, ozone and benzene. The Council also measures radiation, grass pollen count and various meteorological parameters including wind speed and direction, temperature and rainfall.

    Road transport continues to be the most significant source of airborne pollution in Bath and North East Somerset. This is mainly in areas where there are high numbers of vehicles and/or congestion.

Nitrogen dioxide results show that the air quality objective will be exceeded at roadside locations on busy roads in Bath. Results from ozone monitoring show pollution episodes during the summer months caused by meteorological conditions.

8. Bath & North East Somerset Council, *Stage 4 Review and Assessment of Air Quality, Consultation Draft*, February 2003, Executive Summary.

This Stage 4 review and assessment report summarises the work undertaken as a further review and assessment as required under the Part IV Environment Act 1995. This follows the declaration of an Air Quality Management Area (AQMA), which Bath and North East Somerset Council made on 1 February 2002. The order was made in relation to the nitrogen dioxide annual mean objective, for an area on the London Road from Bathwick Street to the Batheaston bypass for a distance of 7 metres from the centre of the road.

The review and assessment has been carried out in accordance with guidance set down by Department for Environment, Food and Rural Affairs.

The report is supplementary to the Stage 1, 2 and 3 review and assessment documents.

From the results of the monitoring and modelling carried out as part of the Stage 4 review and assessment, it is recommended that the AQMA is extended. The recommended area includes Bathwick Street, and the original area is widened to 70 metres from the centre of the road, along London Road from London Street to Hanover Place, and 20 metres from the centre of the road from Hanover Place to the Batheaston Roundabout. The existing AQMA is 7 metres from the centre of the London Road.

9. 'Memory effect' is discussed in Mary F. Striegel, 'Materials and cultural resources', in *Acid Rain: Are the Problems Solved?*, May 2001 Conference Proceedings, Session III, Acid Rain Impacts – State of the Science, Center for Environmental Information, www.ceinfo.org (accessed 9 October 2003).

10. McLaughlin, 'Acid rain and the cleaning and conservation of stonework in Bath'(1993) is an earlier version of this chapter and includes comparative mapping of Lower Lansdown, including the Circus, Brock Street and Royal Crescent, for 1975 and 1992. An earlier version of that essay was published in Robin G.M. Webster (ed.), *Stone Cleaning and the Nature, Soiling and Decay Mechanisms of Stone*, Proceedings of the International Conference held in Edinburgh, UK, 14–16 April 1992.

11. http://www.cosis.net/abstracts/EAE03/05066/EAE03-J-05066.pdf (accessed 9 June 2004).

12. Nimbus Conservation Group, 'Cleaning and Conservation', p. 3.

13. This technique was demonstrated at an ASCHB study day at Christ Church, Spitalfields, in the late 1970s.

14. Allen, *et al.*, 'Role of NO_2 and SO_2'.

SANDSTONE
Ian Williams

Sandstones derive from sediments of previously existing rocks and consist of particles of quartz naturally cemented together by either silica, calcium or iron. The different colours and grain sizes of the many building sandstones are partly a result of this varying geological composition (Figures 2.6 and 2.7). Changes in the environment during deposition and variations in the incoming sediment and later geological activity produce layers or beds of rock of differing characteristics. Sandstones formed from sediments laid down under water contain salts which affect their weathering characteristics and therefore the uses to which they can be put.

A lapse of time between the different layers of sediment being laid down results in the creation of bedding plains. In quarrying, these beds are natural breaking points which determine the size of blocks that can be produced. Within a bed there can be further internal laminations which may render stone unsuitable for use as a polished ashlar block but fit for a squared rubble block. Ashlar blocks can be produced from large blocks of medium- to thick-bedded sandstones which have no internal laminations. Relatively thin beds of sandstone with internal laminations can be used for paving stones, such as the flagstones produced from Caithness.

Sandstones have varying colours and degrees of durability, largely due to the cementing or binding material between the particles, the age of the stone and the level of compacting undergone while it was still in the ground. A pure silica sandstone would be white, while oxides of iron create buff, brown and red sandstones, and the presence of clay produces grey tints (Figure 2.8).

The colour is significant when repairs are carried out to a wall. Stone fresh from the quarry is likely to change colour as it weathers with exposure and this change has to be carefully estimated. Different considerations apply when reusing a stone from another building or structure: an assessment must be made of how much weathering the stone has already undergone and how much further change in colour can be expected. Reusing stone is usually the least expensive means of repairing rubble walls, provided the existing and replacement sandstones match. It is not acceptable for a mason to be given the instruction to use any second-hand stone which happens to be available, without checks being made. Given that the objective is to achieve a colour match between replaced and original stone once an appropriate weathering period has elapsed, the replacement stone will initially stand out and may not appear visually pleasing, so the reasons why

Figure 2.6 Crisp detail at St. George's Hall, Liverpool, by Harvey Lonsdale Elmes (1841–54).

Figure 2.7 Acton Burnell Castle, Shropshire: the remains of a thirteenth-century fortified manor house built of distinctive red sandstone.

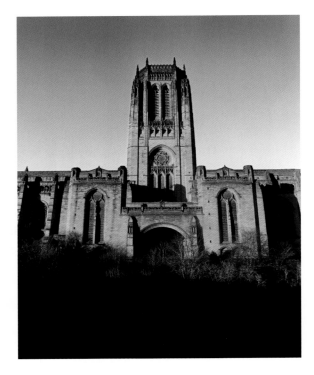

Figure 2.8 Liverpool Anglican Cathedral, by Sir Giles Gilbert Scott (1904–78), is built of red sandstone, mostly quarried at Woolton, south-east of the city.

a particular stone is selected for a repair must be explained to the owner.

However, Dr Ewan Hyslop in his study of the performance of replacement sandstone in the New Town of Edinburgh makes it clear that finding suitable matches for replacement stone is complicated:

> It is unlikely that new stone from the same quarry as the original will undergo the same combination of processes of soiling, cleaning and decay and it is therefore unlikely to obtain a similar colour and appearance. Equally, the selection of replacement stone in order to match the present-day colour of the original stone could result in future problems as the original stone continues to decay, or the colour produced by the previous chemical cleaning continues to change. It is clear that stone has to be regarded as a dynamic natural material whose appearance will continue to change through time.[1]

In reality it is likely that there will be a limited choice for replacement stones, which means that differences between the two are unavoidable.[2]

Rates of decay

The cements which bind the sediments affect not only the colour of the stone but its resistance to weathering and the ease or otherwise of working it. The cement within the stone thus affects repair decisions and should be identified before any decision is made. The types of cements, from most durable to least durable, are as follows:

siliceous   containing silica and known as secondarily deposited silica.
calcareous   containing calcium carbonate.
dolomitic   containing the double salt calcium-magnesium carbonate.
ferruginous   containing iron oxide.
argillaceous   containing clay.[3]

Argillaceous stone would not normally be suitable for building as the clay easily washes out, releasing the sediment particles and causing rapid decay, unless there is some mix of cements including silica. In urban environments, dilute acids and atmospheric carbon dioxide attack the carbonate in calcareous and dolomitic sandstones, but small amounts of calcium carbonate (lime) in the stone have little effect on its resistance to weathering. The combination of substantial calcite content and poor compaction indicates the likelihood of a short life. Slight decay over a long period may be expected and is not problematic but substantial and rapid decay may require urgent repair and replacement.

Thin clay beds may be present within beds of solid stone, sometimes quite frequently, and weathering of these produces surface furrows where the sections of clay erode faster than the adjoining stone. Unless the erosion has reached quite deep levels, this weathering is not likely to be a structural problem requiring urgent repair because erosion slows down as it progresses into the stone as the overhang of intact stone provides some protection. It may be that little or no remedial action is required. However, if these clay-bedded sandstones are used in certain situations, such as for lintels or overhanging cornices, the likelihood of failure must be considered.

Before decisions are made concerning stone repairs, likely weathering patterns must be considered on the basis of either experience or tests which show the composition and therefore probable rate of decay.

Faults

Cracks as a result of ground movement usually follow the lines of the beds in the stone, but may be invisible and only detectable if the stone has a dead sound when tapped with a hammer or when it is being worked. If the crack is far from the surface it may be ignored, but if it is filled with calcite the stone may weather at varying rates; the differential will increase where there is a high water content. In the case of replacement repair using second-hand stone, such potential problems obviously have to be considered and stone with this source of weakness should ideally be rejected.

More serious cracks may occur as a result of quarrying with high explosive, which causes numerous cracks running in all directions. It is inadvisable to use any stone extracted close to an area where such methods have been employed. Stone affected by blasting weathers rapidly, even if it stays in one piece on the mason's banker. A small charge of low-level black powder explosive, however, only shocks the stone sufficiently to split it, without shattering it entirely. Careful handling in the quarry during and after extraction is important too, because if a stone is dropped or knocked small fractures may occur which may develop with weathering.

A stone's characteristics – its natural faults and variations in texture and structure which can vary greatly even within the same quarry – and the methods of extraction both past and present all determine its suitability for repair. Some blocks will be sound while others should be rejected. The selection of individual blocks is usually best left to the quarryman who is thoroughly acquainted with the stone and the quarry, though contractors and professional agents should determine which type of stone is best for their purpose before approaching the quarry.

Processes of weathering and decay

Weathering can be both physical and chemical. The physical processes are those where the disintegration does not involve alteration to the chemical composition of the mineral constituents – wind erosion, freeze–thaw action, thermal expansion and contraction, and friction damage at the foot of a building. Chemical weathering results from elements being washed off or leached from the stone by rainwater, or from atmospheric pollution or the by-products of biological growths (Figure 2.9).

Figure 2.9 Detail of the weathering, rugged Pennant sandstone at Bush House (1830–31), Narrow Quay, Bristol, by R.S. Pope, now the Arnolfini Arts Centre.

Weathering is likely to have begun while the stone was still in the ground or exposed in the quarry. In the ground, physical disaggregation and chemical alteration may take place. Some sandstones harden after being quarried, and if the hardened surface is damaged or removed during preparation work prior to its installation in a building, the weather-resisting properties will be reduced. Contractors therefore need to be familiar with the particular stone that is being worked.

The effects of water and salts

When assessing the processes of decay, it must be remembered that stone in a building has been removed from the ground and its related groundwater setting and placed in an artificial position. Sandstone may be highly porous – owing to voids between the individual sand grains – and water ingress aggravated by poor maintenance may result in decay through freeze–thaw action (the water expanding as it freezes and causing spalling).

Salts in a stone may originate from leaching within the stone, or from materials in the mortar or rising in groundwater. Chemical weathering can also be accelerated by pollutants in the air. Many sandstones have a calcareous cement binding, which is susceptible to chemical attack.

A salt-free stone expands while becoming wet and contracts while drying. A salt-contaminated stone does the opposite, though the expansion following the wetting and drying cycle is not reversible and the amount of expansion increases from cycle to cycle. The more salts are released, the greater the resulting chemical reaction and level of decay. The moisture distribution within the stone is dependent on the properties of the stone itself and on the surrounding drying conditions. The salts become enriched as further dissolved material leaches to the surface or migrates into areas of a pore system that are wet; as moisture evaporates, they precipitate and expand.

Different types of stone and even different sandstones within the same building elevation can lead to chemical decay when rainwater, having absorbed components from one stone, then runs by gravity onto a different stone and is absorbed.

If the damage is on the surface then **sanding off** will occur; if the damage is slightly below the surface then **scales** form. Exposure to wind and sun, with a correspondingly quick wetting and drying cycle, tends to result in scales and a slow cycle in sanding off. **Flakes** and **exfoliations** occur between the extremes of conditions which give rise to the other two types of decay. Flakes only occur if moisture penetration does not draw too far into the stone. Exfoliations occur parallel to the layers of a stone and particularly when boundary layers are weak. The detachment of black crusts follows the same principles, in that beneath the crust the original surface is the area of maximum moisture, and is where acidic pollutants are neutralised and gypsum and other salts precipitate. A further variation is **honeycomb weathering** – surface corrosion pits instead of an even recession – where there are isolated zones of high moisture and trapped areas of salts that normally would be distributed over the entire surface of stone.

Incorrect bedding

Delamination of stones can take place where they have been 'face bedded' so that the bedding planes are not restrained by adjacent stone. Surface veneers and contour scaling may occur despite the fact that the stone could be correctly aligned on a natural bed. Sandstones are particularly susceptible to this problem.

Inappropriate repairs

If the ability of stone to breathe moisture is inhibited, damage will occur. A patched impermeable cement repair to flaking stone will result in the decay spreading around the edges of the repair and the cement eventually exfoliating. Similarly, the use of a consolidant compound which does not penetrate sufficiently into the stone, and which, in any case, traps both salts and interstitial moisture, will result eventually in serious exfoliation of the stone. An inappropriate or aggressive cleaning method can damage both the surface and the interior of the stone and leave it more susceptible to weathering because of excessive acid or water penetration. It can also change the colour of the stone.

Most evaporation in masonry using permeable lime mortar will occur through the joints, whereas impermeable cement mortar forces moisture to evaporate through the stone itself, causing a build-up of salts and consequent decay. For about three-quarters of the twentieth century contractors used Portland cement in buildings almost universally, once it was discovered that it was quick-setting, strong and an easy material to use, without being aware of future damage it would cause.

Damage due to stresses placed upon stone

External factors can affect the performance of even the hardest of specimens. High stress concentrations caused by uneven settlement, restrained thermal expansion or corrosion of iron cramps can all cause failure. Stones which have been placed under a heavy load for a considerable period of time may deform without cracking, resulting in distortion to columns and other elements.

Extensive levels of stress are caused by fire when surface heat – and therefore expansion – does not penetrate far into the stone. When this heat is rapidly dissipated as the fire is extinguished with water, cracking and spalling can take place. Brown and buff sandstones which contain iron oxide are likely to turn to a shade of pink owing to the chemical reaction of hydrated iron oxide.

Biological effects

Microbiological growths are associated with the formation of crusts, which lower the evaporation rate and retain moisture. Swelling and shrinking of organic substances also cause mechanical stress, which aids the detachment of the crusts. Biological organisms, simply by their presence on the surface of a stone, alter the micro-climate and affect both the moisture content and the surface temperature.

Algae contribute to decay because they encourage water retention at the stone surface, which can enhance freeze–thaw damage, and they represent an early stage in the successive colonisation of surface mosses and higher plants.

Bacteria cause decay through secretion of chemicals and acids, including sulphuric acid, which are capable of dissolving compounds in a stone. The **fungal hyphae** – the network of filaments that form the 'body' of fungus – cause decay by physically penetrating around the grains in a stone.

Lichen growth and **mosses** can cause surface pitting and disruption to mortar joints. Larger **plants**, such as ivy, attach themselves to stone with little suckers, concentrating moisture on the surface of the stone, and grow into mortar joints, allowing water ingress into the wall.

Some **biocides** used to kill biological growths can themselves be agents of decay, for example by reacting with other past treatments to the stone. To avoid salt crystallisation damage, some biocides have to be carefully washed out of the stone after being applied. There is evidence, too, that some treatments dissolve both calcite and quartz in calcareous sandstones and have the potential to disperse clays in others.

Available advice

Advice on maintenance procedures is available in Planning Policy Guidance 15 (1994) and/or the *Memorandum of Guidance on Listed Building and Conservation Areas* (1998) published in Scotland. Although these documents are aimed primarily at listed buildings, the advice given within them is also applicable to other less historic or less significant buildings. The following advice from Appendix 1 of the *Memorandum of Guidance* (1998), sections 1.12, 1.13 and 1.14, is of equal importance to sandstone buildings whether they are 'listed' or not:

> The original masonry surface, which will sometimes be polished or tooled in a distinctive pattern, should always be carefully respected. Cheap repairs and poor workmanship only accelerate decay and usually result in long-term problems which lead to much higher costs later on.

> Mortars should not be cementatious or synthetic as this will lead to further damage to the stonework. Cement patching must never be permitted.

> Repointing which is poorly executed or makes use of the wrong materials can cause physical damage to the fabric of a building. It can also radically alter the appearance of a building and thus substantially detract from its character and quality.

> Pointing should always be weaker than the surrounding stone. Hard dense mortars generally have the effect of increasing rather than decreasing the risks of water penetration and stone decay. Lime pointing should therefore be used in most instances, never hard grey cement. Original mortar is frequently lighter

in colour than the stone, and this should be reflected in the new work . . . Raking out should be done carefully with hand tools. Power tools are difficult to control accurately and can, and frequently do, cause irreversible damage to masonry . . . Any new pointing should accurately match the original work in all respects and should not spill over onto the face of the masonry.[4]

Information about rock description and classification and building stone resources can be obtained from the British Geological Survey website: www.bgs.ac.uk/bgsrcs/home.html

Further reading

Amoroso, G.G. and Fassina, V., *Stone Decay and Conservation, Atmospheric Pollution, Cleaning, Consolidation and Protection* (Elsevier, Amsterdam, 1983).

Ashurst, J. and Ashurst, N., *Practical Building Conservation. Volume 1: Stone Masonry* (Gower Technical Press, Aldershot, 1988).

Ashurst, J. and Dimes, F.G., *Conservation of Building and Decorative Stone*, 2 vols (Butterworth-Heinemann, London, 1990).

Ashurst, N., *Cleaning Historic Buildings. Volume 1: Substrates, Soiling and Investigations* (Donhead, London, 1994).

Ashurst, N., *Cleaning Historic Buildings. Volume 2: Cleaning Materials and Processes* (Donhead, London, 1994).

Building Research Establishment Digest 177: *Decay and Conservation of Stone Masonry* (Building Research Establishment/Department of the Environment, Watford, 1990).

Building Research Establishment Digest No. 280: *Cleaning External Surfaces of Buildings* (Building Research Establishment/Department of the Environment, Watford, 1989).

Building Research Establishment Digest No. 370: *Control of Lichens, Moulds and Similar Growths* (Building Research Establishment/Department of the Environment, Watford, 1992).

Building Research Establishment Digest No. 418: *Bird, Bee and Plant Damage to Buildings* (Construction Research Communications with HMSO and the Building Research Establishment, Watford, 1996).

Building Research Establishment Digest No. 420: *Selecting Natural Building Stones* (Construction Research Communications with HMSO and the Building Research Establishment, Watford, 1997).

Building Research Establishment Digest No. 421: *Measuring the Compressive Strength of Masonry Materials* (Construction Research Communications with HMSO and the Building Research Establishment, Watford, 1997).

Cameron, S., *et al.*, *Biological Growths on Sandstone Buildings: Control and treatment*, Technical Advice Note 10 (Historic Scotland, Technical Conservation, Research and Education Division, Edinburgh, 1997).

Hill, P.R. and David, J.C.E., *Practical Stone Masonry* (Donhead, London, 1995).

Hunter, C.A. and Berry, R.W., *Control of Biological Growths on Stone*, Building Research Establishment Information Paper, IP 11/95 (Construction Research Communications with HMSO and the Building Research Establishment, Watford, 1995).

Hyslop, E., *The Performance of Replacement Sandstone in the New Town of Edinburgh: Evidence from grant aid repair schemes of the Edinburgh New Town Conservation Committee* (Historic Scotland, Edinburgh, 2004).

Jones, M.S. and Wakefield, R.D. (eds) *Aspects of Stone Weathering, Decay and Conservation* (Imperial College Press, London, 1999).

Leary, E., *The Building Sandstones of the British Isles* (Building Research Establishment/ Department of the Environment, Watford, 1986).

McMillan, A.A., Gillanders, R.J. and Fairhurst, J.A. *Building Stones of Edinburgh,* 2nd edn (Edinburgh Geological Society, Edinburgh, 1999).

Prentice, J.E., *Geology of Construction Materials* (Chapman Hall, London, 1990).

Ross, K.D. and Butlin, R.N., *Durability Tests for Building Stone* (Building Research Establishment, Watford, 1992).

Shadmon, A., *Stone: An introduction* (Intermediate Technology Publications, London, 1989).

Shore, B.C.G., *Stones of Britain: A pictorial guide to those in charge of valuable buildings* (Leonard Hill, London, 1957).

Sowden, A.M., *The Maintenance of Brick and Stone Masonry Structures* (E & FN Spon, London, 1990).

Warland, E.G., *Modern Practical Masonry* (Pitman Books and the Stone Federation, London, 1953).

Winkler, E.M., *Stone in Architecture: Properties, durability* (Springer-Verlag, Berlin and London, 1994).

Endnotes

1. E. Hyslop, *The Performance of Replacement Sandstone in the New Town of Edinburgh: Evidence from grant aid repair schemes of the Edinburgh New Town Conservation Committee* (Historic Scotland, Edinburgh, 2004), p. 21.
2. As part of his Edinburgh study, Hyslop studied thin sections of stone through an optical microscope, using blue dye to highlight the stones' porosity and taking observations of grain size and mineralogy to assess the varying stones' compatibility. He suggests that to achieve the best results a replacement stone must have similar grain size, porosity characteristics and mineral composition, 'so that it has a similar response to wetting and drying cycles, attraction to organic growth and soiling, and contaminants and pollutants (such as salts)' (*ibid.*, p. 73).
3. E. Leary, *The Building Sandstones of the British Isles* (Building Research Establishment/Department of the Environment, Watford, 1986), p. 2.
4. *Memorandum of Guidance on Listed Buildings and Conservation Areas* (1998), Appendix 1, sections 1.12–1.14, pp. 92–4.

GRANITE
Robert Cotta

Introduction

Among the various natural stones used in construction, granite has a history different from that of other building stones. Historically, limestone and sandstone were commonly used, being easily worked materials that were available in populated areas. Granite landscapes were remote from the great cathedral-building areas of France, England and the Germanic countries. Nonetheless, where granite was the locally available stone, churches and civic buildings were built of the material and survive today in areas such as Cornwall, Scotland and Spain, providing examples of the performance of granite over a 500-year history.

The majority of granite buildings, however, date from after the application of steam technology in the early 1800s, which allowed the rapid development and exploitation of bedrock granite. Its strength, hardness and durability were assets that led to escalating demand in bridge, waterfront and civil engineering works. The large-scale operations of granite-producing areas such as Scotland, Cornwall and New England inevitably led to its use in buildings in the nearby commercial centres, with a stylistic adaptation to a simplified monumentality that accommodated the 'intractable' nature of the material.

In the 200-year history of the extended use of granite, the material has demonstrated greater durability than other natural building stones (and concrete) in comparably aged structures and, indeed, its reputation is one of virtual indestructibility. This, however, is not entirely well-founded and issues of deterioration do become apparent with age, especially in the polluted urban environments of the modern world. Some of the modes of deterioration are untypical of other building stones owing to their differing chemical composition, while methods of treatment may be required that are different to those used on sandstones and limestones.

The solidity, durability and monumentality of granite buildings and their associated historical significance make them prime candidates for conservation and continued use. The nature of the material and the issues associated with the conservation of granite buildings are discussed here with a transatlantic slant, highlighting the scattered and limited history of the material's use.

Granite is an igneous rock formed when molten magma deep within the earth's crust forms a dome and slowly cools into a crystalline mass. In order for this slow cooling to occur, there must be a very thick overlying mass of rock and soil, and thus, when formed, no granites are within recoverable distances from the earth's surface. Granite outcrops that occur around the world are typically found in the eroded remnants of ancient mountain ranges such as the Appalachian mountains in North America and the mountains of Scotland and Scandinavia. Past glacial action is usually also a contributor to exposing granite intrusions on ancient mountain ranges (e.g. in New England and Scandinavia) and in combination with major tectonic uplifts, such as in the Sierra Nevada of California, the European Alps and the Andes mountains of South America. Historically, stone for buildings was obtained from local sources and thus historic granite buildings in Britain, especially prior to 1800, are limited to areas near sources in Cornwall and Scotland. Canal and railway networks, however, facilitated wider distribution of all building stones and thus granite can frequently be found in nineteenth- and twentieth-century buildings in most parts of Britain and most world cities.

The granite family has a fairly limited range of composition. Its members contain varying proportions of quartz, acid plagioclase feldspar, potash feldspar, a dark-coloured ferromagnesian mineral which is generally either biotite mica or hornblende, and for some granites muscovite mica. Other accessory minerals may be present, but never in great amounts unless as purely local concentrations.[1]

Feldspar is the predominant mineral in granite. The relative proportions of base minerals and/or presence of accessory minerals give different characteristic colours. Quartz is relatively colourless, although it can take on a grey 'smoky' colour. Orthoclase feldspars range from white to pink and occasionally red. Plagioclase feldspars are typically white to grey, occasionally ranging into a brown, yellowish or pink colour. Hornblende and biotite give the stone a dark colour. Muscovite is a clear reflective mineral that when present gives the stone a 'sparkle' from light reflecting off the muscovite grains. A range of colours and textures may be available from a single quarry.

The chemical composition of granite is primarily silicon dioxide with varying amounts of other mineral oxides, primarily aluminium oxide and to a lesser extent potassium oxide, sodium oxide, calcium oxide or iron oxide, that determine the uniqueness of the particular granite mass. Granites with more than 65% silicon dioxide are termed acid and those with lesser amounts of silicon dioxide are termed intermediate (55–65%), basic (45–55%) and ultrabasic (<45%).[2]

Granite is known to most people as a very hard, dense stone with a deserved reputation for extreme durability, although like most building stones there is some variation in these characteristics that is dependent on the specific source; however, there is less variation in its properties than in those of other building stones. In general, granite is denser, less porous and has a higher compressive strength than other buildings stones. Along with marble, it also has a reliable flexural strength that is comparable to that of timber.

Hardness is dependent on the hardness of component minerals. Each mineral has a specific hardness. In granite, the mineral quartz has a hardness of 7, feldspar of about 6, and mica of about 2.5. Since quartz and feldspar predominate, a typical piece of granite will test to a hardness of 6 to 7, but pieces of mica may easily be flaked out depending on size and exposure.

Granite quarries do still operate in the traditional areas in Britain, Europe and the United States, although current operations typically produce only crushed stone for road building. In Britain, granite quarrying in the past was primarily in Cornwall and Scotland, with smaller production areas in Leicestershire and Cumbria. Scottish granite production was focused in three areas, with by far the largest production coming from quarries along a circle of granite extrusions running south from Inverness to the Cairngorm mountains, east to Aberdeen and then north-east to Peterhead. Aberdeen was probably the earliest centre for granite production in the world, developing a high-volume industrial production in the mid-1800s, from which it came to be known as the 'Granite City'.

Accessible granite is widely distributed across the United States, with historic and current operations in Atlantic coast states from New England to Georgia, several states in the Midwest, and in Texas and California. Production in the early part of the nineteenth century came primarily from Massachusetts and Pennsylvania, where quarries near the ocean or navigable inland rivers and canals had coastal water transport to Boston and Philadelphia and the fast-growing cities of New York and Washington DC.

Operating quarries in the present day are those that have access to large, easily worked outcrops, have stone with desirable colours and patterning, and are either technologically advanced to minimise labour costs or in areas where labour costs are minimal. The proximity of quarries to metropolitan areas with major buildings has not been a factor in the distribution or use of specific stones in recent decades owing to (comparatively) cheap transportation costs. The industry currently operates on a global scale, with stone quarried in North or South America, Scandinavia and Africa being finished in China, India, Italy or Scotland for use around the world (Figure 2.10).

History of technology and building use

Throughout history, the tools available to work granite were comparable, with some modification, with those used to work other stones. However, the techniques for working granite form almost a different trade.[3] Finishing tools for granite, such as chisels and hammers, need to be more substantial and have flatter faces for better durability in working the harder material and because of the limitations in detailing due to the brittle, granular nature of granite.

Figure 2.10 Fletcher Granite Company's Westford Quarry, 40 miles west of Boston, Massachusetts, has been in continuous operation since 1810, supplying white Chelmsford granite for buildings and engineering works.

Until the 1800s, the granite that was used for vernacular building work was very roughly hewn, if hewn much at all, and the material source was typically small-sized field stones that had been created and deposited by past glacial activity. Granite has two perpendicular planes of cleavage; this results in roughly rectangular fieldstones being formed as a result of frost and glacial weathering, which can be used 'as is', with little dressing, in wall construction. A fairly simple, unadorned style of building developed in areas such as Cornwall and parts of Scotland for cottages and churches; other buildings constructed in granite areas were typically solid and simple.

A notable exception to this simplicity is the church of St Mary Magdalene in Launceston, Cornwall, built in the sixteenth century of elaborately carved Dartmoor granite – an incredible achievement for its time. The building is also testament to the ability of granite to stand up to the elements and maintain a level of detail over centuries that is superior to that of sandstone and limestone. Otherwise, major pre-1800 granite buildings are scarce in Britain, and those that do exist, such as the fifteenth-century Cathedral of St Machar and the Town House (1787) in Old Aberdeen, Scotland, have simplified detailing. Early granite construction is rare, too, on the European continent and is primarily limited to the northern Iberian Peninsula – for example, the Cathedral of Santiago de Compostela.

Until the late eighteenth century, field stones were worked with hand tools and in some cases by using a process of rough dressing: the granite was first heated, then iron balls were dropped onto the heated stone to provide cleaved plane surfaces. This process was used in the construction of King's Chapel, Boston (1749–54), the first building of 'dressed' granite in America. The stone was finished by hand-hewing techniques brought to America by German immigrants in the second quarter of the eighteenth century. It would be another half century before the construction of Aberdeen's (and Britain's) first fully dressed ashlar granite building, James Burn's Aberdeen Banking Company Office (1801–02) in the Castlegate.

Advances in technology around 1800 allowed the material to be used in civil engineering and building works. The application of wedge-splitting in America, reported by Brayley to have been commercialised in the Quincy, Massachusetts, granite industry in 1798, led to a drop in production costs of almost a half and opened up the exploitation of vast resources of granite bedrock in quarries around Boston in Quincy, Rockport and Westford. The newly available sources facilitated large-scale works such as the Middlesex Canal and the fort on Castle Island in Boston Harbour. Wedge-splitting facilitated the finishing of granite sufficiently that it could be used as ashlar masonry in crisply detailed classical buildings from the early 1800s.

Steam-powered granite-cutting further revolutionised the industry in the 1830s in Scotland, New England, Cornwall and elsewhere, allowing quarries in these regions to expand their production to supply markets that could be reached by waterways and the new railways. The primary markets were civil engineering works – paving setts and curbs, wharf structures, bridges and railway embankments – but the expanded production of the 1830s also resulted in granite's use in commercial and institutional buildings in Boston, Penzance and especially Aberdeen. Recognising the intractable nature of the material, the Scottish architect Archibald Simpson produced a dignified, minimal classical style – the 'granite classicism' – that defines the streetscape of Aberdeen.

Steam power was used to cut and lift stone in the quarry and later in the mid-nineteenth century in Aberdeen to machine-dress the stone (a technique introduced in America in 1853, at Quincy, Massachusetts). Polishing techniques, using beach sand and Turkish emery, were also developed in Aberdeen in the mid-1800s and were introduced in America by John Westland in 1869 when, in partnership with two other Scotsmen, Gordon McKenzie and George S. Patterson, he founded a firm in Quincy. Cutting technology was refined by Henry Parker and Sons in Rockport, Massachusetts, where a sawing machine utilising iron globules was developed in 1877. Extraction, cutting and finishing technologies continued to evolve into the twentieth century.

Competition between New England quarries provided the incentive to import, refine and develop efficient technologies from 1870 through to the end of the nineteenth century in order to supply an increasing demand from expanding cities in the north-eastern United States, especially for rebuilding after fires devastated Chicago (1871) and Boston (1872). The influence of European technologies and techniques in the New England industry was extensive from the latter part of the nineteenth century into the twentieth century, as exemplified in the ownership of a majority of Quincy quarries and granite-finishing businesses by European immigrants in the early 1900s.

The economic boom for the granite industry ceased with the primacy of steel and reinforced concrete as building materials in the first part of the twentieth century and the depression of the 1930s, leading to the closure of most traditional source quarries of the nineteenth century. Nonetheless, the material had become characteristic in towns situated in a granite landscape – predominantly Aberdeen but also towns in Cornwall, such as Penzance.

The railways had also made economical the possibility of transporting building stone from widely divergent sources to widely scattered building sites. No longer limited to sea and river ports for shipping the material, architects in the late 1800s increasingly specified stone based on material qualities, such as strength, durability and colour, rather than local availability. The combination of granite with brick was common in the Federalist style in the United States in the early 1800s, frequently as ground floor and foundation base course material and also as lintels and sills in brick buildings. By the latter part of the nineteenth century granite had become a common component in the architect's palette, used in combination with other stones and materials not only at the bases of buildings and for window trim but also to define strong architectural elements: for example, the polished red granite columns in Harvey Lonsdale Elmes's Concert Hall at St George's Hall, Liverpool (1841–54), and the elaborate mix of Longmeadow brownstone (sandstone) and Dedham, Quincy, Westerly and Rockport granite in H.H. Richardson's Trinity Church in Boston.

Assessment techniques and deterioration issues

The primary items of deterioration in historic granite structures include cracks in masonry walls (including cracks through individual units), penetrating dampness, staining and soiling of the granite faces, deterioration of mortar joints and decay of the individual masonry units.

When assessing the overall condition of granite structures, it is best to start with an evaluation of the overall macro-behaviour, where problems will be manifest by cracks and staining. This provides indications of moisture paths over the surface of the wall and of breaches in the wall's outer protective skin. Assessment of the patterns of decay can then be put in a proper context by knowledge of the source of moisture. Almost all granite decay is due to moisture working in combination with chemical constituents in the air and in the masonry wall system to exploit the micro-fracture structure between mineral grains in the granite and thus cause decay conditions.

The approach for assessing cracks in granite masonry will typically be the same as for other stone and brick masonry walls, since the overall behaviour of masonry walls is essentially the same for all stone or brick materials.

Diagonal cracks that follow mortar joints, typically originating at the corners of window and door openings, and particularly those that have an increasing width along the length, are usually indicators of differential settlement along the length of the wall. Vertical cracks adjacent to the ends of walls are frequently indicators of thermal expansion and contraction, particularly when present in end walls perpendicular to walls with a long horizontal dimension and no provision for expansion. Cracks at the upper portions of walls immediately below the roof line and with an associated outward bulge can indicate an outward thrust load imposed by the roof structure or be a sign of moisture penetration and possible freeze–thaw damage between the face stone and the back-up rubble or brick wall. For all these generic conditions it is important to ascertain whether the cause is active or static in order to determine the necessary course of action. Cracks identified as settlement cracks, in particular, can frequently be non-active and will require only repointing of the cracked mortar joint to prevent infiltration of moisture into the wall.

Corresponding interior inspections are particularly relevant to help identify the likely source of exterior deficiencies. Interior crack patterns can corroborate observed exterior conditions and help to identify whether the root cause conditions are active or static, since interior finishes are typically restored on more frequent cycles than exterior restorations. Interior dampness, indicated by stains or damp areas on the interior face of exterior walls, can help identify specific problem areas. Dampness that is limited to the upper levels of buildings is frequently an indication of blocked or damaged gutters, defective roofs, or failed parapet or chimney flashing. Dampness that is limited to the lower portion of a building is frequently an indicator of groundwater saturation, although this condition is less common in granite masonry than in other stones owing to its low permeability. Dampness encountered in other areas of the building should be assessed on the basis of specific conditions at the locations. Frequently the cause is due to more extreme exposure conditions (e.g. on exterior walls facing prevailing winds) or to inferior mortar repairs, such as the use of cement mortars, inadequate cleaning of the joint prior to pointing or the use of ribbon pointing and other projecting mortar profiles.

Assessment of soiling patterns in conjunction with evaluation of cracks and the nature of any granite decay is critical to understanding the likely cause or causes of deterioration, particularly along mortar joints. The presence of local orange or 'rust-coloured' stains that run down the face of the wall, particularly when in conjunction with cracks through granite units or spalling of pieces of granite, is usually an indication of corroded iron ties or reinforcements in the wall that have been exposed to moisture – most likely entering through deteriorated mortar joints.

Black crusts or soiling along mortar joints in granite masonry are typically an indication of the formation of gypsum salts from the reaction of sulphuric acid in polluted air with calcium in the mortar and the trapping of soot in the gypsum matrix. Lime mortars are higher in soluble calcium than cement mortars and over time will react with atmospheric sulphur to form gypsum crusts that entrap airborne soot and grow on the granite surface along

Figure 2.11 Gypsum salt and soot crust along mortar joints at the fifteenth-century St Andrews Church, Plymouth, Devon.

mortar joints (Figure 2.11). Frequently the granite adjacent to the joint will be discoloured, indicating either future or actual spalling and loss of detail at the arrisses. The gypsum is thought to deteriorate the granite either by reacting with the feldspar in the granite and converting it to erodible clays or through pressure derived from crystal growth within mineral cleavage planes and other cavities in the stone. The simplified detailing on most granite buildings tends to work in favour of controlling this phenomenon, as areas where the stone is washed regularly by rain or run-off tend not to form the gypsum crusts.

Research at Robert Gordon University, Aberdeen, found that a significant factor in the decay of granite in building walls is the interaction at the interface of the mortar joint and the stone.[4] This would tend to indicate the desirability of minimal exposed mortar joint interface and the advisability of avoiding tuck-pointed, ribbon-pointed or wide convex mortar joints. Research in Rio de Janeiro by Neill and Smith does not explicitly cite mortar joints as contributory to granite decay, but does note that micro-fractures that can accumulate urban atmospheric pollutants, as are likely to be more present for over-extended joints, are a factor in the deterioration of granite-type stones in urban atmospheres.[5]

Although cement-based mortars have less soluble calcium than lime mortars, the known disadvantages of Portland cement mortars still apply to its use in granite masonry. These include the impermeability of cement mortars and their tendency to shrink and crack, providing openings in the

Figure 2.12 Custom House Tower, Boston, Massachusetts, by Peabody and Stearns (1913–15).

overall wall system where moisture can enter but not necessarily escape once it gets into the wall. Research at Robert Gordon University found that moisture that enters through cracks in the cement mortar joints of granite wall systems can have a tendency to migrate to the interior of the building, as the combination of the impermeable granite and impermeable cement mortar does not provide an easy path for the evaporation of moisture to the exterior.[6]

The use of cement-based mortars was a likely factor in deterioration in one of the largest restoration projects on a major granite building. In 1977, the Custom House Tower in Boston, Massachusetts (Figure 2.12), required restoration for conditions where the existing blocks were reportedly damaged by 'settling of the stones and moisture getting into the granite'.[7] Given that the older 1840s Custom House base did not require such extensive replacement, a likely cause is that the use of cement-based mortars in the tower (given the date of construction) provided less flexibility in the masonry construction and a more detrimental condition for trapped moisture to go through freeze–thaw cycles, resulting in spalling of the granite. This scenario of cement mortar deficiencies is not much different from what is commonly encountered in buildings of other stone materials.

In some limited situations, the use of granite in exterior wall designs along with other building stones can result in accelerated stone deterioration due to the interaction of chemicals or differences in porosity between adjacent building stones. Granite has been noted to be adversely affected when it is below limestone or calcareous sandstones. Calcareous stones, similarly to lime-based mortars, will slowly dissolve over time when subjected to rain, to provide the calcium that reacts with sulphur in atmospheric pollution and is deposited as calcium sulphate (gypsum) on the surface of the granite, where it develops gypsum crusts and deterioration similar to that noted above at mortar joints.[8] Where granite on a facade is in contact with sandstone, and especially where sandstone overlies granite, there can occasionally be some decay of the sandstone close to the contact plane. In this case it appears that the impermeability of the granite, perhaps in conjunction with an impermeable mortar, causes moisture in the wall to evaporate through the sandstone, which in turn causes the sandstone to spall as a result of vapour pressure and/or freeze–thaw factors.

Once the macro-behaviour of a granite wall system, based on evaluation of cracks and staining, is understood, a detailed assessment of any stone decay can take place as the specific nature of decay can usually be tied to specific identified causes.

It is always important to evaluate the particular granite, as granites with larger mineral grains, especially of mica, appear to be more susceptible to chemical and molecular processes that cause decay. Some types can have higher porosities or particular chemical compositions that make them more vulnerable to deterioration in aggressive or even routine weathering environments. Even the best granite, though, can be susceptible to pollution and salt-laden environments and over time will experience deterioration in urban environments. Research at Robert Gordon University found that micas and feldspars can be converted to clays when subjected to acid rain with pH values under 5.0.[9] These converted clays will, over time, swell and contract under fluctuating moisture conditions, leading to micro-fracturing that allows moisture to penetrate and making the stone susceptible to freeze–thaw deterioration.[10] This effect is typically not visible for years but can reach a point where there is sudden deterioration at the stone surface following numerous freeze–thaw cycles.

Research conducted by the Masonry Conservation Group of Robert Gordon University identified four general types of decay in granite stone:

- spalling or flaking
- scaling similar to contour scaling of sandstone with plate-type detachment
- loss of detail at arrises
- granular disaggregation (granulation), often associated with mortar joints[11]

Spalling typically occurs along the mortar joint and was identified in research in conjunction with a **loss of detail at the arrises**. In these cases, the growth of gypsum salt crystals along the joints leads to deterioration resulting from pressure in micro-crevices between the mineral grains in the granite. Corrosion in past installations of metal anchors also causes local surface spalling or splitting as iron oxide expands to a larger size than the original metal. Local spalled areas are usually not detrimental to the overall building fabric provided the contours are not of a profile that can lead to accumulation of soot and calcium and the growth of gypsum salts.

Scaling is identified by the detachment of thin surface sheets of stone and is much less common in granite than in more porous stones such as sandstone and limestone, although scaling on granite buildings was reported in locations that include Scotland, Hungary, India, Ireland, Portugal and Spain. Research in Rio de Janeiro, Brazil, has found that scaling does not appear to be due to chemical interactions between minerals in the granite and pollutants, but rather to the trapping of chemicals that can form expansive gypsum salts in pre-existing micro-fractures in the granite and propagate along inter- and intra-granular fractures, particularly in mica grains, to cause the scaling.[12] It appears that susceptibility to scaling is probably more common in coarse-grained granites with a distinct orientation of the grains, which may explain the minimal occurrence in areas where the local granite is relatively fine-grained and homogeneous, such as the Quincy and Chelmsford granites that are prevalent in Boston.

Disaggregation is a surface crumbling, quite often identified by a 'sandy' texture (Figure 2.13). Research appears to have conclusively connected

Figure 2.13 Granular disaggregation below lower horizontal joint in rusticated granite, Castle Street, Penzance, Cornwall.

most granular disaggregation in granite with the exploitation of micro-fractures between minerals and within the mica (where present) at the surface of the granite. Research in Aberdeen by Urquart and others has noted an association between granular disaggregation along mortar joints and chemical analysis that shows a high concentration of gypsum salts in the mortar along these joints.[13] There are also indications that grit blast cleaning methods will cause micro-fracturing of the granite, making it more susceptible to disaggregation-type decay.[14]

The processes causing granular disaggregation, spalling and loss of detail at arrises are quite similar, and when occurring along mortar joints the terms can almost be used interchangeably. To differentiate, the following general distinctions can be made:

- Granular disaggregation will typically progress to a stage where the surface of the decayed stone develops a sandy, friable texture.
- Spalling describes local conditions of surface fracture where the remaining stone has the typical hard non-porous granite consistency.
- Loss of detail at the arrises will typically extend along a linear edge of the granite unit, either at a carved edge or along a mortar joint.

Conservation techniques

The two primary areas in granite conservation are the repair of individual stone elements and the repair of overall wall systems. Owing to the stone's durability, the majority of repair work involves attention to mortar joints on masonry walls.

The composition of mortars recommended for conservation work on historic granite buildings typically includes cement in equal portions with lime to provide a denser, less permeable mortar than would be used with brick, limestone or sandstone.[15] Such mixes are more compatible with the lower porosity and higher strength of granite, while still providing some 'breathability' in the mortar joints. The workmanship of the repointing, as with any masonry, is the key to the success of the performance of the overall wall system. It is important that joints be cleaned of debris prior to repointing to ensure that moisture does not bridge to the interior. The preference for flush or slightly recessed mortar joints in most historic building stones can generally hold for granite. Finely cut ashlars with thin mortar joints are typical of early limestone and sandstone buildings but such construction in granite buildings is 200 years old or less. Older granite construction is rustic rough-cut or random rubble, usually in rural areas not exposed to polluted urban environments for any extended period of time and, in the case of Cornwall, not in an area of severe freeze–thaw conditions. It is thus difficult to judge the relative merits of different mortar joint-tooling techniques.

Where individual stones have been damaged by exposure to harsh urban environments, by physical damage from impact sources, or by faulty or deteriorated joints, roofs and detailing that have allowed moisture to

41

penetrate, the most typical restoration techniques are to replace complete stone units or to replace the face portion of the existing stones, typically to a depth of approximately 100 mm (4 inches). Face replacements of stone should be bonded to the backing stone with non-corrosive anchors and a solid setting of mortar behind the new stone. Since it is such a non-porous and non-permeable stone, there is no need to provide a protective bituminous barrier at the back of the face stone to block migration of moisture or salts from the backing stone, as is advisable in some other stones in certain conditions. Patching mortar repairs, as are used for limestone, are not generally feasible with granite owing to colour-matching difficulties and its non-binding chemical nature.

Finding matches from available sources for replacement materials can be difficult where the original stone, particularly for post-1800 buildings constructed of quarried stone, can have a remarkably uniform consistency that will make a poorly matched stone more visible than in the dressed fieldstone buildings of pre-1800. Frequently original quarries have long closed or the particular area of certain colour and texture has been worked out. The broad range from worldwide sources, though, does provide alternatives that may provide a good match.

The finishing of replacement stones is generally done by traditional hand-tool methods on site. Some finishers, such as Fletcher Granite in Westford, Massachusetts, are able to provide hand-tooled finishes that match existing finishes in the finishing mill based on assessment of the existing buildings. These are worked by a select group of masons trained in the traditional stone mason techniques handed down through a system of apprenticeship that is still maintained, on a limited basis, in areas of the United States with a historic masonry tradition.

Since granite does not typically have the variation of dressed finishes found on historic limestone ashlars, and much of the more finished stone has a documented tradition from 1800 onwards, it is easier to reproduce either the split face or smoother ashlar finishes that are typical of almost all historic granite work using traditional hand tools or comparable power tools. The challenge is in finding comparable stone, especially for split face work, where the appearance of the finish is affected by the natural texture of the stone that is exposed by working with the natural cleavage planes. In some cases, refinement is possible by specification of a bush-hammered finish to an appropriate number of points (two-point through to eight-point or higher), where the lower number of points corresponds to a rougher finish.

One conservation aspect that departs from recommended practice for limestone, sandstone and brick masonry is the cleaning of walls. Like limestone, granite masonry will soil in sheltered areas, but it may also soil in areas exposed to rain, most notably at the mortar joints, where calcium salts react with oxides of sulphur in the air to form gypsum. These gypsum crystals trap soot and bind to the granite by growing in microscopic crevices (usually at the mica grains). Research in Aberdeen appears to indicate that the gypsum salts will cause decay in the granite, particularly along mortar joints, and thus a no-clean approach may be harmful in the long term.[16] These gypsum salts will typically not wash away with just water, and thus a mild acid cleaner is recommended, preferably using a process that limits the contact time between the chemical and the granite. Although granite generally will not absorb chemicals to the extent of some sandstones, it is advisable to limit exposure so that minimal, if any, traces of chemicals are absorbed by the granite. Any chemical methods should always be tested on a small patch of hidden stone to ensure chemical compatibility, as the components of granite, particularly feldspars and micas, can react with certain chemicals. Mechanical methods, such as pressurised water jets, abrasive cleaning and grit blasting, should be avoided on granite as these can cause micro-fractures in the surface resulting in a reduced durability and later contour scaling and flaking, particularly on weathered granites.[17]

Sourcing the material

In the later decades of the twentieth century, granite experienced a revival of use in harsh urban environments as problems with comparable materials, especially concrete and some marbles, heightened an appreciation for its superior durability. Continual advances in cutting and polishing technologies have reduced the relative production costs for granite and allowed granite cladding – the primary market for granite on modern buildings – to be cut to ever thinner panels, resulting in reduced building weight, reduced shipping costs and reduced overall material costs. This has indirectly benefited the building conservation field in that there is a wide range of granite colours and textures being actively quarried around the world. This availability means it is likely that matching material for a conservation project requiring limited quantities can be found among available supplies without the need to reopen dormant quarries – an important consideration for most projects where the amount of required replacement stone is small. Thus Chelmsford granite from Massachusetts, with its light grey colour and fine grain, being similar to Cornish granites used in London, was sourced in the conservation of the Church of St Martin in the Fields.

Further reading

Ashurst, J. and Dimes, F.G., *Stone in Building: Its use and potential today* (The Architectural Press Ltd, London, 1977).

Ashurst, J. and Dimes, F.G. (eds), *Conservation of Building and Decorative Stone, Volume 1* (Butterworth-Heinemann, London, 1990).

Brayley, Arthur W., *History of the Granite Industry of New England* (The National Association of Granite Industries of the United States, Boston, MA, 1913).

Directorate: Mineral Economics, *A Review of the Dimension Stone Industry in South Africa*, (Department of Minerals and Energy, Republic of South Africa, Pretoria, 2002).

Erkkila, B.H., *Hammers on Stone: The history of Cape Ann granite* (TBW Books, Woolwich, ME, 1980).

Hill, P.R. and David, J.C.E., *Practical Stone Masonry* (Donhead Publishing, London, 1995).

Ireson, A.S., *Masonry Conservation and Restoration*, 2nd edn (Attic Books, Builth Wells, Powys, 1993).

Masonry Conservation Research Group, *Causes and Remediation of Deterioration on Granite Building Stone* (Scott Sutherland School, Robert Gordon University, Aberdeen, 2007).

Masonry Conservation Research Group, *Dampness in Granite Buildings in Aberdeen* (Scott Sutherland School, Robert Gordon University, Aberdeen, 2007).

Neill, H.L. and Smith, B.J., 'Background controls on stone decay in polluted environments: preliminary observations from Rio de Janeiro', in B.J. Smith and P.A. Warke (eds), *Processes of Urban Stone Decay* (Donhead Publishing Ltd., London, 1996), pp. 113–24.

Urquart, D.C.M., Young, M. and Cameron, S., *Stonecleaning of Granite Buildings* (Historic Scotland, Edinburgh, 1997).

Urquart, D.C.M., Young, M.E., MacDonald, J., Jones, M.S., and Nicholson, K.A., 'Aberdeen granite buildings: a study of soiling and decay', in B.J. Smith and P.A. Warke (eds), *Processes of Urban Stone Decay* (Donhead Publishing Ltd., London, 1996), pp. 66–77.

Endnotes

1. I am indebted to J. Ashurst and F.G. Dimes (eds), *Conservation of Building and Decorative Stone, Volume 1.* (Butterworth-Heinemann, London, 1990) for much of the technical information in this section.

2. The terms 'acid' and 'basic' refer to the chemistry of the rock and are not indicators of the corrosiveness of the rock.

3. P.R. Hill and J.C.E. David, *Practical Stone Masonry* (Donhead Publishing, London, 1995): 'There were traditional tools, however, critical in the production of softer stones, that were ineffective or unusable for the working of granite. These included the frig bob saws used to cut stone blocks in quarries (e.g. limestone) and the drag and the wooden mallet, all of which were ineffective on granite owing to the hardness of the stone.'

4. D.C.M. Urquart, M.E. Young, J. MacDonald, M.S. Jones and K.A. Nicholson, 'Aberdeen granite buildings: a study of soiling and decay', in B.J. Smith and P.A. Warke (eds), *Processes of Urban Stone Decay* (Donhead Publishing Ltd, London, 1996), p. 76.

5. H.L. Neill and B.J. Smith, 'Background controls on stone decay in polluted environments: preliminary observations from Rio de Janeiro', in Smith and Warke, *Processes of Urban Stone Decay*, p. 121.

6. Masonry Conservation Research Group, 2007. *Dampness in Granite Buildings in Aberdeen.* http://www.rgu.ac.uk/sss/research/page.cfm?pge=33374

7. M. McLean, 'Local granite helps restore landmark'. *Gloucester Daily Times*, 26 July 1977: 748 blocks (2 ft × 3–4 ft) of Rockport granite were supplied to replace original blocks installed in the 1915 tower.

8. D.C.M. Urquart, M. Young and S. Cameron, *Stonecleaning of Granite Buildings* (Historic Scotland, Edinburgh, 1997), p. 6.

9. Urquart, Young and Cameron, *Stone cleaning of Granite Buildings*, p. 13: 'Research has shown that both feldspars and micas can be dissolved and altered to clays by rain water at pH 5. Rainwater in Scotland at present has a pH of about 4.8. The formation of clays and other minerals may lead to micro-cracking due to volume changes on wetting and drying. Once micro-cracks are formed, they will allow the deposition of gypsum which may be the cause of further decay.'

10. Ashurst and Dimes, *Conservation of Building and Decorative Stone*, p. 162.
11. Urquart, *et al.*, 'Aberdeen granite buildings', p. 68.
12. Neill and Smith, 'Background controls on stone decay', p. 117.
13. Urquart, *et al.*, 'Aberdeen granite buildings', p. 76.
14. Urquart, Young and Cameron, *Stonecleaning of Granite Buildings*, p. 17.
15. Ashurst and Dimes, *Conservation of Building and Decorative Stone*, p. 89 [Table 4.1].
16. Urquart, *et al.*, 'Aberdeen granite buildings', p. 76.
17. Urquart, Young and Cameron, *Stonecleaning of Granite Buildings*, pp. 17 and 21.

3 Brickwork

Mike Stock

Perhaps the simplest way of classifying brickwork faults is to divide them into those associated with failures of the bricks themselves or the mortar between them, and those that result from a problem with the structure of the building, leading to cracking or distortion of the fabric. In both cases it is essential that the reason for the failure is fully understood before a repair strategy is decided upon. It is important to remember that in the latter case the observed movement is not the actual failure but the consequence of a building disturbance that may be of far greater significance than the outward symptoms. Repairs to the structure are the domain of the structural engineer, and unless the failure is clearly of a minor nature engineering advice should always be sought. Further reasons for failure are deficiencies in design and failure to maintain.

Material failures

Bricks can fail for several reasons. When bricks were an expensive commodity, or where building was being carried out on a speculative basis, the temptation to use cheap inferior bricks in unseen locations must have been great. Bricks made of poor-quality brickearth or containing harmful impurities and incompletely fired bricks are liable to premature failure. Both bricks and mortar are also vulnerable to the action of frost and the recrystallisation of migrating soluble salts, and joints can fail through progressive disintegration of the bedding or pointing material as a result of natural weathering. Even good-quality brick will fail if used in an inappropriate manner.

The quality of bricks

The quality of a brick is dependent on a number of factors, including the composition of the brickearth, the way in which the material is prepared for moulding and firing, and the degree of burning achieved during firing. A good brickearth contains approximately 60% silica in the form of sand or flint and 20% alumina, which is present in common clay, with lime, soda, magnesia, iron and potash forming the remainder:

- **Silica** produces hardness, durability and resistance to the action of fire, but an excess of the material causes brittleness.
- **Alumina** is responsible for the plasticity of the brickearth in its moist, green, unfired state, but on the application of heat it contracts and warps.
- **Lime** acts chemically during firing, causing improving cohesion and, in small quantities, reducing contraction. An excess of the material results in distortion.
- **Iron** influences the colour of bricks, but if occurring as pyrites the material must be removed before firing as oxidisation during firing will cause local expansion and result in splitting. In modern brick-making, this is achieved with powerful electromagnets prior to moulding.

Very few brickearths can be used without additives to counter the destructive effects of some of their natural constituents or to achieve the preferred ratio of principal elements.

In traditional brick-making the preparation of the brickearth includes weathering, during which the excavated material is heaped up during the winter months and broken up by the action of frost. Any small fragments of limestone, occurring either naturally or present as a modifying element, must be either removed or crushed.

The purpose of firing is to create a component capable of withstanding the effects of frost and capable of supporting the structural loads that may reasonably be imposed upon it. The manner of burning, and the conditions that prevail in either kiln or clamp during this final stage of the manufacture of the brick, will also greatly affect the final colour.

Symptoms of poor materials and poor firing are similar. The most common sign is disintegration of the exposed face, often seen in isolated bricks within an elevation but sometimes affecting large areas of brickwork. Historically, crushed chalk in slurry form was often added to the brickearth to act as a firing flux, and to produce a more coherent pre-fired brick. The inclusion of any uncrushed material that finished up near the surface of the moulded brick resulted in its conversion to quicklime during the firing process. Absorption of moisture, sometimes during the building process, resulted in slaking of this material and bursting of the brick face.

Failures resulting from poor design or neglect

Bricks which may otherwise have performed satisfactorily will sometimes fail if conditions are created within which the material cannot cope. In particular, soft red bricks will fail if a protective cornice or string course deteriorates or is otherwise damaged, allowing saturation of the unprotected elements. Neglect of maintenance of gutters and rainwater goods also leads to local saturation and consequent damage through frost or salt damage. Raising the ground level on one side of a free-standing wall will create conditions where soluble salt migration to the exposed face can lead to spalling. Frost damage is also characterised by extensive spalling

Figure 3.1 Spalling brickwork.

of brickwork, following prolonged saturation. It is a progressive action, and can lead to the complete disintegration of bricks (Figure 3.1). The fault is often exacerbated by the use of strong, dense mortars for repointing in earlier repairs. Such materials not only constrain the brick face, resulting in the local stressing of the arrises of the bricks, but also create a series of horizontal shelves within the brick face. Rainwater percolating down through the open texture of the brick accumulates on these ledges, making the lower arrises vulnerable to localised frost attack. Deterioration of the arris results in a widening of the joint, making repointing difficult from both a practical and a visual point of view (Figure 3.2).

Chemical damage is often characterised by efflorescence appearing on the surface of brickwork. Soluble salts, typically sulphates, are carried through brickwork with migrating moisture under the influence of both osmosis and drying from the exposed surface. These salts may be derived from either the brickearth from which the bricks were made or from contaminated sand used in the manufacture of the mortar. It is also possible for sulphates to be carried by absorbed groundwater, most noticeably where the wall is acting as a retaining wall. Evaporation of this moisture allows the salt to recrystallise. When this occurs superficially the result is surface efflorescence, a visually dramatic but normally benign phenomenon. When recrystallisation occurs within the body of the brickwork, forces created by the formation of the salt crystals can be sufficient to cause surface spalling. Sulphate attack is probably the most common cause of brickwork deterioration. Apart from damage to individual bricks, expansion of whole brickwork panels resulting from sulphate attack on the bonding mortar can lead to the formation of vertical cracks near quoins, lifting of

Figure 3.2 Failure due to dense cement mortar.

brick copings and the oversailing of parapets. An extreme case is often seen in chimney stacks where mortar joints on opposite sides are subject to differing exposure conditions. The south face of such structures dries at a much higher rate than the north, resulting in greater shrinkage on the south side, and a typical curling of the stack is observed towards the south.

Contamination of the surface of brickwork with sea water, either by direct contact or by wind-carried spray, will often cause failure in coastal locations, the culprit in this case being dissolved chlorides.

The use of brick in conjunction with limestone dressings and weathering elements, while visually attractive, can result in surface deterioration caused by the absorption of dissolved calcium salts. Acidic atmospheres will take calcium into solution. The resultant salt – most commonly the sulphate – unless effectively prevented from coming into contact with the brickwork below the soluble stone, is absorbed, resulting in pore-blocking of the otherwise porous brickwork, leaving it vulnerable to the action of frost and sulphate attack.

The traditional use of iron together with brickwork is a further source of problems. Sir Christopher Wren used structural iron in both stone and brick buildings, and in some cases insufficient attention was paid either to surface protection of the embedded iron or to adequate separation from the actions of weathering. During the nineteenth century 'hoop iron' – long flat strips of wrought iron produced initially for barrel hoops – was used extensively to reinforce brickwork, the material being laid in continuous lengths within brick courses with simple hooked connections between individual lengths. In some buildings, for example Charles Fowler's Central Market

Figure 3.3 Jacking of brickwork caused by oxidation of embedded ironwork.

Building in London's Covent Garden (1830), there is a sophisticated secondary iron support system linking the stonework and brickwork of the upper external walls and providing lateral support at the level of the heads of the supporting columns. Iron is often seen embedded directly into brickwork where there are abutting railings, or as part of the support for some attachment to the building such as a finial or a weather vane. Corrosion of the iron resulting from the action of moisture and atmospheric oxygen results in the production of an oxide component which occupies a much greater volume than the original material. The forces generated by this action are great, and are capable of causing very severe disruption of the surrounding brickwork (Figure 3.3).

Mortars

Mortars used in brickwork are susceptible to the same destructive agencies as the bricks themselves. Much research has been carried out into the performance of historic lime mortars,[1] but an understanding of the causes of failure is still far from complete and lime mortar failures in recently repaired or restored structures regularly occur. The disintegration of old lime mortar in old brickwork may result from natural weathering of the exposed face of the bedding material or from loss of material from the core as a result of either poor detailing or failure to maintain.

These 'non-structural' failures require a rigorous process of identification, assessment and evaluation. Where necessary these enquiries should be supplemented by appropriate laboratory examination. Some problems can be easily identified but require further examination. Others, particularly those associated with environmental pollution or deficiencies of the construction materials, may demand a more detailed procedure.

Assessment objectives

Assessment objectives include:

- identification of the provenance of the brick
- determination of the material constituents of the mortar
- careful noting of the nature of the failure
- determination of the degree and any pattern of material degradation
- assessment of the degree of current activity (the failure may be historic)
- assessment of the residual performance capability of the damaged material
- review of options (intervention may accelerate decay)

Site examination will normally involve visual and non-destructive examination, together with the selection of samples, which should be both representative of the failure and highly selective. A detailed record must be taken of the site context of the samples. Photographic recording, both before and after sampling, can be valuable for later off-site assessment. The continuity between site and laboratory examination can be a significant factor in the success of the research. Where possible the tester should be the sampler, as the context of the site samples will influence laboratory procedures. Laboratory examination techniques will include stereo microscopy, optical microscopy of thin sections and infrared spectrometry. There are a number of specialist laboratories that can provide this service.

Once the cause of failure has been determined, it will be possible to programme repairs. These will fall into one or more of the following categories:

- cutting out and replacing whole bricks, either singly or in groups
- removing defective brick faces only, followed by the insertion of brick slips
- cutting back the decayed face of the brick and carrying out 'dentistry' repairs
- repointing

It must be appreciated that unless the cause of the failure is fully understood and appropriate steps taken to respond to that cause, it is unlikely that long-term successful repairs will be achieved. If damaging salts remain in retained material, and water can still reach these salts, it will be only a matter of time before the problem recurs.

Brick removal calls for great care and the use of selected tools that will not damage adjacent retained material. The selection of replacement bricks also requires full consideration. If the original brick is no longer available, it will be necessary to source a replacement of similar size, colour and texture that will perform satisfactorily in use. Brick slips may be an appropriate solution where localised failures have occurred and it is feared that removal of the bricks to their full depth may cause further disturbance of the fabric. Slips must be a minimum of 30 mm thickness, and must be bedded in a mortar similar in character to the bedding mortar. It may be advisable to use bronze or stainless steel pins to improve security. Resin fixing adhesives should not be used as these produce an impermeable layer that may encourage failure at the resin interface.

Localised failures are sometimes repaired using 'plastic' repair techniques. Here the decayed brick is cut back, cleaned, wetted and built up in thin layers. The surface is finished level with the adjacent brickwork, and in more sophisticated systems the texture of the original brick is impressed onto the surface.

The need to repoint must be carefully considered. A great deal of damage is caused, and the character of historic brickwork irretrievably lost, through unnecessary repointing work. Where such work is essential, the original style of pointing should be reproduced wherever possible. Preparation for repointing involves the removal of mortar to an adequate depth and to a square base, followed by the removal of dust and debris and damping of the joint to prevent rapid water loss from the mortar.[2]

Structural failures

Brickwork, particularly when laid in lime mortar, has the capacity to accommodate quite major movements. This is due, no doubt, to the small module of the building element, and the yielding nature of the bonding material. A solidly built wall, if sufficiently thick, will withstand those forces that are tending to provoke failure. It is a sad fact that when brickwork does fail the cause is often the ill-considered adaptation of the original structure. The addition of one or more storeys to an eighteenth-century brick shell, originally built in a manner that allowed the loads to be taken onto a core of rubble or poor-quality brick, will often result in redistribution of loads, signalled by cracking, bulging or local failure of the original brickwork. The formation of new openings, without full consideration of load redistribution or without adequate lintel provision, is also a common source of problems.

Failure to maintain can be equally damaging. Water penetration from choked gutters, broken rainwater goods or neglected jointing can result in saturation of the masonry, with consequent decay of embedded timbers. Local loss of support resulting from this deterioration leads to compression of the core, and thus to distortion and failure of brick arches and the separation of the facing brick skin from the rough core work. When dealing with historic buildings, the architect or surveyor may be presented with any of these problems and quite probably all of them together!

It is imperative that any structural deficiency is identified, assessed and if necessary remedied before any superficial brickwork repairs are undertaken. It is also essential that this assessment is based on full and methodical survey, and that the survey is supplemented by additional evidence. As with the investigation of material failure, it may sometimes be possible for the single cause of the failure to be identified quickly and for a course of action to be decided upon. Other problems will demand a more stringent analysis. The trick is to be able to differentiate between signs of a minor disturbance, which requires either no attention or local repair, and symptoms of more serious problems.

The secondary evidence may take many forms. Where the failure appears to be associated with ground movement, reference to geological maps will often provide vital information and clues may be found in historical research or archaeological investigation. Careful survey of the distortion of the building at or near ground level will indicate whether any cracks emanating from ground level are the result of settlement, subsidence or heave. Where bulging of brickwork is apparent, it is necessary to establish whether this results from 'whole wall' movement or separation of poorly constructed masonry. Such information can be obtained from a combination of plumb surveys and close examination of the condition of the wall core, either by the careful removal of individual bricks or by the use of an endoscope.

Having determined the cause of the structural movement and executed any necessary stabilisation work, there will be a number of options depending on the severity of the structural disturbance.

Do nothing

Where the cause of the structural disturbance has been identified and remedied, or where movement is known to have ceased, there may be no need for any immediate action.

Monitor movement

Where investigation is unable to show whether movement has been arrested or is of a historic nature (i.e. is of long standing), the monitoring of movement can be vital in the diagnosis of faults and can help to avoid unnecessary or inappropriate structural intervention. Cracks may be monitored by the use of either a demountable strain gauge (the Demec gauge) or a good vernier gauge. In the first instance 6 mm stainless steel discs with a small central depression are glued to the structure to receive the conical points of the gauge. Where a vernier gauge is used it is necessary to install small non-ferrous location pins. In both cases the recording points are installed in a set pattern across the crack and regular readings taken and carefully recorded. Traditionally, cracks were monitored by the installation of glass telltales cemented over the crack. The system is capable of providing only crude, non-quantitative information, and the telltales are susceptible to vandal damage and frost. They are also prone to becoming detached at one end and thus suggesting by their intactness that no movement is occurring.

Changes to the 'out of plumb' condition of a structure can be measured and monitored by the use of an 'autoplumb', a theodolite or an inclinometer. Where the structure is small-scale and where separation of masonry is suspected, the traditional plumb bob will be of use.

Rake out and repoint

If the structural disturbance has ceased or has been arrested by stabilisation but has resulted in cracks in the bedding material that will allow water entry into the building, the mortar should be carefully raked out and the joint refilled. Mortar with similar characteristics to the existing must be used. Cracks that are shown to fluctuate as a result of seasonal movement may in some instances be repaired using an oil-based mastic that will better accommodate this movement.

Cut out and rebuild

If fine cracks are noted in dense, non-porous brickwork or if wide cracks have occurred, it may be necessary to cut out and rebuild locally in the region of the fault. While not necessarily injurious to the masonry, large quantities of rainwater are drawn into fine cracks with the attendant risk of decay of embedded timbers or damage to interiors. There will be occasions when there is no option but to take down and rebuild substantial areas of the brickwork, but this should only be done in extreme cases.

Use grouting and remedial fixings

Grouting is useful in the repair of cracks in very thick walls or where separation of the facing work has occurred. In either case great care must be taken to ensure that pressures exerted by the grout will not 'burst' the wall. Grouting is used to replace lime mortar that has been washed out by the percolation of rainwater through coping neglect, a problem most commonly associated with freestanding walls. The deterioration of the wall is often, though not always, indicated by cracking of the brick face and bulging. The process requires the utmost care during the period of investigation and assessment, which is likely to involve internal examination of the brickwork or ultra-sonic methods. The full solution is also likely to involve the introduction of a system of through ties to secure the two facing skins from further separation, and these should be installed before the grouting operation begins. Pressure systems are not normally appropriate for such work, and grouting materials should be introduced in controlled lifts by gravity methods.

Conclusion

Properly burnt bricks made from sound materials, laid in appropriate mortar, on adequate foundations, following sound design principles, adequately maintained and not subject to aggressive environmental conditions will last almost indefinitely.[3] These ideal conditions rarely prevail, however, and brickwork will fail. Repair, whether comprising local repointing or major rebuilding or reinforcement following rectification of some structural inadequacy, should only be undertaken following a rigorous investigation of the cause of the failure. A successful, durable repair will be achieved only if repair materials are carefully selected for compatibility and the work carried out in a manner that will result in the minimum loss of historic fabric.

Endnotes

1. The Smeaton Project, an English Heritage Study carried out in collaboration with ICCROM and Bournemouth University, researched the factors affecting the performance of lime-based mortars.
2. See English Heritage's pamphlet *The Pointing of Brickwork* for practical advice on repointing.
3. The use of brick in England probably pre-dates the period of the Roman occupation but expanded greatly during that period. Roman brick was salvaged and reused in many post-twelfth-century churches, where it continues to perform well.

4 Lime-based plasters, renders and washes

Rory Young

Lime mortars are among the oldest man-made products. Traces of lime jointing and coatings are to be found on most archaeological sites and in most standing buildings constructed before the twentieth century (Figure 4.1). Many a visitor might recognise the skilful working of stone, but would they contemplate the equal human endeavour and sophistication of technique that went into the preparation of lime and associated materials for the construction, protection and decoration of the structures of the past? The idea of mortars and plasters rarely catches the imagination and therefore they are mostly ignored in the new universal appreciation of the stones that they were designed to hold together, protect and beautify. No wonder so much knowledge about their function, variety and inherent beauty has been lost, especially since Portland cement has been substituted for lime and has in effect become the vernacular binding material for buildings almost worldwide – and in only four or five generations. The unglamorous reputation that traditional mortars and plasters have of obscuring the stones we value has been further eroded by the growing awareness that the cement substitutes are functionally detrimental and aesthetically displeasing on old, and new, buildings.

What is lime?

The production process

Lime is the product of burning calcium-based rocks (limestones and chalks) of variable purity, and also seashells and corals, in a kiln. In the process of calcining, calcium carbonate (the raw stone) dissociates into quicklime (or lump lime) and carbon dioxide. The optimum temperature for conversion is just under 900°C. Each lump retains its shape after the burning but feels noticeably lighter in the hand (Figure 4.2).

Calcium oxide is very unstable and difficult to store; the term quicklime suggests 'liveliness'. Therefore it is slaked in water. This is known as 'hydration', forming lime hydrate. It can be slaked in gross excess of water to form lime putty, or air-slaked in a damp atmosphere (in covered pits).

Figure 4.1 Doughton Manor, Tetbury, Gloucestershire: silvery-coloured seventeenth-century roughcast.

Alternatively, it can be slaked within a heap of dampened aggregate as a 'hot mix'. Different countries and districts have different traditions.

The quicklime slakes to form calcium hydroxide, and great heat is generated as it expands and boils. This exothermic reaction can be very dangerous, and lime in the eyes can cause blindness. Health and safety advice is given below. Quicklime is most reactive when the purest limestone is used (containing very little clay), when it is fired at the optimum temperature, and when it is slaked straight out of the kiln. Pure limes known as high-calcium limes are derived from carboniferous or 'mountain' limestones and make the fine-textured, fatty white putty traditionally sought by plasterers.

Hydrated lime

There is often confusion between the commonly heard terms 'hydrated' and 'hydraulic' limes. Hydration of quicklime can follow two basic routes.

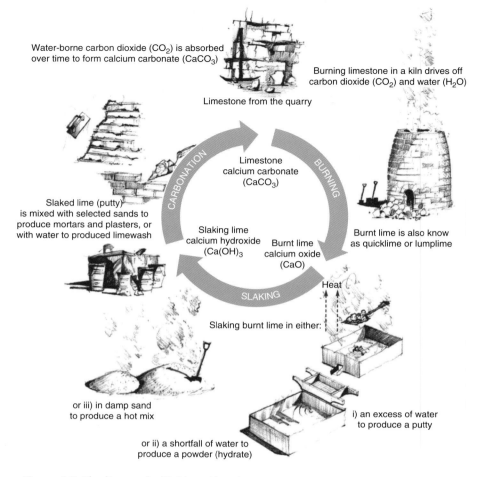

Water-borne carbon dioxide (CO$_2$) is absorbed
over time to form calcium carbonate (CaCO$_3$)

Burning limestone in a kiln drives off
carbon dioxide (CO$_2$) and water (H$_2$O)

Limestone from the quarry

CARBONATION

BURNING

Limestone
calcium carbonate
(CaCO$_3$)

Slaked lime (putty)
is mixed with selected sands to
produce mortars and plasters, or
with water to produced limewash

Slaking lime
calcium hydroxide
(Ca(OH)$_3$)

Burnt lime
calcium oxide
(CaO)

Burnt lime is also know
as quicklime or lumplime

SLAKING

Heat

Slaking burnt lime in either:

or iii) in damp sand
to produce a hot mix

i) an excess of water
to produce a putty

or ii) a shortfall of water to
produce a powder (hydrate)

Figure 4.2 The lime cycle (Ty-Mawr Limes).

Currently most lime produced industrially is slaked with a precisely calculated amount of water, the excess being given off in the reaction to form a dry powder. This dry hydrate, known as 'bag lime', is conveniently packaged as a bulk powder and sold by most builders' merchants. The main disadvantage is that some hard burnt quicklime remains unslaked when bagged up, and this would subsequently cause failure of top coat plaster. Another disadvantage is that the powder can carbonate in the bag – that is, it can combine with carbon dioxide and become 'stale'. (Although carbonated dry hydrate may lose some efficacy, it will still act as a superfine 'porous particulate' addition in a mortar mix.) Bag lime should be used as fresh as possible and should never be used straight from the bag. It should be allowed to soak in water for several days before use to improve its performance and plasticity. In recent times bag lime has been used on site as a plasticiser or extender in cement mixes, to make 'compo'. On its own it might make an acceptable mortar for ordinary interior work, but it is unsatisfactory for limewash.

Lime putty is wet hydrate. Both forms are chemically the same: calcium hydroxide. However, many lime workers recognise that there is a significant difference in handling and performance between putty and bag lime. Putty is considered superior because of its greater stickiness, more readily coating the aggregate in a mix. In solution the hydrate becomes a thixotropic gel. There is a significant liaison at molecular level between the calcium hydroxide and water; the particles break down progressively (to be much finer than those of bag lime) and are held in suspension. This is proof that the inherent quality of putty improves with ageing. The Romans imposed legislation on the building trade about the maturing of lime putty. Much lime putty is still home produced, but a growing number of companies are selling putty at competitive prices in 1 tonne tote bags or in plastic kegs.

Hydrated lime is also known as **non-hydraulic lime** because of its inability to set under water. As well as being termed **pure**, **fat** or **high-calcium lime**, it is also referred to as **air**, or **air-setting**, **lime** because it relies on exposure to CO_2 in the air to carbonate.

This process of 'induration' can only happen above 5°C and at a critical moisture level in the mortar mix – that is, after the majority of the construction moisture has evaporated but while there is residual moisture present. This is because the chemical reaction is between CO_2 in solution, as carbonic acid, and the $Ca(OH)_2$. Saturation only delays induration, but rapid drying at the outset is deleterious to the process. Carbonation can only occur at the surface of new work and travels gradually inwards, setting the mortar incrementally. It follows that the work gains structural competence slowly, often over many years, accommodating settlement meanwhile. In favourable conditions mortar might carbonate 5 mm every month. This phenomenon is the root cause of the perception that non-hydraulic lime is impractical for use in building conservation, but we should remember the old Scots observation:

> When a hundred years are past and gane, then a gude mortar turns tae stane.

Although it cannot be used in all positions in a building – for instance, in the foundations[1] – non-hydraulic lime is the most appropriate lime for the conservation of old buildings as it is the most permeable of all the building limes and also the most workable, and it can be kept under cover for further use (a hydraulic mix 'goes off' overnight).

Hydraulic limes

Hydraulic limes are produced by kilning limestones that contain clay: the more clay, the stronger the resultant hydraulic lime mortar. When burnt, the clay compounds become reactive. The most significant of these compounds are silicates, but there are also aluminates, and sometimes iron oxides. Some of the available lime (calcium hydroxide) will combine with them to form calcium carbonate, calcium aluminates and so on, rather than forming calcium silicate. The degree of burning temperature together with

59

the amount of clay in the stone will influence the strength of the resultant mortar.

Hydraulic limes are so called because of their ability to achieve a firm set, independent of any carbonation, throughout the whole mass of the mortar; they will set in damp conditions, and some will even set under water. This property makes them very useful in marine works – they were known as 'water limes' in the eighteenth century.

This family of 'impure' limes covers a wide spectrum of hardnesses and other properties and makes the link between the soft, slow-setting, pure non-hydraulic limes and the range of natural cements, which contain an even greater proportion of reactive compounds.

They have different physical characteristics from non-hydraulic limes. For instance, they are off-white, grey or buff-coloured. They are not as workable – being 'short' as opposed to fat – and correspondingly they shrink less. Mortars made from them have lower water vapour permeability and porosity, higher compressive strength and greater resistance to salt crystallisation. They have greater flexural strength, and are more suitable for building concrete block walls which have a small bedding area relative to their height. All these characteristics correspond to their degree of hydraulicity. As with non-hydraulic limes, they are all subject to frost damage owing to the fact that they contain a naturally occurring substantial proportion of non-hydraulic or 'free' lime. Thus while they may have an initial set, they will continue to harden over some years. Again, the amount of free lime corresponds to their degree of hydraulicity.

Hydraulic limes are almost always obtained as a dry hydrate. This synchronises with the present 'cement culture' in which people are accustomed to using powder from a bag on site. Even the strongest hydraulic lime shares the beneficial characteristics of the family of limes and is always preferable to cement mixes.

Hydraulic limes can be grouped into three loose categories on the basis of their setting times, although these can vary greatly with temperature, as they can for non-hydraulic lime (Table 4.1).

These three categories relate very approximately to the categorisation of compressive strengths of **natural hydraulic lime** (NHL), which is guaranteed not to contain any additives and is made by burning limestone 'as dug':

NHL-2: 2–7 newtons per mm^2 crushing strength after 28 days
NHL-3.5: 3.5–10 newtons per mm^2 crushing strength after 28 days
NHL-5: 5–15 newtons per mm^2 crushing strength after 28 days

In use, hydraulic limes have in effect bridged the gulf between soft limes and Portland cement. Because of the range of limes now available, we have

Table 4.1 Setting times for hydraulic limes.

Feebly hydraulic	Setting in 15 to 21 days	<12% reactive silicates and aluminates
Moderately hydraulic	Setting in 5 to 15 days	12 to 18% reactive silicates and aluminates
Eminently hydraulic	Setting in 1 to 4 days	18 to 25% reactive silicates and aluminates

reached a point where the use of Portland cement is no longer necessary or justifiable in the repair of historic buildings.

Hybrid mixes

'Hybrid' mixes involving the use of both non-hydraulic and hydraulic limes are now being specified and used, and have been evolving since the re-introduction of hydraulic limes in the last decade of the twentieth century. The idea of blending the two types of lime stems from the desire to move away from Portland cement-gauged mixes, and also from the pragmatism of making lime work successfully in most situations. We have experienced the limits to which the use of putty limes can be pushed, and would now like to make lime mortars that are as versatile, reliable and robust as possible.

The mixes would seem to profit from plasticity and 'breathability' – benefits of putty lime – and also from the more immediate performance and ultimately greater strength of hydraulic limes. There is a desire to create 'complex lime mortars' more akin to historic examples. There have been many successes in using these mixes at lime centres, and many lime practitioners use them routinely. Blends of, for instance, 1 NHL-5 hydraulic lime : 1 lime putty, or 10% of the volume of NHL-3 hydraulic lime comprising lime putty, are commonly used.

Because of some instances of failure, English Heritage has had reservations about the use of hybrid mortars and has not grant-aided such work since around 2000. One anxiety is that there is no historic precedent in the UK for hybrid mortars and we know little about their behaviour; monitoring and more research are necessary.

Pozzolanic additives

The term 'pozzolanic' is derived from Pozzuoli (Puteoli in Roman times), on the Neapolitan coastline near Vesuvius, where deposits of volcanic aggregate were extracted by the Romans for use in their mortars and concretes. Like other pozzolans (see below), this material contains reactive clay compounds. These react progressively with non-hydraulic lime to produce a chemical set, independent of carbonation, which occurs in due course. Pozzolans are reactive in dust form. Any particle over 70 microns functions as an aggregate in a mortar. By adding reactive materials, one is creating an artificial hydraulic lime mortar with properties similar to those of mortars bound with natural hydraulic lime. All pozzalans are carcinogenic if inhaled: use respiratory protection. Pozzolans are as follows:

- crushed low-fired brick or tile; from coarse to fine, from pink to yellow
- Metastar – a fine white ceramic powder from English china clay, a reliable quality-controlled product, specially designed as a pozzolan; used as 15 to 20% of the lime portion of a mix

- HTI – high-temperature insulation – ground fired china clay
- PFA – pulverised fly ash – can contain sulphates, and is a dark grey colour; may be used for internal grouting
- Rhenish trass – a khaki-coloured powder
- volcanic dust, including pumice

Why use lime?

The use of Portland cement instead of lime as the binder for building mortars, renders and plasters in the repair of historic buildings had become commonplace after nearly a century. However, it is clear that this change brought with it disadvantages – in some cases leading to irreparable damage to the very structures that it was intended should be preserved.

Many still use the so-called 'conservation mix' of 1 cement : 1 lime : 6 sand for historic building repair; but this mix is still acting like a cement mortar with lime added to improve its plasticity during application. Even a mix of 1 cement : 2 lime : 9 sand still has properties which make it unsuitable for most conservation work. During the late 1970s and the 1980s, many involved in conservation realised that the presence of any cement in mortars used to repair delicate fabric is potentially harmful.

Cement has little or no place in work on our important and valuable historic structures. We should concentrate upon the proper and effective use of lime-based materials and should develop lime mixes and working procedures. The relearning process will be confused and delayed if cement continues to be used as an additive to accelerate the initial setting and as a general safeguard against poor site practice. For many centuries our ancestors worldwide had little else but lime (with natural additives) to use as their binder in mortars, plasters and washes, and much survives as a result, as explained below.

Choice of mortars and plasters

The choice of mortars and plasters is important in relation to the following three governing factors in the performance of historic fabric: **porosity**, **flexibility** and **strength**.

Porosity

All buildings are easily penetrated by damp from rain, especially those unprotected by a roof. Also, all traditionally built structures are affected by rising damp from groundwater. An equilibrium is maintained in traditionally formed structures because there is a successful relationship between their hard and soft elements; they are complementary. Rain falling on their generally porous surfaces, which may or may not contain cracks, will tend to be evenly absorbed into the body of the wall.

Concentrations of moisture will be diffused by this general absorbency. There will be stress points where severe ingress of moisture into the core might occur, but the porosity of the lime and of most building stones allows the dampness to evaporate freely. In this way, the structure survives the effects of wetting and drying cycles for centuries.

A structure that has been repaired or partially rebuilt using impervious materials will behave differently. Settlement or shrinkage cracks that occur in an area of dense cement-based repointing or rebuilding now pose a threat to the well-being of the structure. Rain falling on exposed impervious areas will concentrate on the surface, and will then be siphoned off by gravity and capillary action through the cracks into the core of the structure. The accumulated moisture will be prevented from re-emerging as evaporation from the surface.

When the structure becomes saturated, soluble salts present within its core will dissolve and be mobilised. Impervious areas of repointing or rebuilding will prevent this solution from emerging to the surface, resulting in a greater-than-normal concentration of salts at the surface of adjacent original fabric which is still porous. These salts will crystallise on drying out by evaporation at the surface and will cause damage.

The individual grains of the various components are also significant, whether they are hard or soft. Old fabric, which may already be in a fragile condition, is thus further damaged. The imposition of inappropriately dense materials upon an old structure will cause this familiar pattern of chronic decay to become acute.

Flexibility

Most older structures do not have monolithic foundations and so are liable to occasional or continual settlement, particularly if their foundations are not placed directly on bedrock. Therefore the binding element must be flexible, to permit relative settlement. Also, it must permit the movements of expansion and contraction due to temperature changes in the various elements. Cement-based mortars and plasters are often brittle and therefore liable to fracturing. As we have seen, cracks of any size are particularly dangerous to structures bound with cement.

Strength

It has now been realised that hardness cannot be equated with durability. In fact, the converse appears to be true in the context of mortars and plasters, especially in older structures. It will be noted that traditional lime-bound structures have often survived for centuries (moreover, frequently with very little maintenance), whereas cement-bound structures develop some of the problems already discussed over periods of less than a quarter of a century. Cement mortars and plasters are often too hard, and adhere too tightly to the various harder elements in a structure, resulting in an overall rigidity. The joints are unable to accommodate any movement within the structure and so the harder components that we are aiming to preserve will be subjected to mechanical stress, resulting in fractures. Destruction of existing stone, brick and mortar can occur if joints are pointed or areas rebuilt with a dense cement mortar. This is because there are differences between the porosity, the specific heat, the thermal conductivity and the coefficient of thermal expansion of the various materials.

Some advantages of cement

- It is relatively cheap.
- It is widely available.
- It is easy and convenient to use, in most weathers and most seasons.
- It is strong: it hardens rapidly and adheres tightly. Therefore large volumes of masonry can be built quickly and the resulting structure will be loadbearing and rigid in a day or so. It becomes frost-resistant far sooner than lime.

Some disadvantages of lime

- It is less easily obtained. As it is not yet commonplace, costs for transport of lime may be high.
- It is more labour-intensive to prepare, to handle and to use.
- It requires different skills and more care, and thus education and a change of attitude.
- It does not *appear* to be as strong, especially at the outset. It does not harden as quickly as cement and it often does not reach the strength of cement.

It is for these reasons that the use of cement became so widespread, to the virtual exclusion of lime as a building agent. Lime was perceived as an old-fashioned and inferior material.

Older structures, even if built with harder elements such as brick and stone, were bound together and covered with a binding element – usually lime-based – which was relatively porous, flexible and weak. These qualities of the binding element are significant to the long-term survival of any masonry structure.

Some advantages of lime:

- It is very workable, ideal for bedding and coating, and is a pleasure to use.
- It allows longer working time. All non-hydraulic lime-based materials have an indefinite shelf life if kept out of the air.
- It reduces wastage on site.
- Its various applications are interchangeable because of its slow set and adaptability.

- It is durable if successfully applied; however, it is also infinitely repairable.
- It allows healthy buildings with evaporative surfaces and a maintained equilibrium of moisture content in the fabric, reducing timber decay and the need for chemical treatment, i.e. damp-proofing.
- It allows healthy living, reducing condensation that causes mould growth and asthma. It is a disinfectant, reducing disease and pests, e.g. woodworm.
- It is aesthetically pleasing, reflecting light beautifully, with a subtle warm, soft, mellow and inviting appearance.
- It has beneficial thermal and acoustic properties.
- It is a fire retardant, protecting structural timber.
- It is the ideal art medium. It can be used to model sculpture or ornament by hand or by mould and cast for 3D and relief decorations; alternatively, it can provide the substrate for fresco painting or the medium for painting in coloured limewash.
- It is environmentally friendly for all the above reasons, being sustainable, reversible and compatible with traditional buildings. Lime production causes 20% less CO_2 emissions than cement production.

The basic ideals of conservation can be achieved by adopting the use of lime:

- It is desirable to repair sympathetically by using materials very similar to or at least compatible with those used in the original structure.
- Whatever the composition of a mortar or a plaster used for repairs, it should be a degree weaker than the material to which it is applied.
- A repair should have maximum beneficial effect upon a structure while causing minimum intervention to its original fabric.
- All repairs to historic structures should be reversible; they should not cause damage to important fabric if they have to be removed.
- All repair materials should be designed to have the capacity to disintegrate and fall away without causing damage to important fabric during any subsequent actions of weathering on, and settlement within, a historic structure.

Such a repair material could be described as 'beneficially sacrificial'. Lime tends to gradually wear away – becoming beautifully 'threadbare' – as it performs its intended function to the end. On the other hand, cement and other modern impervious coatings tend to fail dramatically – becoming tawdry and unsightly.

How to use lime

Health and safety

Before starting to use lime, it should be understood that it is a caustic alkaline material, which like Portland cement can damage the skin or eyes if used carelessly. The more dexterous the user, the less risk there is of accident. Here are a few simple precautions:

- Wear eye protection when close to slaking quicklime, when applying roughcast or limewash and when decanting and pouring lime materials – in effect, any activities that might cause splashing.
- Wear a mask to avoid breathing in the dust associated with the handling of quicklime: it slakes in your throat and lungs!
- When slaking, wear protective clothing, and gloves and/or barrier cream when handling solutions of lime. Avoid getting moisture/lime/ sand *inside* your glove!

First aid treatment should be readily available. Any lime materials in the eye should be removed at once. Irrigate, but not with cold water – this chills the eye. Bathe in lukewarm saline solution (1 teaspoon salt : 1 pint water) or a proprietary eyewash. Then, if irritation persists, seek medical attention.

Planning a project

Careful judgement is needed at all stages, especially at the outset of the repair process, as to how much decayed fabric is to be removed. The greater the intervention, the greater the loss of authenticity and the greater the cost of the work – but the longer-lasting the repair will be. Workmanship must always be competent, conscientious, neat and conforming to the quality of the 'old work'. One must aim to do the best for the building within any campaign of repair work, however short.

Although on large-scale repair projects today there is often an impressive input at an early stage – project management, conservation philosophy, archaeological recording, scientific analysis and advice on health and safety – the quality of the craftsmanship can sometimes be disappointing. More funding, time and thought could have been given to the actual repair work on the fabric. The importance of highly motivated, skilled and careful operators should never be overlooked. Likewise, it should never be taken for granted that all those who handle old fabric will pay it the respect it deserves.

Take into consideration the following aspects of planning a project:

Documentation, recording and assessment of the fabric's cultural significance

Study the 'old work'; discern which mortar or plaster is original to the building and the chronology of subsequent repairs, both at the outset and as the works progress.

Sampling and mortar analysis

Be aware of the expense, limitations and impracticalities of too much scientific input, although some might be very useful. It is pointless, and virtually impossible, to copy a historic mortar exactly. It is more useful, and quicker, to design a replacement mortar that will perform its intended function as a repair material. Compatibility of texture and colour can be achieved empirically.

In order to match a mortar, follow this procedure for simple mortar analysis:

- Remove a piece of mortar from the wall to be repaired.
- Examine the sample using a ×10 lens, noting texture, colour of the matrix and whether there are lumps of lime (indicating a 'hot mix'), ash, coal, charcoal, brick, etc.
- Lightly crush the dry sample to a powder.
- Add water to it in a jam jar; stir and shake thoroughly.
- Allow it to stand for a day, or until the water has cleared.
- Measure and calculate the proportions.
- Assess aggregate sizes and colours.

Planning the detailing

Discern what is original and/or correct, and follow it. For instance, mortars and plasters traditionally abut flush with, or die away onto, freestone quoins, producing seamless surfaces (at once medieval, classical and vernacular). This minimises their surface area, enabling them to withstand weathering. Likewise, traditionally limewash was usually taken across plaster and freestone detailing alike, unifying the elevations.

If Ordinary Portland Cement (OPC) has to be used to perform structural functions, try to contain these repairs in specific zones within the fabric and allow for lime-based materials to surround and/or cover them.

Procurement of materials: limes

We have seen that there are many types of lime – historically, there was a huge diversity – and there are also different ways of preparing mortars on and off site. Different sources of lime are now being explored, in search of variety and character. To effect the best repairs, one should use a palette of limes and mortar mixes and decide which to use when and where at the outset of a repair project. Several mixes might be used on the same elevation, for instance using the two types of lime, with and without pozzolans and at different strengths, with a range of aggregates. Listen to any advice given by mortar suppliers.

One must always be aware of the limitations of lime: fewer liberties can be taken with lime than with cement. Check that lime putty is matured for as long as possible: for example, a minimum of six months for plastering mixes. Likewise ready-mixed mortars, whether 'hot mixes' or of putty/sand, should be allowed to mature for as long as possible to eliminate the risk of as yet unslaked, over-burnt particles of quicklime slaking in situ and 'pitting and popping', disrupting the finished plaster surface.

Procurement of materials: aggregates

Check the source and availability of aggregates, whether for use in ready-mixed or site-mixed mortar, well in advance of the work starting on site. The output of most quarries can change every few months. The choice of correct aggregate is crucial to the success of all lime mortars. Points to check when looking at and feeling aggregates are as follows.

Particle size

Choose a well-graded – 'continuous graded' – sand which contains a wide range of particle sizes so that it locks together as the mortar dries, avoiding shrinkage. Many current sources (conforming to British Standards) are badly graded – that is, 'even graded', and suitable only for a cement binder. It may be necessary to blend different sources of sand. The finer the range of aggregates, the more lime will be needed to coat all the particles. As a general rule, sands <3 mm make adequate mortars at 1 lime : 3 sand whereas <2 mm will work best at 1 : 2.

Particle shape

Choose a 'sharp' sand with angular particles. 'Soft' round-grained sand can be incorporated, to occupy some space between the larger sharp grains, but too much soft sand in the blend will cause shrinkage in the mortar. Corals and crushed seashells make even better sharp aggregate than crushed limestones (see below) and crushed terra cotta.

Particle colour

Remember that the opacity of limes – in particular putty lime, which is powerfully white – will lighten the sand colour in the mortar: for instance, a warm dark red may be lightened up to a pale rose pink, particularly in lime-rich mixes. By adding a strong yellow sand, a mortar colour can be warmed up. Charcoal, coal dust and powder pigments can be added, although there is a risk of the latter fading or migrating within the set mortar.

Particle geology

Quartz and silica sands act purely structurally, although some sands are mildly pozzolanic, being broken-down volcanic rocks. However, crushed limestones act in three ways that are all advantageous for lime mortars:

- as continuous-graded sharp particles, with considerable dust acting as an 'extender' to the lime binder

- in accelerating carbonation by seeding $CaCO_3$ crystal growth on its physically similar (freshly) broken surfaces, a process termed 'impfing'
- as a 'porous particulate', accelerating carbonation by being permeable to carbonic acid; CO_2 can pass through the binder *and* the aggregate to reach more $Ca(OH)_2$ deeper in the mortar, more quickly

Crushed chalk or limestone mortars were ubiquitous in many districts until sand/gravel extraction and bulk road transport, and made very sticky, supple mortars and plasters. One disadvantage is their tendency to shrink, necessitating extra consolidation.

Particle cleanliness

Avoid sea-dredged sand because of the salt content – deleterious to the life of all mortars – and avoid all organic matter (earth etc.) For much high-quality work and for fine top coat plasters it is customary to use clean washed sand. However, it is apparent that many successful mortars contain a high proportion of silts and even loams, giving the advantages described under '**particle geology**' above. Some mortar suppliers are now making excellent mixes to match those found in most vernacular and pre-eighteenth-century structures.

Choosing the right contractor

Invest in contractors who have sound knowledge of the use of lime-based, cement-free materials. Those who have recently discovered lime may lack experience, but if they are motivated, thoughtful and committed and careful, they will learn quickly and have success.

Ensure that all prospective tenderers understand what is required of them. Look at their previous work to assess their standards. Check that all parties share the same priorities.

Training

If first-hand experience is lacking, go with your contractors on a 'Lime Day'; these are organised by various lime centres and organisations such as the Society for the Protection of Ancient Buildings (SPAB). There is no substitute for live demonstrations and hands-on experience. A few hours' practical insight is worth more than any amount of reading; however, theory can then inform practice.

Specifying

The more one trusts a contractor and his capabilities, the less needs to be specified; but never simply issue standard specifications. Each job, however 'regular' it seems at first sight, will be different from the last. Judge each building, and each part of each building, on its own merits. In general be cautious, be specific, and give more information rather than less. Aim to do as little as possible as well as possible. This means striking a balance between having respect for all historic fabric – the 'conserve as found' approach – and adhering to sound traditional building practice and thorough workmanship. Always keep an open mind and be ready to adapt a specification to any discoveries and/or changing conditions, on site.

Seasonal timing

Generally it is not advisable to use lime for exterior works running up to and during the months in which there is a risk of frost. Ideally lime work should cease at the end of September and recommence in March. However, if there is no alternative, work can go ahead under an enclosed scaffolding with means of keeping the temperature of the work above freezing. Extra budget will be required for these precautions.

If the repairs are thin and kept on the surface (i.e. are not deep interventions containing a lot of construction moisture, and therefore uncarbonated mortar), and if the autumn has been dry, there will be less frost risk. Even better, if the repaired building is occupied and heated, the thermal mass of the external walls will stay above freezing in the worst conditions, and this relative warmth will help deep repairs to dry out.

The most risky situation might be a roofless ruin filled with wet uncarbonated mortar which is then saturated by rain and at the mercy of the first bout of frost. A building of this kind might be at risk for several years until the wall has a drying potential such that enough carbonation has occurred for the mortar to become structurally competent. Frost failures are demoralising and costly, and should be prevented.

Public relations

It is worth considering the potential impact on the local community of any proposed works on a salient elevation, such as in a market place or on a church or other local landmark. Alarm, disbelief and even aggressive behaviour can be aroused by a change of appearance, especially from what is often perceived as tasteful 'mellowed grey old stones' to 'garish paint' or 'pale ugly pointing daubed over our stones' or 'a layer of plaster covering up our lovely wall'. Public funding and much research, experience and thought informing some excellent workmanship might be ridiculed by adverse public opinion (as, for instance, when Stirling Castle's great hall was re-harled and replastered). These situations can be avoided, or opinion at least mollified, by diplomacy, dissemination of information and a willingness to explain – perhaps meeting the church congregation, the Civic Society or the Chamber of Commerce and displaying on-site information about the work in hand. If the intentions are sound and the work well done, people will be carried by your vision and the courage of your convictions.

Best site practice

Constant vigilance on site and attention to detail at all stages of a project are essential for successful results with lime. The rate of wear – the performance – greatly depends on the workmanship in preparation and application.

Preparation of substrate

Repairing an ancient wall is similar to dentistry: decay is identified; cavities are opened up and cleaned out, in readiness for filling. Wall surfaces must be clear of all growth and other organic matter, loose material, dust and dirt, in order to achieve a good bond between the lime application and its substrate. If a fungicide is considered for lichen and algae removal, be sure that any water-repelling residue can be completely rinsed off. Even after mechanical removal of lichen and so on, the whole surface should be carefully wet-scrubbed and rinsed clean, avoiding prolonged water penetration into cracks. Any pressure washing should be done with *great* caution.

Preparation of mortars and access to materials on site

For larger-scale works, ready-mixed mortar is often cheaper than site-mixed mortar. Putty and aggregates are best combined by a squashing action. For small amounts, tread thoroughly with gum boots. For larger amounts use a mortar mill which has revolving weighted rollers (with adjustable spring loading and height to avoid crushing the larger aggregates). They range from (stationary) 1 tonne capacity, down to a wheelbarrow's capacity (towable). Pan mixers have paddles producing a turning, kneading action. The tumbling action of ordinary drum mixers is generally not suitable for making stiff yet workable mixes. However, a drum mixer is useful if the putty is not too solid, if damp sand is to be used and if there is time for the resultant sloppy mix to drain and evaporate sufficiently before use.

General-purpose mortar – known as 'coarse stuff' – might be used quite liquid with added hair for plastering (onto a fairly absorbent surface), stiffer with hair for plastering on lath, a little stiffer yet for bedding freestone or brick-laying, firmer still for bedding larger or harder rubblestone, and firmest of all for pointing and consolidation work (i.e. mortar repairs on the face of stones). Thus great versatility can be achieved in most lime mortar mixes by altering the water content.

All non-hydraulic lime-based mortars should be made up well in advance of use. Then they must be 'knocked up' so they regain their plasticity. Avoid adding more than the minimum of water to achieve a workable mix. The more water added at this stage, the greater the risk of shrinkage and the weaker the resultant mortar or render.

Mortars are converted into renders/plasters by the addition of animal hair to give them tensile strength: goat (long, fine) or yak (fine, crimped) or horse (mane and tail, useful in coarse mixes). Calcium hydroxide solution rots hair, so prepared plasters should ideally be used within a week. Add more hair if too much time has elapsed and the hair has been weakened or lost. Once placed and allowed to dry out slowly, the hair in a plaster survives to perform its function for many decades. Synthetic fibre (pale, variable length and width), is now available and is an efficient alternative.

Hair or fibre is teased out over the mortar and folded in either by layering with shallow shovelfuls or by the rollers in a mortar mill. Stated proportions of ingredients are meaningless if the wind blows away the hair or it clogs into useless lumps; therefore judge the hair content in the resultant mix. For maximum performance (as when requiring strong keys between ceiling laths), achieve an even fringe of hairs 1 mm apart in a sample taken out of the mix on the tip of a trowel. A hair every 2 mm is sufficient for plastering solid walls.

The various materials should be identifiable and available at every part of the wall to be repaired. A reliable supply of water at all parts of the wall is convenient for washing and dampening. Very often stone or terra cotta pinnings will be needed for coring out the larger volumes of mortar. A source should be found that matches any original pinnings surviving in situ. Have an ample supply, washed clean and kept damp, in a variety of suitable shapes and sizes, spread along the work site.

Dampening the substrate and keeping the work damp

Before applying any mortar to a substrate, sufficient water must be introduced into the latter to avoid stress at the interface from excessive suction of water out of the mortar; however, a degree of suction is essential. The less water movement, the stronger the bond. Thus mixes should be kept stiff, yet workable and fit for their purpose, and the substrate well dampened by successive wettings in advance of the application, so that the moisture is absorbed back in from the surface.

If the substrate is delicate and precious – say, plaster carrying wall paintings – and sensitive to wetting, the areas to be repaired can be 'primed' with limewash and allowed to carbonate so that it acts as a 'semi-sealant'. Subsequent dampening will be necessary before application of mortar. A damp microclimate can also be created around these repairs to slow down drying.

Assess the absorbency and moisture requirements of the wall to be repaired. The uppermost parts may be very dry (perhaps under eaves), exposed parts may be affected by sun and wind (especially angles and reveals) and parts near ground level may be inherently damp (old buildings do not have damp-proof courses). Also, parts affected by poor rainwater detailing may be regularly saturated, as around broken down pipes.

Anticipate these situations and compensate accordingly by increasing or reducing the dampening. Avoid any run-off at the foot of the wall when using hosepipes. The bottom metre or so can be sheltered from excess wet, and ventilation can be encouraged. Remember that lime-based works carried out to a saturated wall will cause delay and inconvenience, and consequently can be expensive.

As well as dampening in advance of applying the material, be aware of the changing ambient conditions – notably weather – and maintain the appropriate level of dampness. Generally, south and west elevations are more problematic than north and east. Conversely, ambient conditions are easier to control for interior works, where draughts can be prevented or redirected.

Aftercare and protection

Most lime mixes shrink as they begin to dry out. Each application should be allowed to 'settle down'; then, before it becomes solid, it should be consolidated by applying pressure with a trowel or float, pressing in the cracks. Because lime mixes are sticky, it is tempting to build them up too thickly and too quickly.

If lime mixes dry too fast they will fail in two ways: immediately, because carbonation has not begun (as explained above); subsequently, because of 'segregation' in which the fine lime particles, still in solution, are pulled to the surface of the mortar where they concentrate as the moisture evaporates. This results in case-hardening at the surface and a weak interior. Failure occurs at the onset of the first bad weather. It follows that slow drying of all types of lime application produces the best results.

Arrange the work so that there is time at the end of each day to consolidate, and re-dampen, and cover up the work as necessary. Its condition must be checked the following morning. Work should be planned so that it will not suffer over the weekend, unless labour can be provided to tend it as necessary. Do not attempt the impossible. Always provide conditions that enable successful carbonation and hence work that it is safe to leave alone.

On a roofless structure in particular, it is likely that protection will be needed to shield the work from strong sunlight, drying wind, driving rain or frost, depending on the season. Provide ample scaffolding to carry the necessary roof and/or vertical sheeting, and plan to leave it in situ for a sufficient period to allow slow drying out to a moisture content low enough for the work to withstand all weather. Draping damp hessian and/or plastic sheeting is sufficient for short-term protection. Take care not to let the wet hessian or plastic be blown against new work, for it may cause white staining ('laitence') especially on render. Keep the covers taut and 150 mm away from the wall. It is important to provide some ventilation behind protection, especially at ground level. Saturated work cannot carbonate and is vulnerable to freezing.

Ensure that all rainwater detailing is functioning correctly before striking the scaffold.

The various applications

Initial consolidation

It is desirable that any structure is restored to its original state with a solidly filled-up mass of masonry before an attempt is made to repair and/or reinstate its surfaces. It is often essential that some weak areas are consolidated before surface applications can begin. This process may involve underpinning, grouting the opened-out heart of the wall or local voids (see *Structures & construction in historic building conservation*), replacing missing or entirely decayed elements, bridging gaps and stitching cracks with suitable building material (usually thin stone or terra cotta tiles) and, lastly, dubbing out with mortar and pinnings. Consider using hydraulic lime mixes for the deeper repairs; however, putty mixes will work in depths of <50 mm if cored out with pinnings and used in spring/summer.

The need for dubbing (or 'daubing') arises frequently as decay mostly occurs at, or just in from, the wall surface. After preparation of the substrate (see above), best practice involves the following operations:

- Flick a slurry of 1 lime putty : 1 sharp sand into cavities to be filled. This consolidates friable substrates and provides a sticky interface.
- Allow it to become 'cheesy', then accurately throw in stiff workable coarse lime-rich mortar, well haired (to provide tensile strength and flexibility). Do not build up volumes greater than 20 mm^3 (unless the coarseness of the aggregate in the mix allows greater volumes to resist shrinkage).
- Instead, halve the volumes by tapping pinnings (preselected for shape and size) into the mortar, forcing it back tight into the cavity.
- Add more mortar over the coring material so the filling is brought to a 'fair face' level with adjacent surfaces.
- Press in and/or float up and later roughen up the surface. This will provide a stable substrate, keyed to receive the next coat.

Time should elapse for all consolidations to gain a degree of strength before proceeding with surface applications. However, it will be recognised that the wall will continue to regain its structural integrity over many months after the works have been completed.

Plastering

The term 'plastering' usually refers to interior coating systems using haired lime mortar spread with a trowel in two or more coats, decreasing in thickness and increasing in fineness towards the surface. However, the term can refer to exterior coatings, particularly if they are thin and soft. In either case, hair is normally excluded in the top coat. The process is described below. The uncompleted Victorian country house, Woodchester Mansion, near Stroud, Gloucestershire, contains work in all its stages on the interior surfaces, carried out when the traditional lime plastering trade was at its zenith and remaining today as it was left when the project came to a halt in 1868.

Rendering

The term 'rendering' usually refers to an exterior plaster system as described above (Figures 4.3, 4.4 and 4.5) but can also sometimes mean roughcast – often termed 'roughcast render'. It can refer to the application of a first coat of coarse stuff to a solid background, and hence it also refers to the first of any system of coats. It has become associated with modern cement-based external coating. This can be seen as a continuation of **stucco**, which was made from hard-setting natural cements from the beginning of the nineteenth century. Stucco is also the term used (more on the continent) to describe decorative lime-based plasterwork that is modelled in situ (a subject not dealt with in this chapter).

External rendering is often jointed out in imitation of ashlar masonry. If well done it creates the desired 'architectural' effect – the tradition

Figure 4.3 St John the Baptist, Strensham, Gloucestershire. An open-textured hydraulic lime render was applied and finished with a creamy yellow limewash (architect: Tim Radcliffe).

Figure 4.4 Gloucester Street, Malmesbury: smooth render applied to a 'polite' eighteenth-century facade.

Figure 4.5 Market Place, Cirencester: four facades with coloured limewash on new lime render, after rain. The two on the right have render on lath on timber frame.

originates in antiquity. An appropriate iron tool is impressed and pulled (not scratched) along a straight edge, forming 'bed joints' and afterwards the 'perpend joints'. Timing is critical: the top coat must be stable, yet soft enough to be pressed effectively. The work should then be finished with a damp stock brush to soften snags or scuffed edges.

First coat (also termed scratch coat, or pricking-up coat when onto laths)

Do not use metal angle bead; adopt traditional detailing and follow the contours of the wall to be plastered. Vernacular and earlier work is usually thinly applied whereas high-status buildings of the eighteenth and nine-teenth centuries have multiple-coated and accurately levelled work. Decide the 'style' and eventual thickness of the work to be done. Remember that the more coats, the more even the absorption; therefore the easier it is to apply the top coat, which must be of an even thickness. The mix is normally a well-haired 2:5 coarse stuff.

Because lime plaster should be used stiffer than its gypsum equivalent, it may be easier to apply it with a gauging trowel. Press and spread con-tinuous blobs, working methodically from one end of the wall to the other. Allow the plaster to 'take up' – this might be a long time when onto laths as there is no absorption, only evaporation. Then flatten (or 'bump off') with a rectangular plastering trowel, scooping off excess material and smearing it into the hollows (or 'galls'). Do not add too much too quickly; this will cause slumping. Do not overwork, particularly with a steel trowel; this will bring lime to the surface. For best adhesion to dense or smooth substrates (such as concrete blocks), apply in two stages – the first thinly smeared, the second soon following – to achieve a total thickness of 12 mm. If levelling is required, use a featheredge and/or a Derby float. It is not essential to float up this coat, especially when onto laths –it can be left to crack and 'settle down' and even to set hard – but it is good practice to consolidate it before 'keying up' for the next coat. The purpose of keying is to provide a barbed profile on which to hang the subsequent coat(s) and also to encourage CO_2 into the plaster. The most effective method, espe-cially for work on laths, is to scratch with a lath tip (not metal, which cuts the hair) in a 75 mm interval diamond pattern.

Second coat (also termed floating coat, or straightening coat)

The second coat may act as the coarse-textured top coat, or there may be an additional, finer top coat (see below), or the second coat may be (and often is) omitted and a topcoat applied over the first coat. Normally the same mix is used. Old Scots advice is to apply each coat while the previous one 'still has a tear in its eye' – when firm but damp, and as yet uncarbon-ated. It can, however, be allowed to carbonate, but it will require re-wetting and is best followed by limewash as a 'tack coat' for maximum adhesion.

Floating is the priority in this coat in order to achieve a sufficiently lev-elled and compact layer. After the initial floating, allow this coat to 'take up' until it is barely moveable; float again to eliminate any shrinkage. Then, for high-quality work, allow it to firm up to 'green hard' (so it cannot be dented). Wet the surface carefully until nearly saturated, and 'scour' or rub vigorously and evenly in a circular manner with the float, lubricating with more water as necessary to produce a slight lather. Floating can be repeated as often as the quality of the job dictates.

If a top coat is to be applied, key the second coat delicately and evenly with a wire scratcher in wavy horizontal lines, or with a 'Devil float' making circular scratches.

Top coat (also termed setting coat, or finish coat)

Use clean sharp sand (probably silver sand) and an addition of stone dust if required, all at <1 mm. Aggregate/sand ratio is usually 1:1 because fine aggregate has a great surface area that must be covered by the lime binder. The stone dust acts as an 'extender' for the lime. Best practice is to follow the procedure for the floating coat. Maintain a high moisture level in the previous coat(s) for even absorption. A neatly floated setting coat with a texture of finest sandpaper will be the ideal substrate for limewash. However, a more urbane surface can be achieved by allowing that described above to firm up, then painting on very dilute limewash and 'polishing' it with a steel trowel (thereby closing the grain) in the way that gypsum is finished. This porcelain texture is ideal for hard or soft distemper decoration.

Roughcasting (also termed harling, or wet-dash)

There is a long and universal tradition of throwing large aggregate mortar at walls. Roughcast was commonplace because of its technique. Once mastered, it is very quick and efficient, using a material that is versatile, sticks tightly and contains a range of aggregates that resist shrinkage. It is a vernacular feature in most counties of the British Isles and Ireland because it was always recognised that it provides buildings with a long-lasting and effective protection. Roughcast weathers well because of its large surface area, absorbing run-off of rain at vulnerable points on the building, for example under windows, while allowing rapid evaporation from any damp areas. It is robust owing to the largest particles of aggregate shedding rain drops while protecting the softer matrix under them. Moreover, roughcast is resilient while 'green' from the moment it is applied, withstanding showers, wind and direct sun far better than smooth plaster. (See Figure 4.6.)

A wide variety of techniques and textures dictated by period and local tradition are based on the practice of consolidating the newly thrown surface: for instance, 'twigging', in which the wet roughcast is slapped with a birch broom. Also, elevations were enlivened with containing features; for example, quoins and sometimes margins to openings are pressed into the wet roughcast – they may be decorative, like pargetting. Sometimes architectural rustication is achieved by bedding in a grid of battens, then on removal the channels are made good with a suitable tool.

Roughcast is often confused with pebbledash (or spar-dash), which is an early twentieth-century invention involving washed shingle being thrown onto still-wet cement render. It is often hard, dark-toned and ugly. However, it probably evolved from the traditional Scots technique of throwing sieved shingle mixed with lime putty slurry into wet lime render. A more recent

Figure 4.6 Silver Street, Malmesbury: a pair of cottages under one roof, with roughcast render reinstated (left) and repaired (right).

travesty of roughcast is 'Tyrolean render', in which cement-based medium-sized aggregate is applied mechanically, leaving a bland finish. It is no substitute for skilled hand application, which gives visual character as well as the required variation in force and water consistency.

Application

Lime-rich mixes of 2 lime:3 aggregate or even 1:1 (made with a matured 'hot-mix') were traditionally used. Sometimes hair was added – always a good precaution for all the aforementioned reasons. A ratio of 1:3 may be sufficient if the aggregates are well chosen. Continuous grading is imperative, with the largest particle not usually exceeding 6mm.

Weaker mixes will be beneficially sacrificial alongside most fragile ancient surfaces. Roughcasting makes an ideal repair system: friable and loose areas can be strengthened by the addition of new material, then a seamless finish can be achieved by 'blending in' over adjacent areas. Texture can be modified by wet or dry brushing as the roughcast firms up. It is useful to have a sensitive eye and hand, and also a trial-and-error approach.

Before application mask off openings, sheet over any adjacent plants and ensure there is time at the end of the roughcasting session to wipe down rainwater goods and so on. If there is no plinth at which to end the work, take the roughcast down to ground level (and accept that it is likely to be stressed and may decay in this zone). Modern practice is often to leave masonry exposed here; but then the masonry is vulnerable, and the visual effect of a 'floating' elevation is unsatisfactory.

It is convenient to take a stiff mix to the work site, then dilute it thoroughly, stirring it to the desired consistency (anywhere between porridge and thick pea soup). The more dilute, the easier it is to throw and the better it spreads. However, knocked up and with hair added, it is ideal for dubbing out, but it must be thrown with force; then pinnings can be inserted to bulk it out in the deeper hollows (see above).

One recognised method of casting is to hold a half-filled bucket under one arm, dip into it with a dashing trowel – a flattened sawn-off coal shovel will do – and flick the levelled contents with a wristy backhand stroke aimed towards the spot to be covered. The material should fly on a tangent of the semi-circle described by the trowel, and smack the wall. If the action and consistency are correct, nothing will fall off.

The method of casting varies: for example, in Wales a large, worn bricklaying trowel can be used in a vertical sweep, while in Ireland the mix can be scooped off a hawk. Whatever the method, it is important to develop an even, rhythmic, relaxed action that is effective, resulting in the wall being thoroughly and neatly coated. The method of application and the number of coats can vary considerably. For long-term durability it is best to build up to the desired thickness in several thin coats; thereby the contours of the wall are easily followed, complete coverage is ensured and shrinkage is avoided. The first coat provides the body, the second (or third) filling up flush between the lumps, consolidating the rough texture. Subsequent coats should therefore be a little wetter, and with slightly smaller aggregate, so that they spread better. For maximum adhesion between coats, apply them while the backing is still 'green' – leathery . . . and like dessert crumble.

Thus it can be seen that attempting an adequate thickness in a single coat can result in patchiness, slumping and a somewhat shaggy finish.

Sometimes a thick stiff first coat is floated up (to consolidate and level it). Then the next coat is thrown into it after time has elapsed for it to 'take up'. Sometimes cast coats are left float finished. Alternatively, cob walls in Devon, for instance, can be given a roughcast first coat for best adhesion and to provide a good key for a subsequent render coat, which is float finished. Another variant is often seen in the Cotswolds: a first coat of plaster is trowelled on, diamond keyed and allowed to take up before being roughcast. This is the basis of modern cement roughcasting.

Limewash

Limewash provides a protective, permeable and renewable skin of calcium carbonate for the fabric of old buildings. Like our own skin, limewash provides a barrier to infection – acid rain, pollution and airborne dirt. It helps reduce moisture to a harmless level in the fabric by slowing down water ingress, simultaneously allowing transpiration of excess internal moisture (Figure 4.7).

Limewash is a 'low tech', cheap, easily prepared paint but its performance greatly depends on the quality of workmanship. Successfully applied,

Figure 4.7 North Cerney Old Rectory: repairs to early nineteenth-century render with a colour wash.

it beautifies and enhances. However, there is a perception of it being crude and rustic, largely brought about by a faint memory of poor-quality limewashing that survived the practice of the regular disinfecting of cowsheds and the like. Latterly, bag lime was used; this was often applied too thickly, and it caked and peeled.

Additives

Limewash is used for its decorative quality so there is often the need to colour it (Figures 4.8 and 4.9). Lime-fast powder **pigments** should be used. Earth pigments are usually stable, but blacks tend to wash out in situ, and blues must be used on the day of mixing as they rapidly fade in solution. All colours will fade in sunlight; they will sometimes migrate, bleaching in exposed parts and concentrating in the 'rain shadows' of an elevation. Slow drying produces the true colour value; rapid drying pulls the lime to the surface of the coat, resulting in milky colours.

To mix coloured limewash, add water to pigments and shake or stir, then add the coloured solutions to the limewash, stir and sieve to remove any unmixed powder. Make the limewash richer in colour than the required end result. Be aware that the increased burden of pigment diminishes the performance of the vehicle $Ca(OH)_2$. Thus dark hues tend to dust off unless a binder is added (see below). Paint a test panel of at least $1\,m^2$, preferably in situ, and allow to dry fully. When satisfactory, make up an ample quantity for the job, matching against the retained wet sample. Any touching up in

Figure 4.8 Great Badminton, Gloucestershire: warm ochre-colour limewash on lime roughcast render 1.

situ will always show; therefore ensure that each elevation is coated in one session and with the same mix.

Exterior colours need to be 'grounded' – toned down with some umber (brown) so that they look natural and fit into the townscape or landscape. Many a lime project has been marred by too garish a colour, though lime-washes do mellow and improve on weathering.

A wide range of **binders** were used in the past to 'strengthen' limewash, helping it to adhere to its substrate, but they are only necessary for very exposed exterior surfaces of dense materials that require exceptional adhesion and water-resistance. In general, binders should be avoided. They make limewashing easier but can cause subsequent failure, reducing porosity and promoting mould growth (except in the case of pozzolans). There are some confusing Victorian recipes, such as adding common salt, which should be avoided as they could damage the building. Binders that are currently used include the following:

- Tallow, which has always been popular. It must be shredded into slaking quicklime, and the resultant emulsion allowed to cool down before sieving and application.
- Linseed oil whipped into (cold) lime putty or wash. Similarly, various improvisations such as 'chip fat' and engine oil have been used!
- Casein, a protein derived from milk, which has been used for centuries. Added to limewash in powder form, or simply as skimmed milk, it chemically combines with the $Ca(OH)_2$ to form calcium caseinate. 'Casein paint' is a powder containing lime, casein and fillers that is made up with water.

Figure 4.9 Great Badminton, Gloucestershire: warm ochre-colour limewash on lime roughcast render 2. Quoins of smooth render with different coloured limewash.

- Pozzolans can strengthen limewash but they might be heavy, requiring frequent stirring during use, and their inherent colour will modify the limewash colour.
- PVA emulsion (Unibond) is a modern compromise if coloured limewash is required on smooth impervious substrates such as internal emulsion paint; add as 5% of the volume of limewash. Its only advantage will be cosmetic; the potential problems of the emulsion paint substrate will remain. Dead flat acrylic varnish added as 10% of the volume of coloured limewash has been successful in binding to external masonry paint on smooth render while maintaining the authentic appearance of limewash.

Hydraulic limes can be used for limewashing. They are thought to have greater coverage, and less pigment is required to achieve the same depth of colour as in a putty limewash. Add 1 kg of NHL-2 to 2 litres of water; to this, do not add more than 100 g of pigment.

Another powder product, 'lime paint', is available in a range of colours and provides the authentic limewash appearance. However, it contains modern binders so it is wise not to use it on sensitive fabric.

Do not attempt to make limewash by wetting-up dry hydrate; it will probably fail. Instead, scoop out a quantity of lime putty into a clean deep
bucket and macerate with a little water. Use a plaster mixer on a drill for
larger quantities. Gradually add more water until you have a mixture the
consistency of creamy milk . . . or as thin as plain milk. Many thin coats are
better than a couple of thick coats. (Colouring has been described
above.)

Next, pour through a fine sieve – a stainless steel 60 mesh flour sieve is
ideal, or use a muslin cloth if you want the finest finish. Limewash, like lime
putty, will continue to improve with age in storage.

Keep stirring the wash frequently during use and keep the area that is
to be painted well wetted in advance; this is especially important if the wall
is very absorbent. Apply the limewash evenly with a 125–150 mm bristle
brush – difficult, because it is transparent on application; there should be
no noticeable drag. Ideally, the wash should remain on the surface for half
a minute before it begins to soak in. Non-absorbent surfaces must not be
over-saturated; work over any 'rivulets' as they occur. For best results, 'turn'
the whole surface when it has 'taken up' a little, using an empty brush.

Allow this coat to dry out completely – say, for twenty-four hours; damp
areas may take longer – then lightly damp down and apply a second coat,
and later a third.

Limewash may take up to a week to reach maximum opacity. It continues
to strengthen for several weeks if applied carefully and in optimum weather
conditions, with no direct sun, no wind, no direct rain (but very fine drizzle
or mist is possibly even advantageous), cool temperatures but no chance
of frost. It follows that north and east elevations and interiors are easier to
control. Wait for damp conditions, or fully enclose the site, when limewashing non-absorbent surfaces; not being able to hold moisture, the limewash
applied to them might dry before carbonation can occur. The ideal substrate is absorbent lime mortar or plaster, whose residual moisture will
enable optimum carbonation.

Case studies of lime-based repair to historic fabric

All four of the following case studies are small-scale, taking between five
and twenty days to complete and involving only two operators, although
advice was sought before and during the work. They can be regarded as
pilot projects, in which no compromise was allowed. Each job was given
all the time and materials that it demanded. In each case the final amount
of work to the building exceeded the estimated amount, but the consequent loss of income was accepted. The main objectives were to do the
best for the building, and to record the process with a view to returning
at intervals in the future to monitor the effectiveness of the repairs.

None of these studies involved the use of the hydraulic range of limes,
and neither was Portland cement used. Experience with non-hydraulic lime

made from high calcium limestone and matured as a putty, and a confidence in its use on site, were sufficient to make the repairs work successfully in each situation.

Case study 1: Church House, Lechlade, Gloucestershire: repairs to roughcast render

This comprised conservative repairs to the original lime roughcast render to an early eighteenth-century garden building situated adjacent to Church House. The gazebo is in a stable condition and is cherished by its owners. However, the damp level in the basement walls was raised by dense 1960s repairs in Portland cement to the roughcast low down on each elevation. Various repairs were done to the building more recently using lime-based mixes. The owners did not want to restore the mellow grey-coloured patinated exterior surfaces.

When a large plant was removed from against the building, an area of decayed render was revealed. This was the original coating, slowly worn away and unseen for many years. All it required was consolidation of its loose and missing parts and, as holes and cracks were investigated, a day's work seemed necessary to make good the surface so that it would no longer be vulnerable. But despite using nothing more aggressive than small trowels and spatulas, a more extensive pattern of decay was exposed, relating to detachment of the render from its substrate as the building slowly settled on its foundations. Furthermore, poorer-quality stones in the cheaply built rubblework had disintegrated where weather had penetrated through gaps in the render, so these were removed if structurally unsound. After raking out was completed, the cavities were brushed out and washed clean.

Lime mortar had been made up in advance and was blended with different aggregates to make various mixes to suit their context. One of these, rather than the original loam mortar, was used for all deep consolidation, to give strength to the loose rubblework substrate.

The maximum amount of clean, sound stone fragments were tapped into the mortar to provide a core to the repairs, thereby reducing the volume and shrinkage of the mortar. This process was continued in the 'dubbing out' where the surface was levelled up to receive an even coat of roughcast in all the lacunae. This coat is thrown on in the traditional way, at a suitable moisture consistency. Time was allowed to elapse before the addition of the final touches. Visual sensitivity is crucial at this stage. It is possible to blend the repair with the existing surface so that new and old textures are subtly differentiated. Various brushes were used to achieve an appropriate texture. The decorative feature of the render adjacent to the door architrave was repaired with smooth render. Later, several coats of limewash, pigmented to match the general colour of the existing render, were brushed or flicked onto the damp surface. When the render was ready to receive more limewash, various colours were flicked on to harmonise with the patterns of lichen growth. This is *tratteggio*, in which the wall is unified when seen from a distance, but near to the repairs are obvious. Why should old buildings not be considered as artefacts just as precious as paintings or sculpture?

Case study 2: Woolgatherers, Coxwell Street, Cirencester: repairs to rubblework surface

This study is of conservative repairs to an area of limewashed rubblework original to a seventeenth-century wool merchant's house in Cirencester. The work took nine man-days. The wall which encloses the main staircase was selected because its surface was almost intact, having been sheltered by the overhanging roof eaves and having largely escaped the hand of the twentieth century. It survived because it had gone unnoticed. Though once ubiquitous, these authentic surfaces are now rare because they have been misunderstood and are usually destroyed today.

Here was a true and even surface, following the medieval tradition. The wall construction was the same as that described in the previous case study, but it had never been rendered. Instead it was flushpointed, almost 'plaster pointed', with a very resilient lightweight lime-rich mortar – almost pure lime putty – and reinforced with cow hair. Like the mortar used to bed the freestone quoins and the window, it was soft, porous and off-white. The mortar was level with the stones and one could see trowel imprints. The work, though a little crude, had been done with speed, confidence and success. A laminated patina of different coloured coats of limewash survived in the hollows and in the 'rain shadow', but had been worn off the denser and smoother stones. Though not re-limewashed since the nineteenth century, this soft and peeling 'skin' was still providing 'muscle' and 'bone', with a partial containment and a partial barrier to infection from weather and air pollution.

The work on this wall was similar to that described in the previous case study. The minimum of fabric was removed, and that using only small blade tools, except for several isolated hard cement fillings which required a hammer and sharp chisels to free them. Slight settlement within the wall had caused cracks to open up and these contained loose material. Detachment of the pointing mortar was also associated with original shrinkage cracks. The cavities and the surface were carefully brushed down, first dry then wet, care being taken not to let excess moisture penetrate the structure. Only loose flaking layers of limewash were lost in this process.

Mortars similar, but not identical, to those found in situ were used to reinstate the structural integrity of the wall, building up the surface of the mortar joints so that the new work lay precisely in line with the remaining original mortar surface, not overlapping at any point. Areas of decay in the freestone dressings were removed, and these irregular-shaped lacunae were then built up layer by layer with mortars designed to match the colour and texture of the stone. There is a modern convention of executing mortar repairs in rectangular-cut lacunae that no doubt derives from a stone masonry tradition. Straight edges and right angles draw attention to the repairs; they are unnatural to the geology and weathering of stones. Furthermore, it is more effective to place mortar against a curved profile than into corners. Minimum intervention and great visual subtlety can be achieved by filling only that which has decayed.

A day after the mortaring was complete, the whole area was limewashed in a colour related to that of the surviving fragments using traditional iron oxide earth pigments. As always, after systematic and careful dampening the limewash was flooded onto the surface; it was worked into all fissures and granular areas and allowed to partially absorb. The limewash was taken up to the glazing line in the window. It was then 'burnished' with an empty but damp brush to compact it, in the same way that the mortar had been pressed in to counteract shrinkage cracking. The work was protected from sun and wind. Four more coats of limewash were added, no more than once a day, allowing for carbonation to occur. Controlling the moisture under the surface always involves careful attention.

This case study exemplifies traditional maintenance with a genuine historic function and character. If the top surface is regularly maintained, it will protect its substrate – of flush pointing here – which in turn will protect the structure. Thus if minor decay is not halted, it leads to major and costly decay. The wall continues to weather well, becoming beautifully mellow. In appearance, it resembles the walls our ancestors would have seen.

Case study 3: Broadfield Court, Bodenham, Herefordshire: mortar repairs to stone

By contrast, the third and fourth case studies did not involve limewash – although it was used to help bond the mortar repairs to their substrate – nor was there a continuous skin surviving. Instead, only lime mortars were used to repair the fourteenth-century sandstone doorway and surrounding sandstone rubblework in the north elevation. The house has a complex history extending into modern times, and there is a current tradition, perhaps a century old, of expressing all its stonework, rough and smooth together, that had to be respected on this job.

Old limewash was found adhering to the doorway masonry when hard cement patches were removed. Early rubblework in this sandstone district was once finished in similar ways to that found in the limestone district where the previous case studies are situated. Here it might have been flush pointed and limewashed, or rendered.

The aim of this project was to find ways of arresting the decay to the masonry of a doorway without adversely changing its appearance or losing original fabric. Commonplace lime mortars, if used with mastery and invention, as is often the case in 'old work', were considered to be a desirable alternative to unproven – and expensive – chemical 'preservatives', or to conventional masonry practice. Cutting out and replacing so-called 'failed' stone would have drastically altered the ancient character of the doorway, and would have been expensive. On closer inspection the decay, though active, only affected the stone to a maximum depth of 15 mm, and it was mainly confined to the encircling hoodmould which was green-coloured soft siltstone. Apart from ancient wear, the gritstone masonry was in a stable condition. The doorway's decay had two principal causes. One was that the hoodmould was so decayed that it no longer functioned as a water-shedding feature, so the carved voussoirs and jambs suffered unnecessarily. The other was the surrounding rubblework of friable weakened stones in a perished mortar exacerbated by a large area of recent repointing in a dense cement mortar, associated with a once-leaking drainpipe.

It was agreed that the ambient conditions within the fabric must be improved. Therefore its functional equilibrium in the immediate area of the doorway was restored so that it could perform efficiently as a rain-absorbing and evaporating surface. It was hoped that this in turn would alleviate stress in the hoodmould and the masonry below, by reducing direct run-off and avoiding an accumulation of moisture within the wall. It was decided to restore the full architectural form of the hoodmould so that it might once again perform its intended function. The challenge here was to make ordinary lime mortar adhere to the siltstone and endure in this stressful location on the facade.

The work amounted to twenty man-days. Various lime mortars were prepared in advance. Decayed or cementitious material was removed from the doorway and the surrounding rubblework, after which the masonry was cleaned. Joints and voids were filled with the appropriate mortar and subsequently 'finished' by compacting, then paring away, and brushing and sponging the surface to reveal the aggregates which characterise each mix. Because they would be exposed to view, it was important to counteract the inherent light tone of lime. However, the most intricate operation was the consolidation and building up of the hoodmould to its full form. This involved incorporating terra cotta chips, thereby providing a core to counteract shrinkage by halving the thickness of this necessarily plastic mix. It was then limewashed to match the colour of each stone within its length. Lime shelter coats were applied in very localised areas such as the disaggregated ballflower ornamentation. Finally, a rotten stone near the base of the right jamb was replaced with a suitable piece of gritstone.

A mortar repair was not chosen for this position because it might be too weak, being vulnerable to salt decay, frost and mechanical damage. The immediate environmental conditions were controlled so the work would dry out gradually. Fortunately, the autumn was warm and dry. The first frost came seven weeks after completion of the work. The doorway has been inspected every six months since, and it is looking well six years later.

The lime-based materials used on this project did not attempt to compete with the existing materials of the original construction, but to complement them. Although lime was the 'archaeologically correct' substance to use, this in itself was a lesser consideration than that the mortars used should have similar mechanical and functional properties to those in the original construction – both the mortars themselves and, to a certain degree, the soft and hard stones. It was intended that the mortars be 'sacrificial' to the stones, accommodating weathering and decay processes and thereby protecting them. The known benefits of repairing with lime-based materials outweighed any perceived notion that sandstone is damaged by the proximity of lime. Beyond this, the lime-based materials were intended to be aesthetically pleasing. This work of respecting and honouring the doorway did not follow a dogmatic 'conserve as found' approach, but was nevertheless conservative – rather, a 'repair by addition'.

Case study 4: Acton Court, Iron Acton, near Bristol: repairs to paved floor

The fourth case study is of the consolidation of an ancient floor with lime mortars. Here the more strict 'conserve as found' approach was taken. The floor belongs to the cross passage in the centre of the east range of Acton Court. The property was rebuilt by Sir Nicholas Poyntz, who was connected to the Royal Court. Architecturally one of the most important surviving Tudor houses in England, it contains a painted Renaissance frieze and other mid-sixteenth-century features, such as the earlier parts of the cross passage floor. Acton Court was acquired by English Heritage in the 1980s for repair and eventual selling on. Incidentally, the exterior wall surfaces of dark red irony Pennant sandstone rubblework were originally protected with an off-white roughcast render, the remnants of which have been consolidated on the now repointed walls.

The work to the floor, measuring approximately 4 metres by 8 metres, amounted to twenty man-days. The architect's brief was to do as little as possible in order to safeguard the floor and to preserve its integrity. It was established that the majority of the floor would have very low use in the foreseeable future as the only thoroughfare would be across the west end. Therefore it was agreed that non-hydraulic lime mortars would be adequate for the necessary consolidation work. They would allow the maximum transpiration of moisture from the floor, and maximum reversibility. This campaign of work should not preclude any future archaeological, or more sophisticated conservation activities. Having thought that non-hydraulic lime would be sufficiently robust, it was then decided that brick dust should be added to give a pozzolanic set. It would also – along with a range of sands, stone dusts, charcoal and coal dust, all of which were found in different concentrations in the various existing bedding mortars – help to darken the tone of the mixes. The floor was dry-brushed and then gradually wet-cleaned. Only water was used, impacted dirt being softened with repeated mist-spraying. Care was taken not to let excess water sink into the bedding layers as this would activate salts.

In this 'holding operation' the mortar was placed adjacent to the components in place to protect vulnerable edges, and only where absolutely necessary for their survival in situ was it placed under them. The joints between components and only the principal breaks within each component were filled. The work was constantly reassessed, and further filling of secondary breaks was done if it could be justified. It was found that the gradual deposition of dirt in the finer cracks was acting as an effective stabilising medium, and therefore it was left in situ. Shortage of funding and time helped to discipline the extent of the repair activities.

As the work proceeded there emerged a distinct pattern to this rich accumulation of repairs. The oldest flooring of a variety of glazed square tiles was adjacent to the long side walls. By contrast, the areas that had received most wear had been replaced most frequently using Pennant sandstone flags, so the most recent area was down the longitudinal axis of the floor. This included crude patches of mid-twentieth-century concrete. These were removed where possible, on the grounds that they were physically and visually obtrusive, lying proud of the surrounding paving. The concrete was also preventing the floor from performing its function as an evenly evaporating surface.

It was decided not to 'confuse history' by restoring the missing paving with similar materials. Two exceptions were made in front of two door thresholds – areas which would always receive more traffic. Instead, all the other lacunae, both those already existing and those caused by the removal of concrete, were packed with a composite repair material consisting of layers of low-fired tile and lime/brick dust mortar, bulked out with clean permeable stone if the depth exceeded 50 mm (being the approximate thickness of the larger flooring components). The deepest of these areas remained damp and workable for ten days. During this time and subsequently, they were absorbing soluble salts from the ground and the adjacent floor, which were later to effloresce. This phenomenon was expected and accepted as beneficial to the long-term health of the floor. Two months later a crop of salt crystals was removed from the mortar surface which was now hardening steadily. It was hoped that all subsequent efflorescence would be likewise removed from these buffer zones so they can continue to alleviate salt concentrations in the floor. The glazed tiles are particularly vulnerable and precious.

As shrinkage cracks appeared, the mortar was compacted and given a wood float finish, their surface plane being adjusted so it was always between 1 and 3 mm below the adjacent floor surface. When the lacunae and all the joints and larger cracks had been filled, the floor could be read as one continuous surface. Though fragile underfoot, it looked solid and its delicate integrity had been regained.

A warning of the realities of reintroducing lime in building

There are many problems in reintroducing the regular use of lime in today's over-industrialised building industry with its largely de-skilled and poorly motivated workforce. It is difficult to justify the more expensive and time-consuming alternative whose long-term benefits are unvalued in our short-term 'quick-fix' culture; add to this the fact that in life today there are many higher priorities for expenditure than old buildings.

The Lime Revival hardly begins to threaten the vast international domination of the cement industry, while there is no official or government recognition of the long-term damage cement is causing the country's built heritage. Using lime to preserve the authenticity and quality of our older buildings could prove to be one of the most significant investments in the nation's future.

Lime gets a bad reputation when failures occur, but they are almost always due to poor specifying, poor detailing and poor site practice. There is neither sufficient official evaluation of currently available materials nor effective guidance on their application. It is important that those specifying the work, the supervisors and the craftsmen be properly trained. They must accept that lime-based repair is superior to cement-based repair for historic buildings. Then they must understand the properties of lime and how it is used in this context as mortars, plasters and washes. More specifically, they will need to have regard for the composition and properties of historic mortar samples. In this way suitable equivalent mortars can be designed with a view to specifying, preparing and using lime materials correctly.

It is most important that the craftsmen using lime materials are motivated enough to exercise care, judgement and dexterity at all times. They must be committed to achieving success with lime materials, knowing that this greatly depends upon intelligent and thorough preparation, and upon good traditional building practice. These skills need to be relearnt and mastered so that they become almost instinctive to the user. It takes time to acquire experience – that largely empirical knowledge which has been forgotten, or lost altogether. When used correctly, lime is the perfect and most versatile binder in the world.

Endnote

1. This is because carbon dioxide cannot get to the foundations to make it carbonate, or 'go off' (see lime cycle).

5 Concrete and reinforced concrete

Michael Bussell

Introduction

This chapter begins with a short description of the basic properties of concrete and reinforced concrete, followed by a review of the development of concrete as a material from earliest usage to the introduction of reinforced concrete in the 1890s. It then considers the materials and processes involved in concrete construction, which have not greatly altered over the last century other than through the advent of mechanisation and the growth of technical understanding. This chapter aims to give an understanding of concrete as a material, while Chapter 11 in *Structures & construction in historic building conservation* sets out to illustrate the use of concrete in buildings over the last century and a half, and to give guidance on the conservation of concrete and reinforced concrete.

Basic properties of concrete

The terms 'reconstructed stone' and 'reconstituted stone' are commonly used to describe concrete, particularly when it is used as cladding or in the form of blockwork. These terms acknowledge that concrete is an artificial stone, with characteristics often resembling those of natural stone. For example, most sedimentary rocks – many of which find wide use in building, such as Bath and Portland limestone and millstone grit sandstone – comprise particles or grains that have been bound or cemented together over geological time. Likewise, concrete typically consists of stones and sand or other **filler material**, held together by a **binder** (commonly cement or lime, mixed with water) which sets to produce a solid material.

Concrete, like building stone, is strong when subject to compressive forces trying to crush it. Both materials (and also brickwork) are therefore suitable for use in walls, piers, columns, arches, vaults and domes, all of which are essentially structures in compression. However, they are relatively weak in tension, which occurs most commonly in building elements such as slabs, beams and lintels, where the load is carried by bending. This bending produces tension in the bottom face (or in the top face, in the case of a cantilever), and when the tensile stress reaches a limiting value, the element will snap and collapse. This is a **brittle** failure, as happens when plain glass breaks; it is particularly undesirable in a structure as it occurs without warning, unlike the creaking or sagging of overloaded timber or steel.

It was to overcome this weakness in tension of plain concrete that **reinforced concrete** was developed a little over a century ago, followed in mid-century in the UK by **prestressed concrete**. This allows properly designed, properly built, and properly maintained (!) structures to act in a ductile manner and give visible warning of distress if overloaded.

One key characteristic that concrete does not share with natural stone is that, being made as a semi-liquid mass that hardens, it can be poured into forms or moulds whose shape it then takes up. In other words, it can be *moulded* to whatever shape is desired; this capability is a prime reason why architects and engineers regard it as a versatile structural material.

One other important reason why concrete has often been used in place of stone, which of course has to be cut and carved to shape, is that concrete is usually cheaper! Mention of cost may offend some aesthetic sensitivities, but given the choice between two materials that serve the same function, it is a fact of life that the cheaper one will usually be preferred by whoever is paying for the work.

Earliest use of concrete

The Romans probably pioneered the use of concrete on any large scale, although before them the Egyptians and the Greeks used mortar. The Romans were fortunate that deposits of volcanic ash were to be found at Pozzuoli, near Naples, which – when mixed with water – set hard, like modern cement. (The term *pozzolan*, derived from this location, is today applied to any natural material with such cementitious properties.) The Romans used this as the binder in concrete, while the filler was pumice, brick rubble, or other fairly cheap and freely available material. Pumice – a light, porous rock ejected from Italy's volcanoes during eruptions – made a lighter-weight concrete, while brick fragments, and particularly brick dust, added further cementitious material to the mix. With this material, with technical skill and ambition, and with much cheap or slave labour, notable structures were achieved. Of these the c. AD 120 Pantheon in Rome, its hemispherical dome spanning 43 metres, is the outstanding example. A notable feature of the dome is its coffering, by which its overall weight is reduced through a reduction in thickness of panels, leaving a regular pattern of ribs rising to the central lantern ring, intersected and stiffened by horizontal ribs of the same thickness.

Eighteenth-century development of lime-based mortars and Roman cement

With the decline of the Roman Empire, concrete appears to have become a 'lost' material inasmuch as little is known of its use until the mid-eighteenth century, when French engineers were using 'béton', or lime-based concrete, in foundations. At the same time, the British civil engineer John Smeaton began studies of the properties and performance of mortars for use in his Eddystone Lighthouse, to be built in the English Channel south of Plymouth. His concern was to find a reliable 'hydraulic' mortar that could set and harden under water – clearly a necessity for a stone structure whose lowest courses would be laid at low tide but would then be covered over at the next high tide, being subject also to erosion if the mortar were still soft.

His studies, and those by others, showed the way for the development of stronger mortar and concrete using both lime and, later, cement. Pure lime (calcium carbonate), obtained by heating limestone or chalk in a lime kiln at about 800–900°C to drive off the chemically bonded carbon dioxide, produces quicklime (calcium oxide), which is then 'slaked' by adding water. This causes a violent reaction, generating heat and steam, and yielding slaked or hydrated lime (calcium hydroxide). This is then stirred and either stored in water as 'lime putty' or dried and used as a powder. When mixed with sand and water to produce a mortar which is then laid in masonry, the lime will stiffen as it dries out and will then begin to absorb atmospheric carbon dioxide and revert to calcium carbonate. In the same way it can be mixed with larger stones, and possibly sand, to produce lime concrete. This is a slow process, beginning at the outside face of the mortar joint or the concrete's surface, and stiffening and strengthening the mortar as it occurs. Because this reaction cannot occur if the mortar is under water, such lime is known as 'non-hydraulic'.

Lime that is 'tainted' by impurities such as clay, or has clay added when it is heated, undergoes chemical changes by reaction between the elements in the two materials, which means that the ground-up lime powder, when mixed with water, produces a set by further chemical reaction, even when under water. Depending on the clay content, the 'hydraulic' lime is classed as 'feebly', 'moderately' or 'eminently' hydraulic, the latter giving the best set and strength. (Slow carbonation also occurs in hydraulic limes, but this is of secondary importance to the chemical set.)

A particularly well-known form of hydraulic lime was patented by James Parker in 1796 under the name of Parker's Roman cement (reflecting the reputation of Roman pozzolans). This made use of clay-bearing chalk found in north Kent (later a centre of the cement industry). Roman cement was widely used for work where strength and resistance to water were needed, such as in Marc Isambard Brunel's work on the Thames Tunnel in the mid-1820s, and as rendering to external walls. However, it set rapidly and was less well-suited to work such as foundations, where the placing of stone in layers, mixed with a less 'eminent' lime, was more satisfactory in allowing continuous working without a 'flash set' of the lime that would prevent the layers being merged together.

Early Portland cement

Joseph Aspdin took out a patent for the making of Portland cement in 1824, which did not, however, highlight the distinguishing characteristic of modern cement compared to hydraulic limes – it was made by heating the lime-clay raw material to around 1300–1500°C, substantially higher than for making lime, and this further altered the chemistry of the material, which was removed as clinker that was then ground up. Ironically, it was not until 1845 that the first 'real' Portland cement was made in the UK, after numerous trials – and errors – before the key importance of the high temperature heating was understood. (There are interesting parallels with the difficulties Bessemer experienced in making sound steel by his method in the period following his initial announcement of success in 1856, although this was due to problems with the content of the iron ore rather than the temperatures used – see Chapter 7.)

The name 'Portland cement' was probably chosen by Aspdin to convey a favourable impression by comparison with the widely used natural stone from Portland, which was, and remains, a prestigious cladding material. Also, concrete and renders made with Portland cement have a similar colour to the natural stone.

The beginnings of reinforced concrete

The next significant development was in 1854, when William Boutland Wilkinson patented his idea for the use of hoop iron or other iron sections to reinforce floors and roofs of concrete.[1] This was recognition that concrete used on its own was not suitable when subject to bending loads of any magnitude, because of its low tensile strength and the brittleness with which it fails. Iron (and later steel) reinforcement provides the tensile resistance and also permits a beam or slab to deflect or 'sag' if overloaded. The reinforcement has a coefficient of thermal expansion very close to that of most concretes and, when surrounded by hardened concrete, bonds to it. These are two vital properties that ensure that the materials work together.

There were isolated applications of reinforced concrete over the next four decades, but the story of reinforced concrete in the UK does not really start in earnest until 1892, when a French entrepreneur, François Hennebique, took out his first British patent for construction in the material. Additional patents over the next few years laid the foundations for a very successful commercial enterprise led in the UK by L.G. Mouchel. (Examples of these early Hennebique structures, and those of other reinforced concrete pioneers, are described in Chapter 11 of *Structures & construction in historic building conservation*.)

The Hennebique system made use of round mild steel bars for the main steel needed to provide tensile resistance in bending, and also to supplement compressive strength in columns. In single-span beams supported at both ends, only bottom reinforcement was necessary. For multi-span continuous beams and cantilevers, top reinforcement was provided to resist tension forces. The ends of the bars were slit and spread to form Y-shaped 'fishtails', to improve the mechanical anchorage of the bars within the concrete, complementing the frictional bond between the bar faces and the concrete in which they were embedded. Shear, an effect which tries to

Figure 5.1 King Edward Street Post Office, London, 1907–10, during demolition exposing Hennebique system: round bars and flat 'stirrups'.

split a beam or slab vertically, was resisted by flat steel strips or 'links' wrapped around the bars. A Hennebique structure of 1907–10 reveals during demolition a haunched beam with both types of reinforcement visible (Figure 5.1). (It also illustrates that some of the substantial number of tensile reinforcing bars, bundled together, had little or no contact with the concrete, and therefore contributed little or nothing to the bending resistance of the beam!)

Other 'systems' of reinforced concrete were patented around the beginning of the twentieth century, many being imported from abroad. To avoid patent infringement, and in response to the views of the systems' developers on effectively bonding the steel to concrete, numerous differing reinforcement profiles were adopted. For example, the Kahn system from the USA used bars of square cross section with 'wings' rolled onto two diagonally opposite corners, which were bent up to anchor the bars into the concrete. Other bars were of twisted cross section (achieved by cold-working the steel, incidentally increasing its strength), or had indents or projections rolled into them (Figure 5.2).[2]

Cover and the durability of reinforcement

An essential requirement, quickly recognised, was for the reinforcement to be embedded within the concrete at a depth providing adequate **cover**. This was necessary for three reasons: to protect the reinforcement against

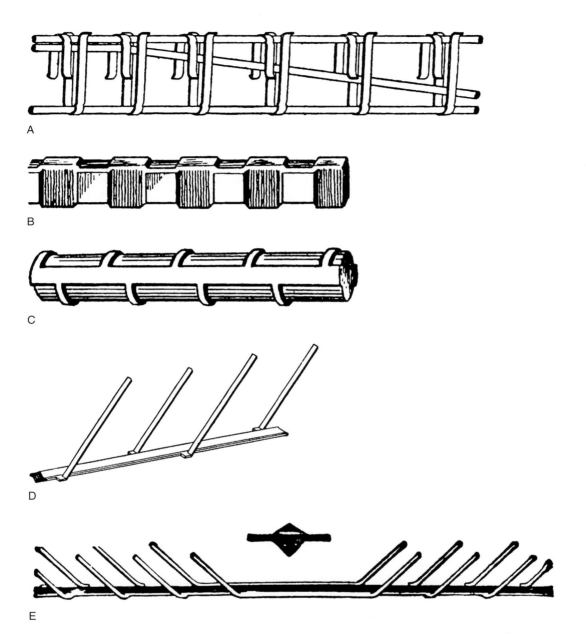

A

B

C

D

E

Figure 5.2 Some common patent reinforcement systems of the early twentieth century: Hennebique (a); Indented Bar (b – square, c – round); and Kahn (d, and e with bent-up 'wings' to improve bond to concrete).

rusting from exposure to atmospheric moisture and oxygen; to ensure an all-round bond between the steel and the concrete so that the two materials work together structurally; and to protect the steel against fire, which causes loss of strength and eventual collapse.

Lack of an adequate cover thickness of dense sound concrete has been the single most important and expensive cause of rusting of reinforcement and damage to concrete structures, and is a particular problem to be addressed when exposed concrete surfaces have to be conserved. This is not just a matter of dimensional thickness of cover. The cement in fresh concrete provides a very alkaline environment, which affords a passive protection against corrosion for the reinforcement. But porous or cracked concrete cover allows atmospheric moisture and oxygen to reach the reinforcement, which will then start to corrode. And, in a slower process, atmospheric carbon dioxide reacts with the lime in the cement to form calcium carbonate, reducing the alkalinity. This process of carbonation starts at the face of the concrete and moves inwards. If the carbonation 'front' reaches the reinforcement then its resistance to corrosion is reduced. Again, pores or cracks allow local carbonation to advance inwards more rapidly.

As the reinforcement corrodes, it forms rust – complex oxides of iron – which occupies a larger volume than the parent iron. The effect of this is to press against the enclosing concrete, and the weakest zone here is clearly the relatively thin cover to the rusting bar. In time the pressure from the swelling rust will 'spall' or crack the cover concrete away from the bar, and eventually it may fall off – leaving the reinforcement directly exposed to the weather, when it will corrode yet more rapidly (Figure 5.3).

Figure 5.3 Co-operative Wholesale Society, Tyne Quay, Newcastle (1897–1901), listed Grade II, with peeling render and corroding reinforcement; since repaired and converted to a hotel.

The essentials of construction in concrete, including reinforced concrete, have not changed greatly since the beginning of the twentieth century, although mechanisation has made labour less tiring, while technical understanding has advanced, so that there is little reason why present-day concrete construction should perpetuate the failings of the past.

Concrete is made by mixing coarse and fine aggregate – the filler material. To this is added cement (formerly lime) and water. The choice of materials and mix proportions are important to achieve a durable and strong concrete.

The typical coarse aggregate is crushed stone or gravel, which should be sound and free of clay or other impurities. (Shingle or other sea-dredged aggregates should be well washed in water to remove salts, particularly if they are to be used in reinforced concrete, where the salts could corrode the reinforcement.) Nineteenth-century concrete often made use of broken bricks, the rubble arising from building demolition, or clinker or 'breeze' (burnt or partially burnt coal), whose sulphur content could also lead to accelerated corrosion. In more recent times, processed coarse aggregates such as fly ash pellets from coal-burning power stations have been used, a useful recycling of waste materials producing a lighter-weight concrete and also reducing the pressure on natural aggregates such as crushed limestone and gravel, whose extraction from rural sites can understandably be contentious.

The typical fine aggregate is sand or stone dust. The grading of this fine aggregate – the distribution within it of particles of varying size – and the proportioning of coarse to fine aggregate are both important because the aim is to produce a dense mix with all the voids between the coarse aggregate filled with a mixture of fine aggregate and the water-cement paste. A dense mix is stronger, and gives better corrosion protection to reinforcement, than a concrete with voids in it. However, unreinforced concrete mixes with only coarse aggregates have been used; for example, 'breeze blocks' with breeze aggregate offered a lightweight product that was of adequate strength for its use in the walls of low-rise buildings and in partitions, and 'no-fines' concrete, when rendered, offered an economical walling material for low-rise structures with better thermal insulation properties than normal dense concrete.

There are nowadays many types of cement, although the 'traditional' Portland cement is probably still the most widely used. Notable varieties of cement include sulphate-resisting (for use in aggressive soils with a high sulphate content), rapid-hardening (for use where rapid strength development is needed) and white (much favoured by architects for use in exposed concrete finishes). A somewhat notorious product, high alumina cement (HAC), may be found in structures built since World War II. It is discussed in Chapter 11 of *Structures & construction in historic building conservation*. (Its structural use is now banned.)

Water should be clean and free from salts. Sea water, rich in sodium chloride, should not be used in reinforced concrete, as the salt will corrode the steel.

The solid ingredients of concrete mixes were generally measured out and batched in proportions by volume. A common mix was 1:2:4 (cement:fine aggregate:coarse aggregate). Stronger mixes were achieved by increasing the cement content while maintaining the fine:coarse aggregate ratio at 1:2, and were commonly $1:1^{1}/_{2}:3$ and 1:1:2. On-site hand-mixing on the ground was the original method for combining the materials – indeed, it is still to be seen widely today for non-structural work – but concrete-mixers were soon on the scene. A 1920 textbook on concrete devotes twenty pages to the different types of mixer available![3] More recently, the ready-mixed concrete plant, usually off site, batches the materials for concrete mixes, weighing and proportioning them automatically for delivery by mixer truck.

Reinforcement

As already noted, the early proprietary systems used a remarkable variety of reinforcing bar profiles. As the patents expired, engineers and contractors became free to use generic types of reinforcing steel, often supplied by companies which themselves provided a design service to architects and general contractors. The round mild steel bar is a common type, complemented by stronger bars, originally achieved by cold-working the steel while forming a twisted or 'deformed' profile and later, from the 1930s, by using alloys which enhanced the steel's strength. These hot-rolled bars were usually rolled with a ribbed profile to improve their anchorage and bond in the concrete, necessary to resist the higher stresses that these stronger bars could take as compared to plain mild steel bars.

Expanded metal was invented in the 1880s, and was another common form of reinforcement. The idea of pre-forming steel into sheets to reduce the site labour involved in fixing it was applied initially in the various types of lattice bar systems, many of which used corrugated rods in one or both directions so that the bars were knitted together. Later, the development of welding led to the production of welded fabric or 'mesh' that remains a common sight on building sites.

More recently, profiled metal decking – usually galvanised steel sheeting – has been widely adopted both to provide permanent formwork to support the weight of wet concrete and, bonded with it, to provide the reinforcement.

Prestressing

In the late 1920s Eugène Freyssinet in France pioneered the use of **prestressing**, in which the concrete is pre-compressed to wholly or partially eliminate the tensile stresses due to bending or direct tension. A simple visualisation of prestressing is to imagine picking up a row of books by pressing hard on the end volumes, which holds all of them together while they are lifted. Prestressing enables the strength of the entire section to be used, and also results in a stiffer element. High-strength reinforcement is needed to retain the prestressing effect, allowing for the inevitable drying shrinkage of the concrete and also for the equally inevitable 'creep' – a long-term shortening under sustained compression. (These reduce the initial stress in the prestressing, so a high initial stress is required to ensure that the concrete remains pre-compressed throughout its working life.)

Prestressing can be applied in one of two ways. The steel can be **pre-tensioned**, typically using small-diameter bars. This method is widely used in mass-produced precast prestressed flooring units cast under factory conditions in long steel moulds. The bars are anchored at the ends of the moulds after being tensioned, and concrete is then poured into the moulds. When the concrete has hardened the bars are released, immediately transferring the prestress into the concrete to which the steel has bonded. The concrete can then be saw-cut to the required lengths for use.

In **post-tensioning**, sheaths are pre-formed in the formwork (see below) before the concrete is placed. When it has hardened, steel – in the form of bundled wires, cable (known as strand) or bars with threaded ends – is threaded through the sheaths and then tensioned by jacking. The tensioned wire or strand is typically locked in place with wedges forced into cast-in steel anchorages, while bars are secured by nuts.

Corrosion-resistant reinforcement

In more recent times, recognition that corrosion of reinforcement is a major concern in exposed structures, such as bridges and marine works, has led to measures to protect the steel. Galvanising was the first remedy, followed by the use of stainless steel in place of ordinary carbon steel. More recently, epoxy-coated steel has found use, the coating providing a tough barrier against moisture and oxygen.

Repair of corrosion-damaged reinforcement in exposed concrete faces (see Chapter 11 of *Structures & construction in historic building conservation*) may well warrant use of one or more of these measures, especially where the replacement reinforcement will have to be closer to the surface of the concrete than is currently recommended for adequate protection in the future.

Formwork

The distinctive characteristic of concrete – its ability to be cast into whatever shape is required – does of course require that this shape is defined before the concrete is poured. This is achieved using formwork – also known as shuttering – to define the *form* of the work. Typically for in situ construction this is made of timber (nowadays often plywood) cut to shape and supported by propping and bracing of timber, steel or aluminium, which has to be designed to support its own weight and that of the wet concrete, and also to resist vibrations and other disturbing effects as the concrete is placed and compacted. Making formwork accurately with tight joints is an important skill, particularly for exposed concrete surfaces where the appearance of the finished work is largely dependent on the formworker's standard of workmanship.

Ribbed and coffered floors are typically formed with polypropylene moulds to define the profiles of deeper ribs alternating with thinner concrete panels. (In such floors, weight is saved by omitting concrete that is mostly in tension, which is of course resisted by the reinforcement in the ribs.)

Precast units made off site may be cast in steel moulds, particularly where many units of the same profile are to be made. Timber moulds have finite lives; indeed their 'stripping' to expose concrete after their first use may cause damage requiring replacement.

Placing of reinforcement and concrete, and curing

Once the formwork has been fixed, the reinforcement can be placed. To provide the necessary cover between the steel and the concrete faces, the steel is supported on spacers of precast concrete or, more recently, nylon or other plastics.

The earliest method of transporting mixed concrete to the formwork was by wheelbarrow, and later by small trucks. More recently, and particularly with the prevalence of ready-mixed concrete delivered to site in trucks, concrete is commonly placed using 'skips' supported from a crane or by pumping directly from the truck.

Placing the concrete into its required location and filling the formwork still often requires the concrete gang to labour hard, and is not the cleanest of jobs. Concreting is a responsible task, and should be considered as much a skilled trade as that of the carpenter or bricklayer.

It is important to 'compact' the newly placed concrete to expel air bubbles and ensure that the concrete fills the formwork to achieve the required profiles. Early concrete was deliberately made to be 'runny', with plenty of water, so that it would flow readily into the formwork, as compaction could be achieved only by using hand tools, some of rather odd shapes like cricket bats and hockey sticks. As is shown in Chapter 11 of *Structures & construction in historic building conservation*, excess water in the concrete mix leads to durability problems, although it has to be said that specialists such as Hennebique exercised close control over their projects, so that many early structures show fewer signs of distress than might be expected.

Freyssinet, whose name appeared above in connection with prestressing, also studied the effects of compaction, and concluded in 1917 that mechanical compaction was essential to produce a dense concrete. This is achieved using either external vibrators, clamped to the formwork, or internal vibrators. Typical of the latter is the 'poker' vibrator, whose moaning drone is a characteristic sound to be heard on a building site.

Horizontal surfaces now have to be levelled and tamped to form the required smooth or roughened finish.

After this, the concrete has to cure as it gains strength. It needs protection against freezing (which will disrupt the setting process), hot weather and strong winds (which remove moisture from the concrete and cause surface cracking), rain, traffic and other disruptive effects.

After a period of time, typically several days, the formwork and later the propping can be removed to leave the completed concrete structure.

Concrete finishes

It was soon realised that concrete had the potential to be used without being covered by another material acting either as cladding or as an internal finish such as plaster. In the nineteenth century concrete was indeed often tinted and formed into ornate shapes to simulate carved stone or terra cotta. Once reinforced concrete had been introduced, allowing the construction of all-concrete structures of greater size and height, its potential to stand exposed was seen to offer a valuable saving in the cost of cladding. It must be said that an early belief among architects and engineers that reinforced concrete was virtually maintenance free was not borne out by performance, and – as now – buildings with externally exposed plain concrete surfaces were often rendered and/or painted soon after construction (Figure 5.3).[4] Nevertheless, untreated exposed concrete was widely used for bridges, functional buildings and other structures such as water tanks and jetties.

In such structures the concrete was commonly cast against smooth timber formwork, although sometimes the rough-sawn timber left a board-marked impression (Figure 5.4) that was later to be widely exploited by architects during the 'Brutalist' period of the 1960s and 1970s (Figure 5.5). Over time, the externally exposed plain surfaces of early reinforced concrete structures have often been 'etched' by sooty rain and frost, exposing the coarse aggregate to leave a surface resembling a flat shingle beach. Present-day concrete should be less vulnerable to such etching, thanks to the lower water content and higher cement content of the mix and the mechanical compaction used in construction to achieve a dense concrete.

Le Corbusier and others took a great interest in the architectural treatment of exposed concrete during the development of the Modern Movement in the 1920s and 1930s, although it was the rebuilding after World War II that provided a major spur to its use in the UK. Architects eagerly designed many treatments of concrete including the board-marking already mentioned (Figure 5.5), lightly or deeply exposed aggregate (Figure 5.6), stepped and profiled surfaces (Figure 5.7) and deep pitting (achieved by pick-hammering to produce a surface more like a rock face) (Figure 5.8).

Achieving neat and visually pleasing results required very careful cutting and fitting of the formwork, and equally careful placing and compaction of

Figure 5.4 Co-operative Wholesale Society interior showing imprint of timber formwork on concrete.

Figure 5.5 The School of Engineering and Science, Westminster University, London, by Lyons, Israel and Ellis (1965–68): external board-marking (now overcoated).

Figure 5.6 Trellick Tower, West London, by Erno Goldfinger (1968–72), Grade II* listed: in situ exposed aggregate and clear delineation of floors and rise of staircase.

Figure 5.7 YMCA, Tottenham Court Road, London, by Elsworth Sykes (1972–77): ribbed concrete weathering well.

Figure 5.8 The Barbican, London, by Chamberlain, Powell & Bon (planned 1959; opened 1982), listed Grade II: pick-hammered 'Brutalist' concrete.

the concrete. The formwork had to be treated with a release agent, such as a light oil, so that the young 'green' concrete did not stick to it as it was eased off, or alternatively – for exposed aggregate finishes – a chemical 'retarder' might be applied to the face of the formwork. This slowed the setting of the surface cement paste, which could then be brushed or washed to remove the cement and sand on the surface and expose the coarse aggregate to the required depth. Alternatively, the hardened surface could be acid-etched or sand-blasted to expose the coarse aggregate. Whatever the method, it had to be applied consistently, otherwise there would be conspicuous 'highs and lows' or local unevenness on the surface.

Precast concrete

The examples of exposed aggregate just referred to and illustrated are notable examples of good-quality concrete finishes achieved in situ – that is, on the concrete already built into the structure. But this is a challenging task. There is only one chance of getting in situ finishes right, unless the concrete can be demolished and recast for another attempt – not usually affordable, and causing constructional delays. Add to this the conditions on a building site – standing on a scaffold in often foul weather conditions and usually working on a vertical concrete face holding a tool of some sort – and it is clear that off-site manufacture of concrete units offers a much better chance of getting a good, consistent result.

Thus **precasting** has been very widely used for concrete when it serves as cladding on the external envelope of the building, loadbearing or non-loadbearing. By casting cladding panels face down with repeated use of moulds, the concrete surface treatment can be carried out more consistently, while the factory environment affords better working conditions and quality control than the typical site.[5] Precasting has also been extensively used for purely structural (loadbearing) elements such as walls, floor panels and the prestressed floor beams previously described. Many precast proprietary low-rise housing systems were developed, mostly after World War II, and so too were systems for high-rise 'tower blocks' – mostly built as part of the local authorities' housing programme. But in 1968 the partial collapse of such a structure following a gas explosion in Ronan Point, a twenty-two-storey tower block in East London, resulted in four deaths. Concern over the safety of system-built tower blocks – and their social failings, too – led to the rapid run-down in such building.

Concrete blocks

Like precasting, concrete blocks were first employed in the nineteenth century. (There is very little that is truly new – only old ideas that have been mislaid!)

Concrete blocks were originally seen as a cheaper alternative to brick in terms of both material cost and labour, as a block takes little longer to lay than one of the several smaller bricks that it typically replaces. Nowadays, the heavy dense concrete block is less commonly used, as energy conservation requirements in building regulations call for walls with increasingly better thermal insulation properties. Dense concrete has poor insulating properties, so today the typical house wall will comprise an inner leaf of lightweight concrete block, a cavity (possibly containing insulation material) and an outer leaf, commonly of brick but sometimes – particularly in areas where the older local buildings display natural stone – precast concrete blocks. These may contain crushed stone and stone dust, with an external face sometimes deliberately profiled to give a rough-hewn look. Containing also cement made from limestone and clay, this is truly reconstructed or reconstituted stone – a thought with which this chapter began and with which it now ends.

Further reading

Hamilton, S.B., *A Note on the History of Reinforced Concrete in Buildings* (HMSO, London, 1956).

Macdonald, Susan (ed.), *Concrete: Building pathology* (Blackwell, Oxford, 2003), foreword by David Watt and Peter Swallow.

Newby, Frank (ed.), *Early Reinforced Concrete,* Studies in the History of Civil Engineering, vol. 11 (Ashgate, Aldershot, 2001).

Sutherland, James, Humm, Dawn and Chrimes, Mike (eds), *Historic Concrete: Background to appraisal* (Thomas Telford, London, 2001).

Information and reference sources include the libraries of the Institution of Civil Engineers (including the Concrete Archive), the Institution of Structural Engineers and the Royal Institute of British Architects, especially for journals such as the *Architects' Journal* and *Concrete & Constructional Engineering.*

Endnotes

1. Brown, Joyce M., 'W.B. Wilkinson (1819–1902) and his place in the history of reinforced concrete', in Newby, Frank (ed.), *Early Reinforced Concrete, Studies in the History of Civil Engineering,* vol. 11 (Ashgate, Aldershot, 2001), pp. 43–60.
2. Others are illustrated in Appendix III in James Sutherland, Dawn Humm and Mike Chrimes (eds), *Historic Concrete: Background to appraisal* (Thomas Teiford, London, 2001), while the Concrete Archive at the Institution of Civil Engineers has a large collection of bar types and original documentation – an invaluable resource for those engaged in conservation work on early reinforced concrete structures.
3. Bernard E. Jones (ed.), *Cassell's Reinforced Concrete* (Waverley Book Co., London, 1920).
4. For 'after' view, see *Structures & construction in historic building conservation,* Figure 11.2.
5. *Ibid.*, Figure 11.3.

6 Stone slate, clay tile and metamorphic slate

Christopher Harris

There are many and varied vernacular roofing traditions across England. Local roofing systems changed over the years as new products were developed or became more widely available owing to improvements in transport and technology. The original pattern of building and roofing was dictated primarily by the local geology, but other factors such as water communications and trading patterns, together with changing fashions, have all played their part.

During the Roman occupation of England, the use of clay tiles and stone slates became common on the more important buildings, with some form of thatch or cleft wooden shingles on lesser structures. After the Roman era the country reverted to its tribal past and, possibly in part because of continual conflict causing insecurity, building construction methods became less long-lived and little other than thatch was used for roofing. Only with the growth of the Christian Church, combined with tribal groupings under Danelaw to the north and east of Watling Street and the Kingdom of Wessex to the south and west, did more stable conditions arise, allowing better-quality buildings to be constructed, which in turn supported heavier roofing.

The Norman invasion, and the subjugation of the whole of England, heralded a period of relative stability that together with the ever growing prosperity of the Church resulted in a golden age of construction.

However, apart from shipping by boat around the coast and along natural waterways, it was not until the Industrial Revolution and the development of the canals, followed by the railway network, that many of our heavier or more fragile building and roofing materials could be economically transported great distances from their places of origin. Before the Industrial Revolution much of the country relied on readily and locally available roofing and building materials, thus producing the vast range of regional vernacular styles we see today.

This chapter will no more than touch on the range of roofing materials and methods that have been used historically, and how, when and why changes occurred. Sedimentary stone slates are introduced first, being more important as a roofing material historically than the other materials that follow. Clay tiles, Welsh slates and other more modern materials were used over a broader geographical area from the beginning of the Industrial Revolution owing to improvements in transport, being lighter and less labour-intensive to produce; placing less of a load on roof structures, they allowed the use of thinner frames and lower pitches. Some of the roofing techniques that were developed for the various random roofing systems (stone slate, wooden shingles and random metamorphic slating – the norm before the growth of Welsh tally slating) were occasionally transferred to clay tiles.

Stone slates

Stone has been used for roofing wherever it has been found to split into thin enough sheets. Across England, different sedimentary stones have been quarried and used to roof many of the lovely buildings in the most outstandingly beautiful areas, producing the distinctive regional architecture for which the country is so famous. In 1890, William Morris's 'On the external covering of roofs' observed: 'If any regard is to be had to the general beauty of the landscape, the natural material of the special countryside should be used instead of imported material.' This holds as true today as it did then.

A **geological map** (Figure 6.1) shows some of England's stone slate varieties. However, there are many additional stones in certain areas, particularly in the Cotswolds, where there were probably more than thirteen geologically different stone slate varieties, and the Shropshire and Herefordshire sandstones along the Welsh Marches, where a similar number of varieties have been recorded. In total, there are more than fifty different varieties of sedimentary stone slate across the country. Unfortunately, owing to a number of factors including past conservation guidance dictating that 'reclaimed' rather than new stone slates should be used in roofing and re-roofing projects, almost none of these stones are now produced on a commercial basis. This has lead to a dramatic increase in theft or illegal removal of stone slates to supply the growing demand, and the subsequent destruction of our rural built heritage. There are now almost no 'legitimate' donor buildings from which stone slates can be removed to supply the demand, so in many areas of the country the majority of the 'reclaimed' material that arrives on the market is illegally sourced, either stolen or removed from legally protected buildings without listed building consent. At the end of the 1980s the Cotswold police estimated that this accounted for more than 50% of the available stone; since then matters have become considerably worse. Planning Policy Guidance 15 (PPG15) states that 'when a roof is stripped it is important that as much as possible of the original covering is reused, preferably on the visible slopes, with matching new materials on the other slopes'. The replacement Planning Policy Statement 16 (PPS16) is expected to further strengthen this guidance.

General random slating method

Stone slates were traditionally holed near the upper edge and had a dry seasoned oak or other peg hammered into the hole (across the country

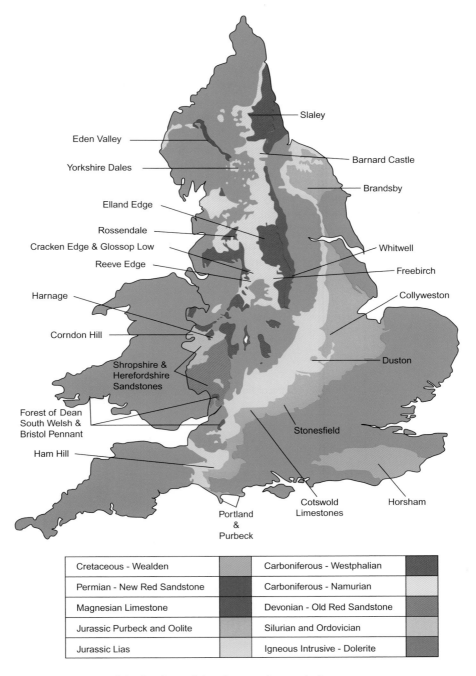

Cretaceous - Wealden		Carboniferous - Westphalian	
Permian - New Red Sandstone		Carboniferous - Namurian	
Magnesian Limestone		Devonian - Old Red Sandstone	
Jurassic Purbeck and Oolite		Silurian and Ordovician	
Jurassic Lias		Igneous Intrusive - Dolerite	

Figure 6.1 Some of England's traditional stone slate varieties.

various materials have been used instead of wooden pegs, including sheep and chicken bones). It is important to use dry heartwood because the wood will expand as it absorbs moisture from the air, tightening it in the hole. Heartwood is less prone to rot or attack by wood-boring beetles. The slates were then hung over cleft laths before being torched on the underside with a combination of fat lime mortar and hair. The quarrymen used every suitable piece of stone that was abstracted from the ground. This meant that the stone slates varied enormously in length and width – in the Cotswolds, stone slate lengths are known to vary from less than 6 inches (150 mm) – 'outrules' in Collyweston drop to 5 inches (125 mm) – to more than 4 feet (1200 mm) in length on a single roof. When the stone arrived on site, the roofers would sort the slates to different lengths before estimating the running widths of each length and calculating how many courses of each size should be used to cover each elevation at the **headlap** necessary to provide watertightness. The largest slates are used near the eaves and the sizes are gradually reduced as work progresses towards the ridge. The slates were generally laid using a double lap system, where the tails of one course of slates cover the heads of the two courses below (Figure 6.2).

It is essential that both the headlap and **sidelap** are kept to an adequate size to avoid water ingress. The sidelap is more important than the headlap

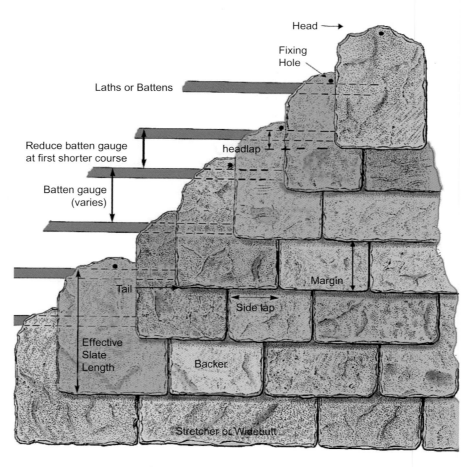

Figure 6.2 Terminology of random slate roofing.

Figure 6.3 Cotswold stone roofs at Arlington Row, Bibury, near Cirencester.

but, unfortunately, it is rarely mentioned in modern roofing specifications and all too often the vertical joints between the slates are allowed to be too close together on adjacent courses, allowing water to run into the roof space. Different stones and conditions may require the stone slates to be spot- or head-bedded in lime mortar to help them to lie flat, or to resist wind uplift.

The ridges of stone-slated roofs vary in different parts of the country. In the Cotswolds it is usual to use more or less ornamental ridge tiles cut from limestone freestone (Figure 6.3); in other areas terra cotta saddle slates have been used. In the northern sandstone regions, a ridge tile may be cut from a piece of stone from the same quarry, or another sandstone may have been used; occasionally, 'wrestlers' – stone slates notched in the sides and interlocked to provide a weathertight crest – are still to be seen in both sandstone and metamorphic slate.

Sandstones

All sandstone slates are produced from laminated deposits which will cleave with the use of a mallet and cold chisel. The majority are fairly regular in thickness and have a reasonably flat surface, but there are exceptions, such as the very shelly, rough-textured Harnage stone, with a size range closer to that of Cotswold limestones.

Generally, sandstone slates are considerably larger than those of limestone. They can be laid at lower pitches (30–35°) but because of their size they do not allow for fine detail, and traditional roofs are rarely built with any more than a simple gable construction.

113

Where two roof slopes meet, either lead gutters were built into the valleys or a chevron valley was formed. The chevron valley uses a downward-pointed valley slate to guide rainwater down the centre. It works reasonably efficiently in light rain, but water may leak into the building in very heavy downpours. It is therefore best to include a lead soaker in each course to guide ingressed water back into the valley.

Limestones

The country's limestone roofing comes almost entirely from the Jurassic limestone belt, from North Yorkshire south to near the Wash, then across the country to the Cotswold belt, and turning south through west Wiltshire and east Somerset, finally meeting the coast in Dorset.

The smaller limestone slates allow for greater variation and intricacy of roof design, with valleys, hips and dormer windows far more common. The traditional **swept Cotswold valley** comprises alternating sets of three and two stone slates (Figure 6.4). This type of valley needs to be carefully constructed to ensure it is stable and weathertight. As with all valley types, it is best to insert lead soakers in each course to guarantee adequate performance.

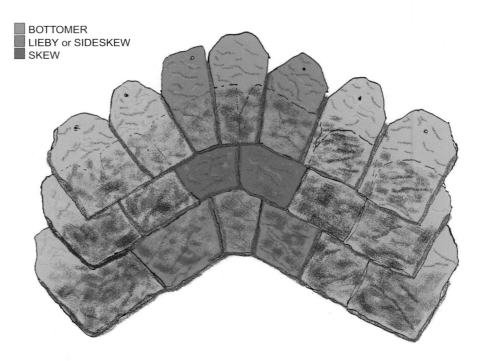

BOTTOMER
LIEBY or SIDESKEW
SKEW

Figure 6.4 Diagram of a Cotswold swept valley.

Clay tiles

Plain tiles

By the commencement of Norman rule in England, clay 'plain tiles' were common on the roofs of more important and urban buildings south and east of the limestone belt across the country. However, until the Industrial Revolution clay tiles were extremely rare almost everywhere else. Due to earlier conflagrations, in 1212 there was an Ordinance that prohibited thatch roofing in London, mentioning the alternatives: shingles, lead, stone slates and clay tiles. Tiles were both locally made and shipped across the channel from Flanders, delivered to coastal towns and along navigable waterways.

It is likely that the basic flat 'plain tile' was developed as a terra cotta version of wood shingles, another common roofing system. Tiles were made in the same kilns as bricks, which were used to shield the less substantial tiles from the ferocity of the heat. Although Edward IV passed a statute in 1477 standardising the size of plain tiles to $10^{1}/_{2} \times 6^{1}/_{2} \times 5/8$ inches, old regional traditions continued, and variations were compounded by the fact that clay shrinks during firing, so under-burnt tiles finished larger than standard, and over-burnt ones smaller. It was not until a statute of George I in 1725, reaffirming the earlier statute, was combined with improved technology that a fairly regular size of tile became the norm.

Spanish and Roman tiles

The plain tile is by far the most common historic clay tile across England, although it is rarely seen outside this country. Around the Mediterranean the Spanish tile is the norm – effectively a tapered cylinder, cut in half lengthways to make two channels which are laid in alternating upward- and downward-facing courses up the rafter line, giving them their common name, 'overs and unders'. Although these tiles are effective and can be laid at a low roof pitch, they are not suited to the complicated roof designs in the UK and were not common until the latter part of the nineteenth century.

In England, the Romans used a system of flat tiles (*tegulae*) with the vertical joints protected by semi-round tiles (*imbrices*). In the nineteenth century, Bridgwater in Somerset started producing a range of tiles copying this design but amalgamating the flat and convex sections to produce 'Roman tiles' and, more commonly and twice the width, 'Double Roman' tiles (Figure 6.5). These interlock, are laid as a single-lap system and have become quite common on historic buildings especially in the south-west, replacing thatch or other earlier roofing materials.

Pantiles

Pantiles are most often seen in the east Midlands and north-east England, originally imported from Holland, and in Somerset, where they were

Figure 6.5 Double Roman tiles replacing Cotswold stone slates.

originally imported through Bridgwater and later made in the town (they were not used in the south-east, where plain tiles were available). They are quite large – approximately $13^1/_2$ inches (340 mm) by $9^1/_2$ inches (240 mm) – and have the shape of an elongated 'S' where the drop on one tile overlaps the rise on the adjacent one. They are laid to a single-lap system, but are not particularly efficient as they tend not to interlock very well and often rely on the underlying roofing felt or straw to offer complete protection. As they are large they do not allow any intricate roof designs, and even dormer windows tend to look awkward.

Metamorphic slate

Slate is a metamorphic mudstone produced when a deposit of fine sediment is heated and compressed due to the movement of tectonic plates, causing the crystals of mica to be compressed and creating new cleavage planes at 90 degrees to the line of compression. These cleavage planes bear no relation to the original bedding planes, which can often still be seen in the material.

Slate has been quarried in areas of Cumbria, with Westmorland being the most famous, in Leicestershire, where Swithland slate is still often seen, and in Devon and Cornwall, where the Delabole slate quarry is one of the largest in England, measuring over 2.5 km in circumference and about 400 metres deep. Historically, each of these areas has had a number of producing quarries, but in England only Westmorland and Delabole are still producing today.

Almost all English-quarried slates would have been random slates, produced in a range of lengths and widths, and hung using similar techniques to the original stone, slate and wood shingle industries. It is only since the expansion and mechanisation of the Welsh slate supply that tally slating (slates sold by the number of identical sizes – tally) has become common.

Welsh slates are the most common indigenous slate seen across the UK today, but they are only one of a number of varieties that have been used historically, some of which are still in production. Indeed, Welsh slates only became very common following the opening of the railway across North Wales to Holyhead in 1848, which allowed the material to be shipped across the country both rapidly and economically.

It is possible to see the historical development of many areas of the country by assessing the roofscape. The oldest settlements have evidence of the local vernacular roofing materials; with the opening of the canals in the north of England in the eighteenth century, sandstone slates were transported greater distances from their quarries, and they are seen along the routes of the canals; when the railways opened in the mid-nineteenth century, Welsh slates travelled nationwide and are to be seen in many places almost exclusively around railways.

Glossary of various roofing terms

Backer: narrow slates laid roughly centrally over a wide slate to accommodate the increasing number of slates in each course as work progresses up the roof. Synonym: bachelor.

Band: head lap.

Ballast: stone (usually rubble) used to support the eaves slating in some systems.

Bachelor: see Backer.

Batten: sawn wooden support for hanging or nailing stone slates. Synonym: lath. In this guide, the word lath is reserved for split supports.

Batten gauge: spacing of battens or laths up the rafter. In random slating it always varies.

Bedding: (of rocks) a plane parallel to the surface of deposition of a rock. The plane along which stone slates often, but not invariably, split.

(of slating) use of mortar in spots or fillets to prevent stone slates from rocking. In some areas, it is used to improve weather tightness.

See also Head bedding, Full bedding.

Bevel: the shape of the edge of stone slates produced by dressing them to size and shape. Bevels take a variety of local or regional forms and are significant to the local distinctiveness of roofs.

Breeze: a mixture of clinker and lime or cement. When used to bed slates it could be crushed down to fill any gaps without excessive separation of the slates.

Cleavage: slaty cleavage is developed in fine-grained rocks following metamorphism. Under the influence of pressure and heat the pre-existing

117

platey minerals are partially re-crystallised and aligned perpendicular to the pressure. Slates cleave parallel to the platey minerals.

Clete: spike bent at right angles and driven into the rafter below thin laths to hold them without splitting them.

Counter-batten: batten laid up the rafter to raise the level of the battens. Commonly used to prevent pegs piercing an underlay or to provide a drainage gap between the battens and an underlay. If the underlay can be installed with a sag between the rafters, a counter-batten to provide drainage will not be necessary.

Course: single row of slates across the roof.

Coursing: setting out the courses of slates. In random slating the coursing has to be adjusted to take account of reducing slate lengths.

Cresting: ridge stones or tiles.

Delph, delve: dialect term for a shallow quarry, especially in the north of England.

Diamond pattern: a slating system using 'diamond-shaped' pieces of stone hung from one corner; the shape is actually hexagonal to avoid three layers where adjacent slates and courses meet. An ancient method found on many Roman sites and in Dumfries.

Diminishing: the system whereby slates are sorted by length and laid with the longest at the eaves, diminishing to the smallest at the ridge. It is essential that the minimum head lap is maintained when there is a change of slate length between two courses. This also ensures that each successive margin is the same size or smaller than those below.

Double battening: the use of two battens to prevent the fixing peg tilting. For conservation the mortar methods (head bedding or torching) are more appropriate.

Double lap: stone slates laid so that each course overlaps the course next but one below. In some regions and in some special applications, triple-lap slating (where each course overlaps the course next but two below) is adopted.

Dressing: the process of shaping the stone slate and producing the edge detail using either a chisel-edged hammer or a bladed tool. Regional differences exist for the edge detail which may be square or bevelled. Synonyms: trimming, fettling (Yorks, Lancs), crapping (Cotswolds), napping (Collyweston).

Eaves: (of stone slates) the short course laid at the eaves under the first full course. The method of placing and supporting the eaves stone slates varies regionally. Synonyms: under eave(s) cussome (Cotswolds).

Eaves tilt: *see* Tilt. Synonym: eaves kick.

Exposure: (to weather) most commonly the conditions of wind and rain which apply to a roof or location. Less commonly the conditions or frequency of frost.

(of slates) the area of the slate or course of slates not covered by the overlying slates or course.

Facies: the sum total of features such as sedimentary rock type, mineral content, sedimentary structures, bedding characteristics, fossil content, etc. which characterise a sediment as having been deposited in a given environment.

Fissile: rock which can be split along bedding planes; cf. Cleavage.

Fixings: nails, pegs or cleats.

Full bedding: setting slates in a bed of mortar at the tail and across the full slate's width. Although common in some regions, the technique is prone to trapping water within the slating with the risk of leaks.

Gallet: small pieces of stone slate or metamorphic slate bedded in lime mortar at the head of a slate to support the slate above. Synonym: shale.

Gauge: the spacing of laths or battens up the roof slope. In stone slating, the gauge is always variable.

Head: the top edge of a stone slate as laid.

Head bedding: setting the head of slates in a bed of mortar across part of or the full slate's width.

Head lap: in double-lap slating (the normal slating method), the amount by which a slate overlaps the slate in the course next but one below. In single-lap slating such as diamond pattern, it is the amount by which each slate overlaps the one immediately below. Synonym: band.

Lath: split wooden support for hanging stone slates. Synonym: batten. In this guide, the word batten is reserved for sawn supports.

Log: in Collyweston slating, the raw stone which is suitable for splitting by frost.

Margin: strictly the area, but more commonly the length, of the exposed part of the slate.

Metamorphism: the process, involving heat, pressure or both, which changes the direction in which sedimentary rocks split. Metamorphic rocks such as true slates split along cleavage planes which are unrelated to their original bedding. Sometimes the cleavage and bedding are parallel.

True slates are formed by low-grade metamorphism – not much heat or pressure involved. Higher grades of metamorphism produce rocks with larger mineral crystals which can be seen without magnification. Examples include schists, quartzite and gneiss. Generally such rocks cannot be split thin enough to use for roofing, but some examples do exist.

Mossing: use of moss or other vegetable material to windproof the joints and gaps between stone slates.

Mossing iron: tool used to force moss etc. between slates.

Oversailing: verges which are carried beyond the outer face of a gable wall.

Overburden: (in quarrying) useless material which overlies a bed of useful material.

Peg: wooden or metal peg used to hang slates from laths or battens. Metal pegs are a modern innovation.

Pendle: generally a quarrying term for any fissile rock. For Cotswolds stone slates it is used specifically for rock which is split by frosting.

Pig: a course with a larger margin than the course(s) below, resulting from poor setting out and a failure to maintain adequate head lap.

Pitch: the angle of the rafters to the horizontal. The pitch of the stone slates themselves will be significantly less because they are resting on each other, but this is taken into account by the traditional rafter pitch and lap relationship for the slate and the locality.

Pointing: use of mortar to fill the vertical joints and to seal the tail gap of stone slating. Pointing may show (undesirable) or be raked or held back. Often associated with bedding.

Presents: stone slates formed by natural, including peri-glacial, weathering in near surface deposits. They are often thicker than hand-split stone slates produced from deeper layers (Cotswolds).

Random: (of stone slate) variable length and width.

(of roofing) slates laid with reducing length up the roof slope and the widths selected and placed so that they provide at least the minimum side lap over the slates in the course below.

Recording: (a roof) compiling a photographic or written record of the construction of a roof. Typically it will involve measuring the slate lengths, margins, laps, and batten gauges and describing the detailing at valleys, hips, ridges, abutments, etc.

Regularly: (of diminishing or random slating) the system whereby each successive margin is the same size or smaller than those below. It does not mean that there are an equal number of courses of each margin size.

Secret gutter: sheet metal gutter – usually lead – hidden by carrying the slating over it. Most commonly used at abutments especially where the use of soakers and flashings is prevented by a coping etc.

Sedimentary: rocks formed from other rocks which have been broken down by weathering, or rocks formed by biological or chemical actions. If they can be split to make roofing (fissile), it will be along bedding planes. *See also* Metamorphism.

Shadow: (1) a thin piece of (usually metamorphic) slate used in the Horsham district to improve the weather resistance of the roofs when, because of a shortage of stone slate, the head lap is reduced to less than the normal minimum. Originally the shadow was a thin piece of Horsham stone. It is always used in conjunction with mortar bedding and pointing. Technically this is an undesirable method because it seals the roof, preventing it from breathing. (2) a thin piece of slate or stone used to block the entry of wind-driven rain where the shouldering of stone slates does not provide sufficient cover with adjacent slates.

Shale: small pieces of stone slate or metamorphic slate bedded in lime mortar at the head of a slate to support the slate above. Synonym: gallet.

Shoulder: (1) to remove the top corners of a stone slate;

(2) the top corners of stone slates.

Excessive shouldering can result in a roof leaking.

Side lap: the amount by which a stone slate laterally overlaps the stone slate in the course below.

Single lap: slating or tiling system where each slate overlaps the slate immediately below. It is uncommon in slating but is the normal system for interlocking tiles.

Slate: There is debate about the correct term to use to describe sandstone, limestone and similar non-metamorphic roofing products. The most frequently encountered traditional and colloquial terms are stone slates or grey slates but they are also called flags, flagstones, thackstones, stone tiles, sclaites or grey sclaites (in Scotland), slats or slatts.

Each of these terms is used to distinguish them from metamorphic or 'blue' slates. The objection to the term stone slate is that sandstones and limestones are not, petrographically, slates; that is, they have not been metamorphosed and consequently they split along bedding rather than cleavage planes. This is certainly true, and some geologists prefer the retronym tilestone to distinguish them from real slates. However, the term slate meaning any flat rectangular roofing product has historical precedence, since it pre-dates the science of geology by hundreds of years and is the term in common use. In this document stone slate is used.

Spot bedding: the use of small spots of mortar to prevent uneven stone slates rocking. The minimum of mortar should be used and should not lift the slates.

Tail: the bottom edge of a stone slate as laid.

Tiering: *see* Torching.

Tilt: (at the eaves course and at back abutments) the lift provided to ensure that successive courses lie correctly without gaps at the tail. On the main areas of the roof slope, the tail of each stone slate rests on two thicknesses of stone slate in the course next but one below. At the eaves, the first full course rests on only one thickness – the eaves slate. Essentially, the tilt replaces the missing thickness. The required amount of tilt can be provided by a tilting fillet, by building up the wall head underneath the eaves course or by setting the rafter back from the outside edge of the wall. Historically, stone roofs usually did not have fascia boards. Although fascia boards can be used to provide tilt, this is not traditional.

(at verges and side abutments) the lift provided by raising a rafter relative to the roof slope or by use of a batten or tilting fillet to tilt the slating into the slope, thus directing water onto the roof slope.

(at valleys) use of a wooden fillet to support the edge of the valley slates and to fill the gap between the lead and the slates, thus preventing water driving into the slating.

Tilting fillet: length of wood used to provide tilt.

Tingle: metal strap fixed to the slating batten or lath and hooking under the tail of the slate as a temporary repair. Typically lead or copper. Many stone slates are too heavy for this to be a successful repair.

Torching: lime and hair mortar applied to the underside of stone slates to render them windproof. Synonym: tiering.

Half torching: application of lime and hair mortar between the top edge of the lath or batten and the underside of the slates. Synonym: single torching.

Full torching: application of lime and hair mortar between the top and bottom edges of the laths or battens and the underside of the slates.

Single torching: *see* Half torching.

Undercloak: slate (or other material) laid under the slating to form a neat finish.

Under course: the first, short course of stone slates laid at the eaves. *See also* Eaves.

Underlay: flexible sheet material laid under slating, primarily to prevent wind blowing through it.

Unweathered: (of stone roofing) rock which is too deep to have been subjected to weathering and consequently has to be split by mechanical action or frosting after extraction.

Valley: the intersecting of two roof slopes forming an internal angle. A variety of methods are used to weather the intersection including, laced, swept, Welsh and chevron.

Weathering: (1) the process by which rocks are broken down and decomposed by the action of external agencies such as wind, rain, temperature changes, plants and bacteria. In the development of weathered stone slates, it is often very thin clay or mica beds which are weathered out.

(2) the use of lead, etc. or stone shales, shadows or shivers to block the entry of wind-driven rain where the shouldering of stone slates does not provide sufficient cover with adjacent slates.

(3) the use of lead, etc. to prevent water leaks at roof junctions.

Widebutt: a wide slate used with a backer.

Wrestlers: notched and interlocking slates used to form a ridge.

Acknowledgements

I would like to thank Richard Jordan of Amber Roofing, Nottingham, and Cliff Beauchamp of Abbey Roofing, Witney, Oxfordshire, for their help and guidance over the years.

Further reading

Bennett, Frank and Pinion, Alfred, *Roof Slating & Tiling* (Donhead, Shaftesbury, 2000; this edition originally 1948).

Clifton-Taylor, Alec, *The Pattern of English Building* (Faber, London, 1987) http://www.stoneroof.org.uk/

7 Cast iron, wrought iron and steel

Geoff Wallis and Michael Bussell

Manufacture of iron and steel

Iron, the fourth most abundant element in the earth's crust, occurs widely in ores (mainly oxides) with a metal content up to 60%. Iron has a strong affinity for oxygen, but fortunately carbon has an even stronger attraction for oxygen. At high temperatures carbon will therefore combine with oxygen in the ore leaving the metal behind, but much heat energy is required.

$$Fe_2O_3 + 3C > 2Fe + 3CO$$

Iron ore Carbon   Metallic   Carbon monoxide
     (Charcoal/coke) iron   gas driven off

Smelting of iron first developed around 2000 BC, heralding the **Iron Age**. It was discovered that when heated in the charred embers of a fire blown by bellows, iron ore could be reduced to a spongy metallic **bloom** which could then be hammered to consolidate and purify it. It was further refined by reheating and hammering, becoming usable **worked** or **wrought** iron.

It was discovered, probably by accident, that the addition of limestone chips helped the purification process by combining with many of the ore's impurities, forming a fluid slag.

Wrought iron is too soft to hold a good cutting edge. Around 1400 BC it was discovered, probably in Asia Minor, that reheating blades with carbon (charcoal) produced a harder and tougher surface that could be sharpened. The carbon combined with the implement's surface, forming iron carbide, or **steel**. (Iron carbide is known as cementite, which later gave its name to the cementation process for the production of steel.) This steel surface could be heated and quenched in water to produce a hard edge.

Wrought iron production in early 'bloomeries' was small scale and expensive, so in pre-industrial times the metal was used where its strength, hardness and malleability were essential, for example in weapons, tools, security applications such as locks and window bars, wearing parts (hinges, bearings, bell hangers and clappers, and parts of machines such as pumps, windmills and watermills), fastenings (nails, rivets, collars, cramps) and ornamentation. Because of its value, it was also used as currency and jewellery, **currency bars** being bent round at their ends to prove that they did not crack, demonstrating their quality as usable iron and therefore their value.

Iron-making remained a rural craft until the development of the blast furnace, probably in the Liège area of Belgium during the fourteenth century. Using air-blast from water-powered bellows, temperatures of 1150°C could be achieved, sufficient to produce a **molten** form of iron which was then **cast** from the furnace into sand moulds to form finished products, or into blocks (called 'pigs') to be refined for subsequent casting or for conversion to wrought iron.

Pure iron melts at 1535°C, a temperature too high to be reached in the medieval blast furnace. However, when about 4% carbon (from the charcoal) has combined with iron, the melting point is reduced to about 1150°C – the lowest melting point of any iron-carbon alloy. As the molten iron cools, much of the carbon settles out in the form of flakes of graphite, giving a characteristic grey colour to a broken surface. These weak graphite flakes act as 'slots' in the iron, making it brittle and relatively weak in tension.

Much pig iron was therefore refined (in a 'finery') to produce the purer, softer, forgeable **wrought** iron, which was considered much more useful than brittle **cast** iron. The process involves heating the iron in the presence of air. Atmospheric oxygen combines with the carbon in the pig iron, resulting in an almost pure iron with, however, some slag. Hammering the hot iron drives off some of this slag, while further heating and hammering improves the quality of the **wrought** iron. The hammering forces the slag into strands within the iron, a distinctive characteristic for the identification of wrought iron.

Blast furnaces increased the availability of iron, but depended on charcoal as fuel. Shortages of timber and competition from other users made charcoal increasingly scarce in the seventeenth century. Coal could not be used directly to make iron because of the deleterious effect of its impurities (particularly sulphur) on the iron. Then, in 1709, Abraham Darby used coke (purified coal) in his blast furnace at Coalbrookdale, Shropshire. Coke is made by heating coal in a closed chamber to drive off the volatile material to leave porous carbon. With sulphur and other impurities eliminated, coke – a strong but porous material – was also able to support a larger charge of iron ore and limestone than could charcoal, and allowed the air-blast to pass more freely through the furnace chamber so that the blast furnace could be made bigger and more efficient.

However, charcoal was still needed in the fineries to convert pig iron to wrought iron, and shortages continued. (As in the blast furnace, coal could not be used in the finery as its sulphur content caused brittleness in the iron at high temperatures.)

In 1784 Henry Cort developed a 'reverberating' furnace at Funtley, Hampshire, using coal burned in a chamber separate from the pig iron, its heat being reflected or **reverberated** off the roof of the adjacent chamber containing the iron, which gradually melted under the heat. The charge was stirred (or 'puddled') until almost all the carbon was burned out by combining with atmospheric oxygen. As its carbon content reduced, the melting point of the iron increased, so that the metal gradually solidified into a spongy lump that was then pulled from the furnace and hammered to remove much of the residual slag and improve its quality. The need to 'puddle' or stir the iron with long iron tools limited the size of charge to what could be worked and handled, typically about one hundredweight (50 kg). After further heating, hammering and rolling the wrought iron was finally rolled to a wide range of finished sections in grooved rolls (also developed by Cort). Figure 7.1 shows some typical 'traditional' rolled wrought iron sections.

John Wilkinson developed a steam-powered furnace blower in 1776, removing dependence on a supply of running water, and in 1794 he designed a cupola furnace to remelt pig iron with coke in foundries away from the original blast furnace site. Pig iron now became a commodity that could be transported by cart or canal from its maker and delivered to an ironfounder anywhere in the country. As a result, many foundries were established on sites in cities and towns, serving local demand for what could be a wide range of castings, from structural beams and columns through railings and gates to cooking pots and boot scrapers.

Thus in the eighteenth century iron manufacture developed from a charcoal-dependent woodland craft into a coal-based industry. Accordingly, blast furnaces now began to be sited in parts of the country with deposits of coal and iron ore, such as the West Midlands. Freed from charcoal shortages, and fuelled by the increasing demands of the Industrial Revolution, the production in the UK of both cast and wrought iron grew dramatically in the eighteenth century with the decline of charcoal as a fuel in favour of coke (Table 7.1).[1]

The nineteenth century saw many further developments and improvements, including the heavy steam hammer invented by James Nasmyth in 1839.

Steel had until now been made in small quantities. In the 1740s, Benjamin Huntsman packed wrought iron and charcoal in crucibles and heated them for a week or more, during which carbon from the charcoal diffused into the iron, producing cementite. The resulting metal was steel, but the slow and small-scale production method led to its use being largely confined to weapons, tools, cutlery and other artefacts that needed to take an edge and be hardened by suitable heat treatment.

The way to the mass-production of **steel** was shown in 1856, when Henry Bessemer, an inventor, developed a method of blowing air *through*, rather than *over*, molten pig iron to oxidise away much of its carbon. The process was rapid and generated much heat, with the metal remaining molten and indeed increasing in temperature as the carbon was burnt off, while the iron was 'converted' to steel, with streamers of slag and flames being

Table 7.1 The growth of UK iron production in the eighteenth century.

| 1720 | 35 700 tons | 99% using charcoal, 1% coke |
| 1796 | 252 500 tons | 6% using charcoal, 94% coke |

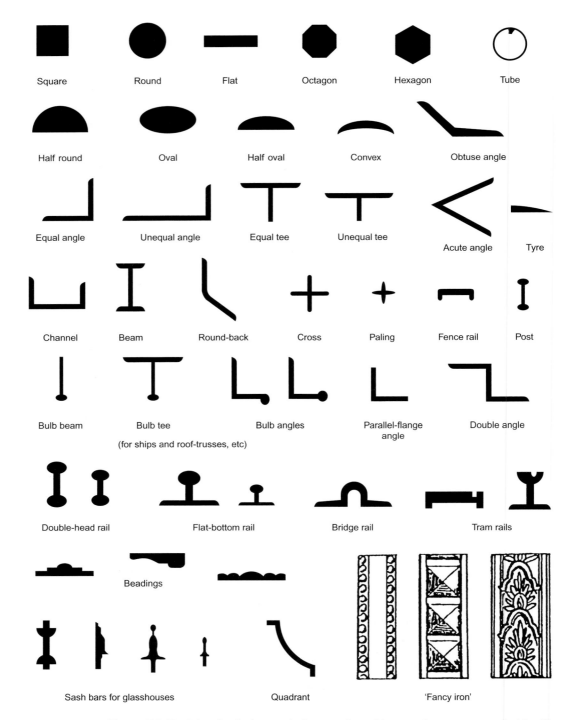

Figure 7.1 Traditional rolled wrought iron sections. Most sections were supplied in different sizes.

Figure 7.2 Bessemer Converter at Kelham Island Museum, Sheffield.

thrown out of the 'converter' vessel. This was made to tilt so that the molten steel could be poured out, to solidify as ingots which could then be recast or rolled into whatever shapes were required. The Bessemer process reduced the conversion time to minutes from the hours required for Cort's puddling process for wrought iron, was on a very much larger scale, and produced steel, whose strength was typically 50% stronger than that of wrought iron. Figure 7.2 shows a later Bessemer converter, now preserved in the open; these could readily produce several tons of steel in a single 'heat' taking less than an hour – a production rate that appeared to render wrought iron-making immediately obsolete.

Difficulties were, however, encountered in making Bessemer steel using British iron ore, which had a significant phosphorus content. (Bessemer had, by chance, used a low-phosphorus ore.) It took some time to establish that using a converter lined with limestone or dolomite, in place of the more commonly used silica-based lining, would allow phosphoric ores to be used successfully. Steel-making was further improved by the introduction of the Siemens-Martin 'open-hearth' process in the 1860s. This was a slower, more controllable, method than the converter and could work using solid scrap metal, whereas Bessemer's process needed molten iron.

With these methods of making steel in bulk, its cost plummeted. Early uses included railway track (where steel's 'toughness' gave longer life in

Figure 7.3 The Forth Rail Bridge, the first major structure built in steel (1890).

Table 7.2 The eclipse of wrought iron by steel in the UK during the late nineteenth century.

	Wrought iron	Steel
1870	c. 3 000 000 tons	220 000 tons
1900	1 160 000 tons	4 900 000 tons

service) and shipbuilding (where a lighter hull could be built with the same strength as a heavier one in wrought iron). Structural steel found little use before the 1880s, when rolled steel beams began to be used in buildings, while the first major steel structure, the Forth Rail Bridge near Edinburgh, was opened in 1890 employing over 50 000 tons of open-hearth steel connected together by some 6.5 million rivets (Figure 7.3).

The decline of wrought iron was then inevitable, and by 1900 its usage was waning, whereas steel was in the ascendant (Table 7.2).[2]

Further developments in steelmaking took place in the twentieth century, first with the electric arc furnace, which (like the open-hearth furnace) could melt solid scrap steel, and more recently with the basic oxygen steel converter, a 'high-tech' version of the Bessemer converter in which oxygen is blown from a water-cooled pipe through the molten iron. These two methods are now responsible for virtually all the steel made worldwide.

The last wrought iron puddling furnace in the UK, Thomas Walmsley's Atlas Forge in Bolton, Lancashire, finally closed in 1973. Its furnace, shingling hammer and rolling mill are now preserved at the Ironbridge Gorge Museum in Shropshire, an area associated with some of the world's most important developments in the manufacture and use of iron. Wrought iron is occasionally rolled for demonstration purposes, using salvaged material. A Bessemer converter has been relocated as a landmark at the Kelham Island Museum, Sheffield (Figure 7.2), while at the Magna Centre between Sheffield and Rotherham no fewer than six electric arc furnaces are housed in the huge shop of the former Templeborough steelworks. One of these has been adapted to simulate the process of charging with scrap metal, melting it and discharging the molten steel by an ingenious use of 'son-et-lumière' that gives some idea of the scale and noise of steelmaking.

Properties of iron and steel

Cast and wrought iron and steel have widely differing properties which complement each other, although wrought iron and steel are similar (Table 7.3).

Strength of materials

Cast iron is strong in compression but relatively weak in tension; it 'snaps' in a brittle way rather than stretching or 'yielding' as with wrought iron and steel.

The strength of cast iron is influenced by several factors including carbon content, rate of cooling in the mould, and size and shape of the cast element. Thick cast iron sections are less strong than thin sections.

The yield strength and the ultimate (breaking) strength of wrought iron are increased during the working and rolling process, and the same applies to steel. Wrought iron is generally more ductile than steel, but excessive

Table 7.3 Comparative properties of cast and wrought iron, and mild steel.

Cast iron	Wrought iron	Mild steel
1.8–5%C	Almost pure iron (<0.1% C, silicate slag content up to 4%)	0.1–0.4 %C
Crystalline structure	Fibrous wood-like structure (thin 'laminae' or layers of slag alternating with iron)	Crystalline structure
Brittle, poor resistance to mechanical or thermal shock	Ductile, malleable (forgeable)	Ductile, malleable
Good in compression, weak in tension	Good in tension and compression	Good in tension and compression
Difficult to weld	Readily forge-welded	Readily welded
Good corrosion resistance	Better resistance than steel	Corrodible
Can chill hard in the mould; brittle	Ductile	Ductile, tough
Formed by casting in mould	Rolled or hammered to shape	Rolled to shape

Table 7.4 Typical ultimate strengths of cast and wrought iron, and steel.

	Tension	Compression	Shearing
Cast iron	7.5–15 (116–232)	38–50 (587–772)	Same as for tension
Wrought iron	18–38 (278–587)	16–20 (247–309)	12–25 (185–386)
Steel	25–32 (386–494)	Same as for tension	19–24 (293–371)

Table 7.5 Permissible stresses in cast and wrought iron, and mild steel, as tabulated in the London (General Powers) Act of 1909.

	Tension	Compression	Shear
Cast iron	1.5 (23)	8.0 (124)	1.5 (23)
Wrought iron	5.0 (77)	5.0 (77)	4.0 (62)
Mild steel	7.5 (116)	7.5 (116)	5.5 (85)

working can reduce the ductility of both materials while increasing their strength. The strength of wrought iron is somewhat lower at right angles to the 'grain' – the parallel layers of slag alternating with iron – compared with strength parallel to the grain.

Typical ultimate strengths of the materials are given above. They are in tons per square inch (tsi), with the present-day SI values of newtons per square millimetre (N/mm^2) in brackets (1 tsi = 15.44 N/mm^2) (Table 7.4).

Structural iron and steel were originally designed on the basis of a 'permissible' stress, which was not to be exceeded in service under the applied loads. Typically, this permissible stress was based on the ultimate strength divided by a factor of safety – commonly 4, although a higher factor was often recommended for cast iron. This factor allowed for variations in material strength and quality as well as providing an adequate 'comfort' margin. The first 'official' figures for permissible stresses appeared in the London (General Powers) Act of 1909 (by which time cast iron was in minimal use for structural purposes) (Table 7.5).

The last British Standard for wrought iron, BS 51 of 1939 (now withdrawn), specifies test procedures and properties, and usefully highlights the lower strength across the grain.

Present-day structural assessment still takes a permissible stress approach for cast iron, as the material lacks ductility and so cannot 'yield'. However, both wrought iron and steel can be assessed using modern 'limit state' principles, based on the yield strength of the metal. Fortunately, the suggested yield strengths to be taken for assessing wrought iron and older steel can be taken as effectively the same, so it is not too critical to be sure which metal is present. But it is essential that cast iron is distinguished, and assessed appropriately![3]

Shape and design

- Iron castings are often heavier and coarser than wrought iron or steel sections, and may form recognisable components such as columns, beams, monolithic panels, etc.
- Profiles that are ornate and/or vary along the member length are cast iron; wrought iron and steel, being rolled sections, are of constant cross section although additional elements may be bolted, riveted or welded on.
- Cast iron is used in compression for columns (typically of hollow circular or cruciform '+' section) and for beams (usually with a larger bottom tension flange than the top compression flange, in view of its relative weakness in tension). Wrought iron and steel are found in I-beams, angles, tees, channels and tie rods, and as girders built up from plates or beams and angles, riveted together and often with additional flange plates over their middle section.
- Mould lines may be visible on cast iron sections, particularly as diametrically opposite lines on hollow circular columns, cast horizontally, where the upper and lower halves of the mould meet. There may also be a mismatch between the two halves of a pattern for a casting.

Surface appearance

- A sandy or rough surface, blowholes, porosity and inclusions all indicate cast iron.
- A hammered or incised surface is probably wrought iron.
- A smooth surface with sharp outside corners and radiused internal corners is probably wrought iron or steel.

Connections

- Cast iron is joined using only bolts because riveting could lead to fracture of the casting as the hot rivets cooled and contracted.
- Fire- or forge-welded joints indicate wrought iron.
- Riveting indicates either wrought iron or steel.
- Arc welds indicate steel unless made to earlier wrought iron, as the technique was not available when wrought iron was in use.

Dating

- Dating, if known, is a valuable aid to identification, particularly for distinguishing between wrought iron and steel. Later alterations may, however, mislead!
- Cast iron was in structural use from the late eighteenth century until c. 1900, although decorative castings and functional elements such as railings continue to be made up to the present day.

- Wrought iron was in structural use from c. 1840 to c. 1900. Steel was in structural use from c. 1880 onwards, so there are about two decades when it is difficult to distinguish the two metals without sampling.

Testing

- A sliver cut with a cold chisel gives a curled shaving for wrought iron, whereas steel does not produce such a curled shaving and cast iron breaks in chips.
- When partially cut and then bent, cast iron breaks with a crystalline fracture; wrought iron bends, showing a fibrous wood-like structure.
- When a sample is placed against a power grinder, cast iron gives ragged reddish sparks; wrought iron and steel give narrow straw-coloured sparks.
- Laboratory tests may be used to distinguish the metals and establish likely properties. Metallurgical tests will analyse element content and microstructure. Mechanical properties such as yield and ultimate tensile strength and percentage elongation may be determined by stretching a test piece to destruction.

Shaping and working cast iron

Pig iron (ingots cast from the blast furnace – see above) forms the raw material for foundries to recast into architectural and structural components. The process as developed in the Middle Ages is still widely used today, with some modifications. Originally developed by John Wilkinson around 1794, a coke-fired **cupola** furnace was used to melt the iron; modern equivalents are fuelled by gas, oil or electricity. Molten metal is run into a crucible or ladle and poured into a sand **mould** to fill a void formed from a **pattern** shaped like the final component. After solidifying, the casting is broken out and the runners/risers which fed in the metal are cut off. A ragged edge (**flashing**), often caused by seepage of metal between the two halves of the mould, is dressed off (or **fettled**) and the raw casting is blast-cleaned to remove sand deposits.

Traditionally **greensand** was used for moulds, set in open metal boxes. This is a naturally occurring clay–sand mixture; used slightly damp, it can give excellent surface definition. While this process is still used for small-quantity production, nowadays the more mechanised foundries use resin-bonded sand cured by chemical hardeners or gases to give more consistent and accurate castings. The mould is typically in two parts, the upper part having one or more 'gates' (holes) into which the molten metal is poured. Vent holes must also be formed so that air can escape as the molten iron fills the void.

A **pattern** to form the void in the mould is made slightly oversize to allow for shrinkage of the metal (about 1% for iron). Patterns are usually made of wood, but two-pack resins and aluminium are often used in high-volume applications, and patterns for one-offs can be shaped easily in wax, expanded polystyrene or plaster.

An original component can be used to create a replica casting provided that

- surface detail is sufficiently crisp
- new castings 1% smaller than the original will be acceptable (or the original can be built-up)
- the shape of the original will allow it to be drawn from the mould

Shapes that will not draw from the mould, and hollow castings, require loose mould-pieces called **cores**. These are shaped blocks of sand cast in a specially made box, hardened to become self-supporting and placed inside the mould to form internal shapes. In the nineteenth century hollow circular columns were cast – usually horizontally – with an internal sand core formed around a wrought iron bar. Because the core was less dense than molten iron, there was a danger that it could literally float on the iron unless it was securely held in place at the ends and at intermediate points. The result would be a column with a wall of varying thickness, with possibly adverse effects on strength. In practice, minor variations in wall thickness are common and are not significant.

Shaping and working wrought iron

Wrought iron is highly malleable and ductile, and it forge-welds readily – properties exploited by the blacksmith to create the many delicate and ornamental designs of traditional **wrought ironwork** such as scrolls, leaves and masks.

Processes employed to shape the finished product included punching, upsetting, drawing-down, fullering (shaping with a hand-held form tool), swaging, twisting, cutting and so on. Joints were generally secured not by bolts but by the use of mortices and tenons, collars, wedges, pins and rivets, or by forge welding. The latter entails swelling up the ends to be joined, heating them to white heat, beating them together to fuse and finally truing-up, forming a weld approximately 80% as strong as the original section (see Figure 7.4).

Simple leaves were formed by hammering thin sheet down onto a metal stake. More complex shapes such as large leaves, shields and masks were formed by doming out from the reverse, filling with lead and cutting in detail from the front using fine chisels and punches (*incised* and *repoussé* work). The smith would make many of the tools himself, often developing tooling especially for the job in hand.

For structural wrought ironwork, the starting point was the rolled plate and the billet, and heat. Plates could be sheared and then rolled or pressed to form angles, tees, tie rods, straps and the like. The billet, a thicker piece of iron, was fed into a rolling mill, usually in several passes which progressively reduced and shaped the iron until the finished I-beam or channel emerged.

Larger structural sections such as bridges and roof trusses were fabricated from smaller sections joined by riveting. Both shop and site riveting

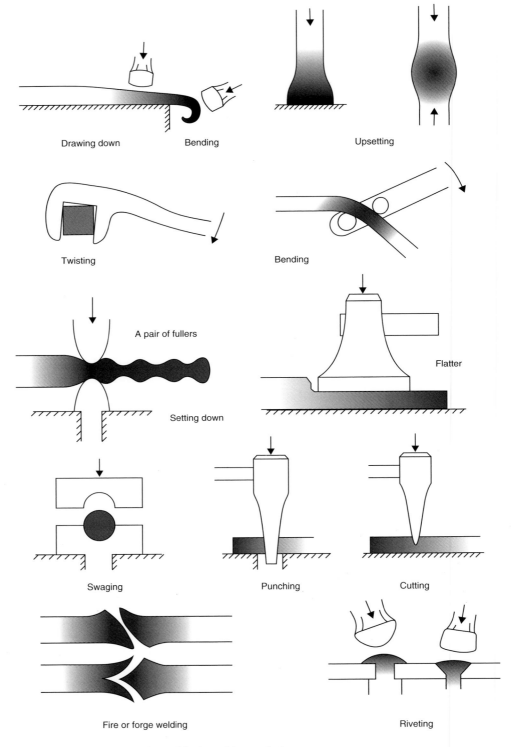

Drawing down

Bending

Upsetting

Twisting

Bending

A pair of fullers

Setting down

Flatter

Swaging

Punching

Cutting

Fire or forge welding

Riveting

Figure 7.4 Some basic blacksmithing techniques.

were usually necessary as the shop-assembled sections were limited in size by transport considerations. Rivets were usually made from a slightly more ductile wrought iron, with a shank and a formed head at one end. The heated rivet was then inserted into a clearance hole in the pieces of iron to be connected, its head being held while the end of the shank was hammered down to form and close the second head. At the same time, this hammering would expand the rivet shank within its hole in the iron, the end result being a firm clamping grip of the joined parts as the rivet cooled. Site riveting was quite a dramatic business, with white-hot rivets being thrown up from a portable forge to the riveter and a deafening sound of hammers (originally manually operated, later pneumatic) as rivets were closed.

In refurbishment work it is important to use the correct traditional materials and techniques, not modern equivalents, if subtle detailing and historic integrity is to be preserved.

Recycled wrought iron is still available commercially, and riveting is still practised by a few specialist contractors. For larger-scale work it is possible to replicate the appearance of rivets using dome-headed pre-tensioned bolts, although this is not an authentic solution!

Shaping and working steel

The change from wrought iron to steel was one of transition rather than innovation, certainly as far as the shaping process was concerned, although from the outset in the 1880s larger sections were rolled in steel than had been attempted in wrought iron. This was partly because steel was made in much larger batches – in tons from a Bessemer converter or open-hearth furnace, compared with the 1/20th of a ton (50 kg) from the finery. More powerful rolling mills were employed. In 1887, the largest steel I-beam rolled by Dorman, Long at Middlesbrough was already 20 inches deep with 8-inch flanges (508 by 203 mm), weighing 100 lb/ft run (149 kg/m).

Riveting remained the major means of connecting steel sections until the mid-twentieth century, being gradually replaced by arc welding from the interwar period. The high-strength friction grip bolt was introduced from the 1950s, pre-tensioned to provide a similar clamping action to the rivet, but nowadays this requires only a spanner rather than white-hot metal.

Non-structural uses of steel proliferated during the twentieth century, with wrought iron gradually declining. Some semi-functional or decorative metalwork is still described, presumably unwittingly, as 'wrought iron', perhaps because this is a more appealing soubriquet than plain 'steel'.

Corrosion

Iron and steel both have a natural tendency to recombine with oxygen, reverting to the more stable oxide forms as found in nature. This process is **corrosion**, from *corrodere* (Latin), meaning 'to gnaw to pieces'.

Metals are made up of atoms which include nuclei and negatively charged particles called electrons. In an electrochemical reaction, iron atoms lose electrons and oxygen atoms gain electrons, becoming **ions** with, respectively, positive and negative charges. Ions then recombine to form more stable compounds. This requires adjacent metallic areas with positive and negative charges, known respectively as *cathodes* and *anodes*. Together these form an electrochemical circuit resulting in the development of **rust**. As can be seen from the formulae below, both oxygen and moisture are needed for iron or steel to corrode. Electro-chemical reactions occur between areas of different charge or energy level; cathodic areas are protected, while anodic areas are corroded.

The most basic electrochemical reactions are:

$$2Fe + O_2 \quad + \quad 2H_2O > 2Fe(OH)_2$$
$$\text{Iron} \quad \text{Oxygen} \quad \text{Water Iron hydroxide}$$

or, with more oxygen:

$$4Fe(OH)_2 + O_2 + 2H_2O > 4Fe(OH)_3$$
$$> 2Fe_2O_3.H_2O + 4H_2O$$
$$\text{Red rust}$$
$$\text{Akagenite}$$
$$\text{Fully oxidised}$$

A similar process produces the partially oxidised black rust or magnetite – Fe_3O_4.

Hydrated iron oxides (rusts) have a greater volume than the iron dissolved, so they can jack components apart.

Areas of positive and negative charge may be formed by dissimilar metals in contact, differing compositions or physical properties within iron, or differential aeration of moisture on the surface.

Corrosion will stop if

- the electrolyte (essentially water) is not in contact with both the anode and the cathode, for example if the metal is kept dry, or is coated with a barrier to prevent an electrochemical action (e.g. an epoxy coating)
- oxygen is excluded (e.g. the metal is coated or submerged in an inert liquid)
- cathode–anode electrical contact is broken (e.g. different metals are insulated from each other)
- the cathode–anode electrical potential is reversed (e.g. a metal is coated with a baser metal, or a reverse current is applied, as described below)

Bimetallic corrosion and sacrificial protection

Metals tend to ionise with either a greater or lesser positive charge than iron or steel, and are called respectively more **noble** or more **base**. Nobler metals attack iron or steel in a corrosion cell, whereas baser metals are sacrificial and protect them.

The commoner metals, listed in order in relation to whether they are nobler or baser than iron and steel, are as follows:

Nobler than iron (so aggressive to iron)
GOLD, SILVER, COPPER ALLOYS, NICKEL, TIN, LEAD

Baser than iron (protects iron)
CADMIUM, ALUMINIUM, ZINC, MAGNESIUM

Coating iron and steel

Paints are commonly used to exclude oxygen and water, and thus protect the surface of iron and steel. It is important that the coating is continuous, as even pinholes allow the formation of corrosion cells in which an anodic area develops under the film around the hole, causing corrosion to spread.

If a sacrificial coating such as zinc or aluminium is applied, the polarity is reversed and the coating sacrificially protects the ferrous metal.

Nobler metals, such as chromium, tin, copper and their alloys, are often used as protective or decorative coatings for 'indoor' metalwork, but in fact offer no electrolytic protection.

Corrosion of exposed iron and steel

Rust is hygroscopic, and of greater volume than the original iron. This usually makes rusted members appear to have lost more of their useful cross section than is the case, although conversely rust flakes can fall off to give the misleading impression that less iron has been lost, so it is always worth scraping back to the uncorroded metal face when comparing corroded and undamaged sections.

Cast iron has good corrosion resistance as cast (except in sea water – see below) because the cast surface chills quickly to form a tough layer which also can take up sand from the mould. However, if the as-cast surface is removed (for example, by grit-blasting prior to repainting) then the cast iron will corrode more rapidly. **Wrought iron** generally is slightly more resistant to corrosion than is **steel**. All three ferrous metal types need protection. Traditionally, this is provided by paint coatings; an alternative for steel is zinc galvanising. All coatings, particularly paints, need regular maintenance by local touching-up or renewal, depending on their condition.

Riveted joints in trusses, girders and the like can collect water in the narrow gaps between the component parts by capillary action or simple run-off. The trapped water is then slow to evaporate, so crevice corrosion can occur, which may eventually weaken the connections.

Where a structural element is embedded in a floor or wall, corrosion may be concealed just inside the painted exposed section where it is often unpainted or lightly painted. Seaside buildings and structures, not just those standing in the sea, are of course more vulnerable to aggravated corrosion from aggressive salt spray and abrasive wind-blown beach material, in addition to the normal corrosion process from atmospheric oxygen and moisture.

Corrosion and mechanical damage in water

Structures such as piers (both commercial and for pleasure), jetties, sheet-piled retaining works and more recently offshore platforms are all targets for accelerated corrosion unless well protected. Apart from the effects on superstructures of the salt spray, salt water adds to corrosion activity. The worst-affected area is potentially the 'splash zone', subject to frequent wetting and drying. Further, abrasion by seabed material such as shingle and sand can quietly reduce the cross section of iron or steel piles, sheet-piles and columns, the damage being invisible and unknown unless regular diving or CCTV inspections are made.

A particular form of corrosion affecting cast iron in sea water and other brackish or acidic water, including groundwater, is anaerobic corrosion, requiring little oxygen. It is an electro-chemical process in which soluble iron salts are leached out in an electrolytic reaction, leaving insoluble iron salts, finely divided free iron and the graphite. (This accounts for the alternative name of 'graphitisation' for the process.) Affected ironwork has a blistered black surface which is fairly easy to dislodge. The section is clearly weakened and may collapse, particularly if hit.

Accelerated low-water corrosion (ALWC) is a relatively recently recognised phenomenon, apparently caused by bacteria with a taste for steel. It has affected sheet piling and other steelwork embedded in shallow water.[4]

Corrosion within masonry

Colloquially often called 'Regent Street disease', corrosion may be found in steelwork embedded in masonry walls. In the 1900s larger buildings began to be erected with steel frames, allowing the floors and roof to be built quickly while the bricklayers and stonemasons followed behind building the walls. Columns and beams of the building perimeter were enclosed in masonry; embedded steel also supported cornices and other masonry features, while iron or steel cramps and ties were used to secure the masonry. Typical construction is shown in Warland's *Practical Modern Masonry*, though some of the techniques shown are no longer regarded as safe methods.[5]

Regulations at the time required no more than a coat of cement wash on the steel, in the belief that a skin of stone, brick or terra cotta several inches thick would provide protection against both fire (which it does) and water ingress (which time has shown it often does not). Moisture and oxygen can pass through joints and porous or cracked units, giving rise to expansive rusting. This often shows first as cracking in the masonry on the lines of the columns and/or beams.

One consequence of this is loss of cross section in the steel frame, with obvious structural implications. In addition, the expansive action of the rust may dislodge masonry, with potentially fatal consequences for a passer-by. Investigation requires access at high level over (often busy) streets and involves opening-up (which will require consent on a listed building).

Corrosion of embedded steelwork can be 'patchy', with damage often confined to the more exposed parts of the facades. A 'total' solution is to expose all of the facade steelwork and then repair and protect it, but this is extremely expensive and disruptive, and it may require planning and listed building consents if elevations are to be altered. The 'piecemeal' solution is to deal with visible problems now, and follow with regular inspection for cracks and evidence of masonry disruption, accompanied by repairs. The strategy must be explained to the client so that action can be agreed.[6]

Cathodic protection

Cathodic protection is one way to prevent or limit further corrosion, using an electric current that neutralises the electrochemical action causing corrosion. There are two methods. The sacrificial anode method uses a metal such as zinc as anode in a circuit that includes as cathode the iron or steel structure to be protected; as its name implies, the anode corrodes while the structure does not. The anode therefore has to be periodically replaced. This method is particularly applicable to marine structures such as piers. The impressed current method passes a small current permanently through the structure, again to suppress its further corrosion, and is being trialled on several masonry-clad steel frames. The method has been used successfully to protect wrought iron cramps buried within stonework, but each application requires a bespoke system design and careful monitoring and control, and suffers from practical constraints, for example locating buried metalwork and making connections to it.

Surveys of metal structures

The need for a survey

Metal structures are often prominent, complex and highly loaded. Conservation work on iron and steel can be intrusive, non-reversible and costly. It is therefore important that metalwork is surveyed expertly before conservation work starts, so as to determine the **method and materials** of construction; establish fully the nature and extent of **defects/deterioration**; facilitate **strength assessment**; and allow the least intrusive and most economical **conservation options** to be planned.

Preparations

Old coatings on iron and steel can be useful indicators of past movement, corrosion in joints, impacts, and water leaks and ponding; their
general removal should be unnecessary, unless they are exceptionally
thick.

It may be necessary to lift or partially remove flashings, claddings, panelling or floorboards temporarily to allow inspection, but extensive dismantling of metalwork should be avoided.

A range of equipment is available for viewing internal spaces, such as
optical endoscopes and CCTV, which require access holes of 12 mm or less.
Figure 7.5 illustrates some typical hidden defects.

Measurement

Much historic structural and other functional iron and steel is often already
exposed, and measurements can readily be made. Embedded structure,
however, usually requires opening up to assess for structural adequacy,
for example cast iron beams supporting a brick barrel-vaulted floor in a
nineteenth-century textile mill. Such beams were often cast with a 'hog-
backed' profile, and with top and bottom flanges of different sizes, reflecting awareness of both the need for increased bending strength in the
middle of the span and the relative strength of cast iron in tension and
compression (see above). It will be necessary to open up at least one typical
beam at the ends and at midspan to record such variations in profile in
detail. Other apparently similar beams should be spot-checked for
variations.

The wall thickness of hollow circular cast iron columns can be determined
by drilling holes – but it is essential that a non-percussive drill be used to
avoid shattering the brittle iron! Three holes should be drilled spaced at
120° around the column's perimeter in case the internal core was not well
supported during casting, leading to variations in wall thickness (see above),
and it may be worthwhile to check wall thickness at both top and bottom
and at mid-height, for the same reason. A wire with a bent end can be
pushed into the hole and then gently withdrawn until the bent end is tight
against the inside face of the wall. After marking the point where the
straight portion of wire emerges from the hole, the wire can be withdrawn
and the distance between this point and the bent end measured; this gives
the local wall thickness to within about 1 mm – an adequate precision for
columns with walls typically at least $^3/_4$ inch (20 mm) thick.

Paint sampling

Almost all historic metalwork was painted from new, and evidence of past
priming, undercoating and finish coats often survives. The survey should

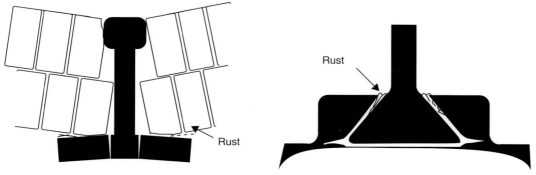

Hidden cracks in structural iron castings

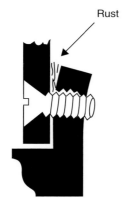

Rust

Rusting behind
panel

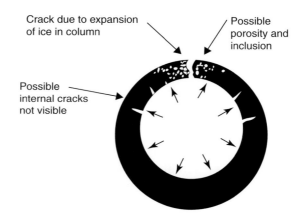

Crack due to expansion
of ice in column

Possible
porosity and
inclusion

Possible
internal cracks
not visible

Bursting of a cast iron column
Note: the core of a column may 'float'
during casting, resulting in uneven wall thickness.

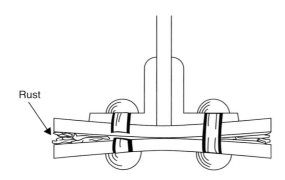

Rust

Defective rivets can often
be detected by hammering
as they emit a duller sound
than sound rivets.

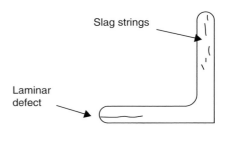

Slag strings

Laminar
defect

An original laminar rolling
defect and slag strings in
wrought iron

Figure 7.5 Some hidden defects.

sample these and an attempt be made to identify original colours. If paint-work has failed generally or little survives, remnants can often be found intact in crevices and protected areas. A full-depth sample from each area of the structure should be dislodged by scalpel or chisel and inspected on edge under a ×20–×40 microscope.

- Layers of paint and dirt should be sketched to scale, and photo-micrographed.
- Samples should be retained and archived.
- Colours should *not* be visually matched to those seen in samples, as binders usually darken on drying and some colours change dramatically with age.
- Pigments should be laboratory-analysed and their formulation used to mix new paint.
- The advice and services of a specialist paint analyst and/or conservator can be beneficial.[7]

Condition

Evidence should be sought for general and localised defects including

- overloading: distortion, rust or frost heave, fractures
- settlement and other induced movements: a survey of levels may assist, but original misalignments may exist
- mechanical shock, such as from vehicle impact
- thermal shock: fire damage, effects of quenching, past weld repairs
- original material or manufacturing defects: voids, inclusions, delamination, cracks
- badly executed alterations and repairs
- corrosion: especially in joints, areas of poor drainage or ventilation, splash zones and around dissimilar metals

Non-destructive investigation techniques

Non-destructive techniques (NDT) are available for inspecting metals on site, to expose small or internal defects on highly stressed parts. Surfaces must be blast-cleaned first. Techniques include **dye penetrants**, in which a low-viscosity coloured liquid is sprayed onto the surface and allowed to enter cracks by capillary action. The excess is removed and a white 'developer' powder applied generally. This draws out any penetrant within cracks, revealing their position.

Magnetic-particle penetrant testing is similar to using dye penetrants, but here the penetrant is a magnetic-particle ink, drawn out of the crack by application of a hand-held magnet.

With the **ultrasonic probe**, a reflected beam of ultrasound indicates the presence of internal flaws.

Survey report

The survey report should ideally include

- description of the structure, identifying its materials
- causes, nature, extent and location of defects and deterioration
- record of active deterioration and estimate of its rate of progression
- structural analysis
- paint sample analysis
- schedule of recommended repairs
- specification for conservation works

Conservation strategy

General conservation principles and options

The general guiding principles in the treatment of historically important buildings are **minimal intervention** and **minimal loss of evidence**. A lightness of touch should be adopted, preserving as much inherited evidence as possible for future generations.[8]

If a metal structure is stable, or has achieved equilibrium, it may simply require cleaning and painting to prevent further deterioration. Settlement, distortion, corrosion and cracking do not necessarily justify intrusive treatment, provided they are not structurally significant; further deterioration can be prevented by surface treatments such as filling and painting. Historic structures that are to be adapted for continued use are often required to carry higher loads than those for which they were originally designed (if indeed they were 'designed' in a formal sense at all).[9]

If the strength of the structure has to be increased, additional components can be introduced either to share the load (for example, by introducing additional beams into a floor to span alongside the existing beams) or to increase the strength of the existing elements. This is preferable to removal and replacement of the existing structure. The assessing engineer has a professional duty to ensure that the structure is safe in future use, although lateral thinking may obviate the need to introduce strengthening, for example by removing non-structural floor finishes against whose surplus weight the required extra loading capacity can be 'traded'.[10]

Dismantling an iron structure clearly offers the advantages of allowing repairs to be undertaken in the controlled conditions of a workshop, where the components can be cleaned as necessary and fully painted all round, and new elements and fastenings can be fitted. However, dismantling can be destructive of brittle or rusted components, and there is a risk of losing parts or reassembling them incorrectly. Riveted metalwork is particularly vulnerable both to damage as the rivets are removed and to the loss of the original rivets, as these cannot be reused. Therefore dismantling should be adopted only as a last resort, be carefully planned and be undertaken by specialists experienced in the conservation of the particular material.

Parts should be double-tagged with metal labels wired on before removal, and re-erected without delay as soon as any necessary work has been carried out. Detailed records should be kept at all stages.

New materials should be distinguishable from old, being date-stamped or embossed. Drawings showing the work done should be provided for the health and safety file that is required to be created and retained by the client under the current Construction (Design and Management) Regulations.[11]

Hot repair techniques

Introduction

Hot processes are used in forming, joining and cutting iron and steel, but are often prohibited in historic buildings owing to the potential fire risk, or are allowed only on the basis of a daily 'hot works permit' where no other process can be substituted.

Coke-fired hearths were the traditional means of heating for manufacture and workshop repairs. On building sites, small portable hearths were employed for heating rivets and suchlike, and hearths are still widely used in workshops for general forgework. More modern methods of heating include the following:

- **Fuel gas and air**: butane or propane stored in portable bottles mixes with air at a torch to provide a flame of several hundred degrees centigrade. Used for low-temperature operations such as heating components to separate them, softening paint and soft soldering.
- **Fuel gas and oxygen**: propane or acetylene and oxygen, stored in heavy bottles, mix at the nozzle of a blowpipe to produce a flame of around 3000°C. Used for forming metals, separating components, flame cleaning, silver soldering, brazing and fusion welding (see below). These gases can also be used for cutting thick sections of wrought iron and steel where excess oxygen is used to blow away white-hot metal (flame-cutting).
- **Electric arc**: the low-voltage/high-current output from a transformer provides a continuous spark or **arc** between the workpiece and an electrode at around 3000°C, instantly producing a localised molten pool. Used mainly for welding processes, principally MMA and MIG (see below). Electric arc welding is not recommended for repairs to cast iron owing to the risk of thermal-shock damage to the brittle material.

Note: the use of gases on site is dangerous because of their flammability and the naked flame and is restricted by the size and weight of gas bottles.

Soldering and welding processes

Iron oxidises when heated, which prevents joining or reduces the strength of the joint. A flux or inert gas shield must therefore be introduced to prevent **oxidation** by providing **reducing** conditions. Common 'hot' techniques applicable to iron and steel repair include the following:

- **Brazing or hard soldering**: surfaces to be joined are cleaned, fluxed and heated by oxy-propane flame to around 600°C. A bronze filler wire (spelter) is melted into the joint, being drawn in by capillary action. Spelter containing silver (silver solder) melts at a lower temperature, providing a weaker joint. Suitable for non-structural applications on thin cast and wrought iron sections, the technique can be applied to thicker cast iron if heated and cooled slowly to minimise the risk of cracking.
- **Gas fusion welding**: components are heated by oxy-acetylene flame to their melting temperature, creating a localised weld pool into which a filler rod of the same metal is melted. Suitable for the structural repair of cast iron which must be pre- and post-heated to minimise thermal shock.
- **Manual metal arc welding** (MMA or 'stick' welding): an electric arc between a consumable electrode and the workpiece forms a small weld pool in which the components fuse. Oxidation is prevented by the vaporisation of a flux coating around the electrode. Widely used for jointing wrought iron and steel on sites and in workshops, but the technique is not recommended for cast iron owing to the risk of thermal shock causing cracks around the weld. Wrought iron should preferably be welded with a full or partial penetration butt weld over its cross section, as the alternative of fillet-welding to the metal's surface can be ineffective owing to the laminar nature of wrought iron.
- **MIG welding** (**m**etal **i**nert **g**as): this is similar to MMA welding, but the weld pool is protected by a shield of argon and the filler-wire electrode is automatically fed into it by a current-sensed servo-system. Suitable for welding wrought iron, and also for cast iron if pre- and post-heated to reduce thermal shock.
- **Fire or forge welding**: two pieces of wrought iron will readily fuse together if heated in a hearth to white heat and then hammered together. A well-executed forge weld should achieve about 80% of the original metal strength and is recommended as an appropriate traditional process for repairing wrought ironwork.

Hot set riveting

This is the commonest traditional method of joining wrought iron components in structural and decorative applications, and should *not* be replaced by welding. A rivet is entered white-hot into a prepared hole, the rivet head is retained by a hand-held gun or jack (a 'holder-up') and the shank is then forged down to form a second head, fill the hole and grip the components. Grip is further tightened as the rivet cools and shrinks, resulting in a strong, watertight joint. Rivet heads are commonly spherical (round-head), conical (snap-head) or flush with the surface (counter-sunk). Small rivets are set by hand, and larger ones by pneumatic or hydraulic tools which allow large numbers of rivets to be set quickly.

Removal of rivets must be undertaken with care to avoid damaging plates and holes. Heads may be ground off, shanks drilled and the rivet punched out. A quicker traditional method is to shear off the head with a **rivet buster**, a long pneumatic gun operated by two persons. Its chisel is placed under the rivet head to shear it off, and a punch in the same gun is used to drive out the shank. Appropriate safety precautions are essential.

Cold repair techniques

Cold repairs avoid the thermal stresses and fire and fume hazards of hot processes, and so are safer and particularly suitable for use in historic buildings. Cold processes also generally employ simpler and cheaper equipment than hot techniques, so should be adopted where possible. All the techniques described in this section are commonly used for repairing cast iron, which contains flakes of graphite that lubricate cutting operations such as drilling and tapping (threading) holes. Figure 7.6 illustrates typical cold repairs to cast iron.

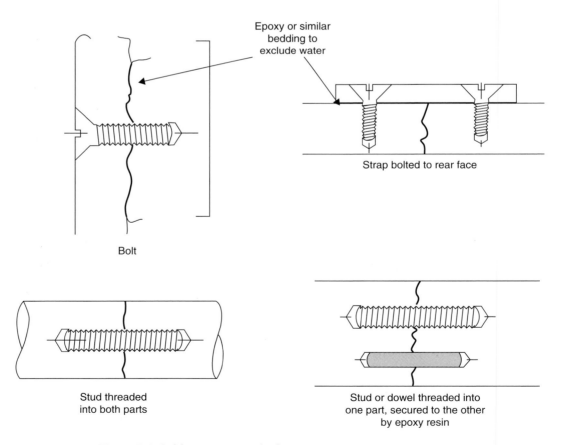

Epoxy or similar bedding to exclude water

Strap bolted to rear face

Bolt

Stud threaded into both parts

Stud or dowel threaded into one part, secured to the other by epoxy resin

Figure 7.6 Cold repairs to cracked iron castings.

Plating

A strong and discreet repair can often be achieved by bolting a steel or brass plate across a cracked cast iron component on a hidden face. Plates must be bedded on red lead or on a two-pack epoxy putty to exclude water, and can be secured with countersunk screws flush with the surface for a neat appearance. If stainless steel plates or fastenings are used, they must be physically and electrically isolated from the casting to prevent bimetallic corrosion (see above). Stainless steel bolts and nuts can be isolated by plastic washers or by being painted with a two-pack epoxy primer and assembled before the paint cures.

Studding

Broken rod-shaped components can be repaired by drilling and tapping both parts and screwing together onto a threaded bar (studding), bedded on red lead or two-pack epoxy putty. If components cannot be rotated, the studding can be screwed into one part and secured by epoxy putty into the other.

Carbon- or glass-fibre repair and strengthening

In some situations, strips of carbon- or glass-fibre matting bonded with two-pack epoxy resin onto a blast-cleaned surface can repair a crack or strengthen a component. Pre-formed pre-tensioned plates may also be used to upgrade structural strength, and have been used on a number of cast iron bridges and beams. As this is a relatively new technique long-term performance has yet to be proved, but the technique is worth considering for conservation work as it is reversible and affects existing fabric only minimally.[12]

Stitching

Stitching is a modernised traditional technique for repairing cracked cast iron. Holes are drilled across the crack and slotted, and then a ferrous lock or 'stitch' is driven into the slot to tie the sections together. Further slots and stitches are installed across the crack, which is then sealed with interlocking studs screwed in along the crack (see Figure 7.7).

The advantages of this method are:

- It is a cold process requiring only portable hand tools.
- It is safe on site.
- The repair is hermetically tight, with no sealants used.
- The repair is heat-resistant.
- The repair is invisible on completion.

The disadvantages are:

- It is not suitable for thin sections.
- It cannot be applied near edges and corners.

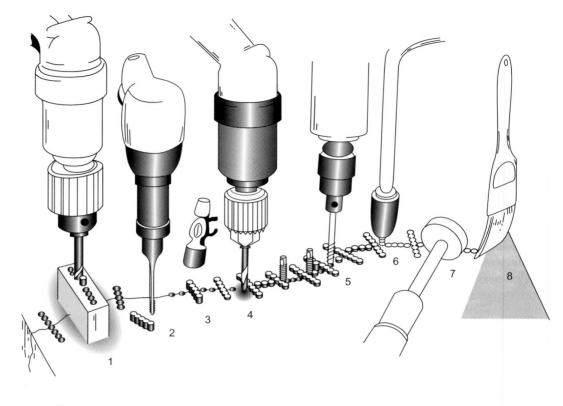

The process

1 A jig is used to drill holes in a line across the crack.
2 A pneumatic chisel cuts away part of the webs between holes.
3 A steel stitch or lock is hammered in and spreads in the slot.
4 Interlocking holes are drilled along the crack.
5 Holes are threaded (tapped).
6 Interlocking studs are screwed in.
7 Excess metal is dressed off and the surface smoothed.
8 Paint coating is applied.

Figure 7.7 Stitching cast iron.

Surface preparation

Surface preparation aims to provide a physically and chemically stable surface with a micro-profile suitable for adhesion of the priming coat – one of the most important factors determining the long-term success of a paint system. Surfaces must be free of loose material, grease and oils, which can be removed by degreasing compounds, solvents, or steam-cleaning if necessary. If rust or existing paint are to be removed, care must be taken not to damage surface detail, decoration, tooling marks, arrises, edges and so on.

Traditional cast iron usually carries a thin burnt-on foundry skin which is protective and should not be removed. Similarly, millscale is often found on wrought iron, and should not be removed if adhering. The least intrusive and risky method of cleaning, consistent with achieving a stable, clean surface, should be selected and trialled before use.

Preparing existing paint

Where historically important coatings survive and adhere well they should be retained. Bare patches should be rubbed back with abrasive cloth, primed, undercoated and again rubbed back to blend, before final finish-coating. On thick coats, damaged areas may be brought forward with a filler such as red-lead putty or polyester resin after priming. The chalky, powdery surface of lead paints provides a poor substrate, but can be re-coated with linseed or alkyd oil paint after rubbing back (see below).

Many early paints contain lead, which is toxic and cumulative in the body. Cleaning methods must be chosen to minimise the dispersal and loss of toxic material, with appropriate personal protective equipment used and measures taken to contain the paint fragments. Where lead paints are being removed, their debris (together with spent abrasive etc.) must be collected and disposed of to a certified waste-management contractor.

Loosely adhering millscale, rust and paint can be removed by **hand tool cleaning** – wire-brushing, scraping, and chipping – but these methods will not fully remove tightly adhering material. **Power tool cleaning** – wire-brushing, sanding, needle-gunning and descaling chisels – is more effective, quicker and less laborious, but is more likely to cause damage. Wire-brushing tends to polish rather than remove adherent rust, reducing the adhesion of subsequent paintwork. Descaling chisels and needle guns are slow but effective and remove paint in relatively large pieces, a safety advantage if lead-bearing paint is present.

Flame cleaning, being non-abrasive, is particularly suitable for the soft surface of wrought iron, and is effective in dislodging rust packed behind scrolls, water-leaves and so on. An oxy-propane flame is passed over the surface to scrape and burn off paint, and to spall away rust. Surfaces are left warm and dry, which helps passivate rust-promoting compounds, but they must be wire-brushed before priming. However, the process is not suitable for use in historic buildings because of the risk of fire.

Chemicals may be applied in the form of a gel or poultice to soften paint which is then scraped and washed off. Products often contain dichloro-methane (methylene chloride), sodium hydroxide or other toxic or corrosive chemicals, which must be treated with care and the appropriate precautions taken. Smaller items may be pickled in acid to remove rust and paint, before thorough washing. There is a risk that porosity in castings and 'traps' in wrought iron work may retain chemicals or wash water, promoting future corrosion, so thorough rinsing and drying are essential.

The British Iron and Steel Research Association advise that paint on a **blast-cleaned** surface can last up to five times as long as that on one prepared by wire-brushing, owing to the adhesion achieved with a good roughened surface profile (normally 50–70 microns) and the cleanliness of

149

the surface. Soluble salts can exert a strong osmotic pull, drawing moisture through a paint film, causing loss of adhesion and possible blistering through re-rusting.

For outdoor metalwork the preferred method of preparation is therefore

- dry or wet abrasive cleaning to remove all rust and paint
- pressure-washing to remove salts
- testing for salts removal
- further washing and blasting if necessary
- drying
- priming before re-rusting occurs

Dry abrasive cleaning uses several media. Copper slag or aluminium oxide powder is commonly used in a 'once-through' process. In a workshop, chilled iron shot can be filtered and recycled. A softer blast can be achieved with abrasives such as marble dust, but silica sand must not be used, for health reasons. Abrasives are stored in a pressurised pot at about 6 bar and fed via reinforced hoses to a ceramic nozzle.

The process is fast, effective and widely available, but is potentially hazardous, both to personnel and to adjoining materials. The work area must be properly enclosed and protected from over-blast, and operatives must be fully encased in suitable protective gear, with positive-pressure helmets. Spent grit contaminated with paint dust must not be allowed to build up, and must be collected and disposed of to a certified waste-management contractor. Trials must be carried out to establish non-damaging levels of air pressure, grit size and hardness. On wrought iron, low pressure and fine grit must be used with great care to avoid the risk of damaging its relatively soft surface.

Some common abrasives are detailed in Table 7.6.

Wet abrasive cleaning is similar to dry abrasive cleaning, but a water-abrasive slurry is used. Specialised systems, including vortex blasting, are available for applications requiring close control, such as the removal of individual layers of paint and cleaning of soft metals.

The advantages of this method are:

- Airborne dust is much reduced, and hence cleaning is less hazardous.
- Soluble salts and corrosion products may be washed out of crevices.

Table 7.6 Some common abrasives.

Type of abrasive	Mesh size	Typical maximum surface profile height (microns)
Fine aluminium oxide	80	37
Coarse aluminium oxide	12	70
Iron shot	14	90
Copper slag (1.5–2.0 mm grains)	–	75–100

The disadvantages are:

- The method is much slower than dry blasting, and hence is more costly.
- Collecting and disposing of spent slurry is more difficult.
- Wet iron surfaces re-rust within a few minutes in damp conditions, although this can be slowed by the use of a corrosion inhibitor (maximum concentration 0.2%).
- Visibility is poor for the blasting operative.

Pressure-washing and testing for salts removal is applicable for metalwork in polluted or coastal environments, which should be spray-washed at pressures up to 200 bar with clean water containing a maximum of 0.2% of a corrosion inhibitor, to remove salts. Blotting-paper treated with 10% potassium ferricyanide solution applied to damp iron surfaces will turn dark blue in contact with ferrous salts. Washing should be continued until salts are removed, and primer applied once the surfaces are dry and before visible re-rusting (gingering) can occur.

Ultra-high-pressure water-jetting at pressures up to 800 bar may be used to remove rust and paint without abrasives. The advantages of this method are:

- It is relatively fast.
- It is non-scouring.
- Salts and corrosion products can be washed out of crevices.
- No airborne dust is created.
- There is minimal slurry.

The disadvantages are:

- Equipment is costly and requires special operator-training.
- It is potentially hazardous to personnel and adjoining materials.
- Wet ironwork rusts quickly.
- There is a risk of water being forced into joints and porous castings.

Traditional coatings

Ironwork has been treated from antiquity for decoration and protection. Indoors, architectural metalwork was usually finished by painting, surface-colouring or (later) plating. Outdoors, protection was paramount so painting was usual, or (from the late nineteenth century) cathodic metal coating.

To form **surface colouring and patination**, the simplest traditional form of decoration was colouring of the surface itself by heating and dipping in various liquids to create a range of colours, principally dark blues, or light or dark browns. The process is cosmetic rather than protective so it was generally used for indoor metalwork only.

An improved level of protection was achieved by **electro-plating** iron with a more corrosion-resistant metal, often chosen for its decorative qualities, such as copper, brass or chromium. Most of these metals are more noble than iron (see above), and hence provided no cathodic protection; thus they too were generally confined to indoor metalwork. For external use zinc, a sacrificial metal, was used as a coating from the late nineteenth century. Wrought ironwork was chemically cleaned, dipped in a bath of molten zinc and then hung to drain.

'Hot-dip' galvanising was common on iron roof sheeting and was used occasionally in aggressive environments such as kitchens, conservatories and plant-houses. Early examples of galvanising are now rare and must be preserved. Hot-dip galvanising is still widely available, and has been used as a cheap treatment for decorative wrought iron, but this is not recommended nowadays in conservation work as the dipping process forms an uneven coating thickness, voids often form in 'trap' areas and the surface appearance is non-traditional. Hot-dip galvanising is of course widely used for steelwork, from exposed structural frames to the ubiquitous (and now misnamed) corrugated 'iron' sheet.

Galvanising must not be used on cast iron, which can be porous and can retain the acids used for cleaning prior to hot-dipping.

Paints comprise three components:

- **pigment:** powdered solid providing the paint's colour
- **binder:** the base or medium that carries the pigment and bonds it to the surface
- **thinners:** solvent or diluent

Historically, colour was provided by crushing and blending natural **pigments** into a suitable medium and mixing with a binder. Many pigments would not mix easily with binders, so grinding and incorporating was undertaken by specialised paint makers, and paints were blended and sold by 'colourmen'. Common sources were raw or burnt earth colours (such as ochres, umbers and siennas), as well as the products of chemical processes, especially the corrosion of metals. The commonest of these was white lead (lead carbonate) produced by the enforced corrosion of lead sheets by acetic acid (vinegar). Less stable colours were obtained from vegetable and animal sources such as plants, berries, logwood and – in the case of cochineal red – the dried bodies of a South American cactus beetle. Black was obtained from soot or lampblack, but was *not* commonly used on outdoor metalwork until the advent of alkyd oil paints in the 1930s.

All the above pigments have been used on *indoor* metalwork. The pigments that have most commonly been used on *outdoor* architectural and structural iron and steel are the following:

- **White lead:** this provided white and white-base for other colours, and was used from antiquity for priming and finishing timber and metalwork. Added pigments produced creams, 'stone' colours (sometimes tinted to blend with a building's walls) and greys, including 'lead' colour. Today, paints containing *white* lead may only be used on Grade I and II* listed buildings after authorisation by English Heritage.

- **Red lead or minium orange (lead tetroxide):** this has often been boiled with linseed oil to improve its drying properties. It has been used from antiquity as a primer, and may still be used for that purpose without prior authorisation.
- **Red oxide:** this is a cheap, hard-wearing paint for priming and finishing.
- **'Invisible' or Brunswick green, and bronze greens:** these form a range of greens often used in garden settings. They are made by mixing lemon chrome, Prussian blue and trace pigments.
- **Smalt (cobalt glass blue):** this, together with other rare and costly pigments, was occasionally used by the wealthy for prestigious metalwork on prominent facades from the seventeenth century. Paint with such rare pigments must be conserved if found, and not overcoated.
- **Varnish:** this is a clear or pale yellow resinous lacquer used as a gloss finish coat.
- **Coal tar and natural bitumen:** these, often mixed with solvents, were used as thick protective coatings in functional applications.
- **Gilding:** this was commonly applied to decoration on fine ornamental ironwork.

The commonest traditional **binder**, used from the eleventh century, has been linseed oil – made by crushing flax. It has a light yellow tint, and dries by absorption of oxygen (oxidation) over several days. Drying time can be reduced to about one day by boiling, or by adding a 'dryer' often containing lead, manganese or cobalt. To reduce skinning and cracking, 'extenders' including chalk and mica can be added to bulk up the paint, forming a paste which is easier to apply and covers arrises more effectively.

Thinners are mixed with the binder to change its working properties and to vary the final level of gloss. More thinners in the final coat gives a higher gloss. A gloss finish on metalwork was not uncommon, often being achieved with a varnish coat; but lead-based paints soon weathered to a matt and chalky surface. Turpentine was the most common traditional thinner (distilled from pine-tree sap) until 1885, when synthetic 'turps substitute' (white spirit) became available.

Modern coatings

Theory of painting

Paints cure to a dry film ranging in thickness from a few microns for a thin traditional paint, to over 100 microns per coat for modern high-build coatings. The film's thickness and uniformity depends on the paint's formulation and viscosity, the method of application and the skill of the painter. The wet film tends to recede from arrises and thicken in crevices. To ensure adequate protection it is therefore necessary to apply several coats, normally at least three. Coatings must be compatible with one another, of differing colour, and all should be purchased from the same manufacturer for best performance. Nowadays paints are formulated to perform specialised tasks:

- **Primer**: this wets the metal surface, providing adhesion for subsequent coats; the primer is often zinc- or aluminium-rich to provide cathodic protection.
- **Intermediate coats**: these provide thickness, opacity and colour.
- **Finishing coat(s)**: these provide colour and texture, and are the first defence against the aggressive effects of the environment.

Modern paints

In the twentieth century, petrochemical-based resins with synthetic pigments effectively replaced linseed oil paints. The first of these (in the 1920s) were alkyd resins, which were stronger, tougher and faster-drying than linseed oil, and provided intense white (using titanium oxide pigment) and black, both of which became common on metalwork, and are still used widely today.

Provided traditional oil-based paint coats have dried fully and are adhering well, they should be recoatable with a modern single-pack water-based system. Alkyd systems have also been used successfully, but should be trialled well in advance to check for the substrate's susceptibility to solvent attack, and allowed to weather to check medium-term adhesion.

A wide range of paint types is now available for metalwork, and specialised manufacturers devote considerable resources to developing complete paint systems for specific applications, for which their guidance should be sought. They will guarantee their products only if applied in accordance with their own instructions. The current industry tendency is towards water-based paints and high-solids technology.

The characteristics of paints currently available for use on metalwork are summarised in Table 7.7.

Rust converters

Rust converters are low-viscosity tannic acid products which convert a thin layer of rust to a stable dark blue or black tannate. On lightly rusted surfaces they provide, on their own, limited protection suitable for indoor use. They can be overcoated with paint systems, although paint manufacturers prefer all rust to be removed.

Paint application

On ferrous metals the thickness of paint can readily be measured with a dry film thickness meter. Coat **thickness** should therefore be specified, and checked after application of each coat and on completion. Dry film thickness of at least 250 microns is normal for outdoor metalwork.

Table 7.7 Characteristics of currently-available paints.

Paint types	Strengths	Weaknesses
Alkyd or modified alkyd oil	Ease of application; Good decorative appearance; Good salt spray resistance; Low cost; Can be formulated to give reasonable surface tolerance.	High film build not generally possible so multicoat system required; Poor water immersion resistance; Moderate/poor chemical resistance; Poor solvent resistance; Not recommended on zinc (saponifies).
Acrylated rubber, vinyl, chlorinated rubber	Good water resistance (especially if coal tar modified); Good salt spray resistance; Fairly good weathering properties; Good chemical resistance; Generally flexible with good inter-coat adhesion; Application generally good, but may appear 'liney' by brush; Can be formulated to give reasonable surface tolerance.	Poor handleability and damage-resistance rules out shop application; Very poor solvent resistance; Low solids and low film build – multi-coat systems required; Fairly expensive; High volatile organic (solvent) content, not environmentally friendly.
Water-based acrylics	Low volatiles content, so safer than solvent paints.	Relatively poor corrosion protection; Relatively expensive.
Epoxy and modified epoxy	Can be formulated to give high or low solids, thick or thin film versions; Very good salt spray resistance; Very good alkali resistance; Moderate acid resistance; Very good solvent resistance; Very good water resistance; Good handleability and damage resistance when cured; Can be formulated to give good surface tolerance; High-build versions give savings by reducing number of coats needed.	Poor gloss and colour retention, when exposed to sunlight and weather; Prone to chalking; Appearance best when sprayed; Two-pack, so can be difficult to handle; Curing is temperature-dependent, can be slow in winter months; Fairly expensive; Coal-tar modified versions require specific skin protection due to carcinogenic hazard.
Polyurethane and moisture-cured polyurethanes	Very good weather resistance; Very good salt spray resistance; Very good chemical resistance. Very good solvent resistance; Can be formulated to give reasonable surface tolerance; Generally good handleability and damage resistance; Good low-temperature curing; Good application characteristics and high standard of appearance.	Moderate water resistance (against immersion); Over-coatability poor to good, depending on type. Two-pack can be difficult to handle (moisture-cured versions are single-pack, but may give prob-lems due to moisture sensitivity in the can); Subject to strict health & safety and environmental controls; Generally expensive.

Table 7.7 *Continued*

Paint types	Strengths	Weaknesses
Zinc silicates	Hard and abrasion-resistant; Generally good solvent resistance; Withstands immersion and salt spray.	Very poor acid-alkali resistance; Two-pack can be difficult to handle; Difficult to overcoat; Spray application only; High standard of surface preparation required; Salts form on exterior exposure; Prone to 'mud-cracks' and 'pinholing' if over-applied.
Other zinc-rich coatings	Strengths as for particular binder type.	Poor acid-alkali resistance; Salts formation on external exposure; High standard of surface preparation required.

Finish colour for traditional paints is specified by detailed recipe, and for modern paints by the appropriate British Standard or RAL number.[13]

A range of application processes can be used, depending on the metalwork's size and shape and the properties of the paint. Brush, roller and conventional spray are suitable for most architectural applications and are often used together, with brushing being employed for edges and areas of difficult access.

Traditionally paint was thinned and applied by animal hair or bristle **brushes**. The skill of the painter was paramount in achieving a coat of full coverage, uniform thickness and good final appearance. Modern paints contain additives to ease the transfer of paint from the brush to the workpiece, and the spreading and curing of the paint. These paints are applied to tightly defined specifications, but the skill and integrity of the painter remain critical.

The advantages of brush-painting are:

- Minimal equipment is required.
- Good coverage is achievable on 'difficult' shapes.

The disadvantages are:

- It is relatively slow.
- The individual coats are thin.

Roller application is faster than brushing, but is suitable only for applying modern paints to relatively large and flat surfaces.

In **conventional paint-spraying**, compressed air (at 3–4 bar) draws paint from a hand-held pot, atomises it and propels it onto the surface. The paint requires thinning – typically by 10%, which reduces dry film thickness by up to 50%, making more coats necessary.

The advantages of the method are:

- It is relatively fast, especially on complex shapes.
- Moderate coat thickness is achievable.
- It produces a good surface finish.

The disadvantages are:

- There is poor coverage on 'shadow' areas.
- Coat thickness is uneven.
- It is non-traditional.

High-volume low-pressure spraying (HVLP, or pressure pot) is similar to conventional spray, but a larger quantity of paint is held in a pressurised pot and forced via a hose to the atomising spray gun. This method is suitable for large, complex areas.

In **airless spraying**, paint is pumped to a tungsten-carbide-tipped atomising gun by a specialised high-pressure pump at 200–450 bar.

The advantages of the method are:

- Application rates are high.
- Coat thickness is also high, with no thinning needed.
- There is reduced over-spray and bounce-back.

The disadvantages are:

- It is relatively complex.
- It is expensive.
- The equipment used is potentially hazardous.
- Specialised training required.
- It is not suitable for complex shapes.
- It is non-traditional.

Zinc or aluminium **metal-spraying** is a modern process using an oxy-propane flame to melt and blast the coating metal onto steel or wrought ironwork. It provides a uniform coating with good cathodic protection, and a rough substrate suitable for subsequent painting. Metal-sprayed coatings cannot easily be applied to thin edges, tend to mask fine detail and must be etch-primed before painting.

Further reading

Adamson, Simon H., *Seaside Piers* (Batsford, London, 1977).

Angus, H.T., *Cast Iron: Physical and engineering properties* (Butterworth, London, 1976).

Appraisal of Existing Structures (Institution of Structural Engineers, London, 1996).

Ashurst, J. and Ashurst, N., *Practical Building Conservation: Vol. 4: Metals*, English Heritage Technical Handbook (Gower Technical Press, Aldershot, 1988).

Ayrton, Maxwell and Silcock, Arnold, *Wrought Iron and Its Decorative Use* (Country Life, London, 1929).

Bates, W., *Historical Structural Steelwork Handbook* (British Construction/Steelwork Association, London, 1984).

Beaver, Patrick, *The Crystal Palace, 1851–1936* (Hugh Evelyn, London, 1970).

Brough, Joseph, *Wrought Iron: The end of an era at Atlas Forge, Bolton* (Bolton MBC Arts Dept, 1981).

Bussell, Michael, *Appraisal of Existing Iron and Steel Structures*, Publication 138 (Steel Construction Institute, Ascot, 1997).

Campbell, Marian, *Decorative Ironwork* (V & A Publications, London, 1997).

Conservation of Metal Statuary & Architectural Decoration in Open-Air Exposure, ICCROM Symposium, Paris, 6-8 October 1986 (ICCROM, Rome, 1987).

Cossons, Neil, *The BP Book of Industrial Archaeology* (David & Charles, Newton Abbot, 1975).

Doran, D. (ed.), *Construction Materials Reference Book* (Butterworth Heinemann, Oxford, 1992).

Gale, W.K.V., *The British Iron and Steel Industry* (David & Charles, Newton Abbot, 1967).

Gale, W.K.V., *Iron and Steel* (Longman, London, 1969).

Gardner, J. Starkie, *Ironwork* (Chapman & Hall, London, 1893).

Gayle, Margot, Look, David W. and Waite, John G., *Metals in America's Historic Buildings: Uses & preservation treatments* (HCRS Publications, Washington DC, 1980).

Gibbs, P., *Corrosion in Masonry Clad Early 20th Century Steel Framed Buildings*, Historic Scotland Technical Advice Note 20 (Historic Scotland, Edinburgh, 2000).

Gloag, John and Bridgwater, Derek, *Cast Iron in Architecture* (Allen & Unwin, London, 1948).

Harris, John, *English Decorative Ironwork, from Contemporary Source Books, 1610–1836: A collection of drawings and pattern books, etc.* (Tiranti, London, 1960).

Hix, John, *The Glasshouse* (Phaidon Press, London, 1996).

Kempster, Maurice Henry Albert, *Materials for Engineers* (English Universities Press, London, 1964).

Mallory, Keith, *Clevedon Pier* (Redcliffe, Bristol, 1981).

Mandel, Gabriele, *Wrought Iron* (Magna Books, Leicester, 1990).

Millar, John, *William Heap & His Company 1866* (Hoylake, Heap and Partners, 1976).

Minter, Sue, *The Greatest Glass House* (HMSO, London, 1990).

Raistrick, Arthur, *Dynasty of Ironfounders: The Darbys and Coalbrookdale* (Longman, London, 1953; 2nd rev. edn 1989).

Rivington's Notes on Building Construction (London, 1892; reprinted, Donhead, Shaftesbury, 2004).

Robertson, E. Graeme and Robertson, Joan, *Cast Iron Decoration: A world survey* (Thames & Hudson, London, 1977).

Rolt, L.T.C., *Victorian Engineering* (Allen Lane, London, 1970).

Stratton, Michael and Trinder, Barrie, *Industrial England* (English Heritage, London, 1997).

Sutherland, R.J.M. (ed.), *Studies in the History of Civil Engineering: Vol. 9: Structural iron, 1750–1850* (Gower, Aldershot, 1997).

Swailes, T., *Structural Appraisal of Iron-framed Textile Mills*, ICE Design and Practice Guide (Thomas Telford, London, 1998).

Swailes, T., *Scottish Iron Structures*, Historic Scotland Guide for Practitioners 5 (Historic Scotland, Edinburgh, 2006).

Thorne, R. (ed.), *The Iron Revolution: Architects, Engineers and Structural Innovation 1780–1880: essays to accompany an Exhibition at the RIBA Heinz Gallery* (RIBA Heinz Gallery, London, 1990).

Thorne, R. (ed.), *Studies in the History of Civil Engineering: Vol. 10: Structural iron, 1850–1900* (Ashgate, Aldershot, 2000).

Trinder, Barrie, *The Making of the Industrial Landscape* (Weidenfeld & Nicolson, London, 1982).

Twelvetrees, W.N., *Structural Iron and Steel* (Fourdrinier, 1900).

Tylecote, R.F., *A History of Metallurgy* (Institute of Materials, London, 1992).

Walker, B., *Corrugated Iron and other Ferrous Cladding*, Historic Scotland Technical Advice Note 29 (Historic Scotland, Edinburgh, 2004).

Westhofen, Wilhelm, 'The Forth Bridge', *Engineering*, 28 February 1890; repr. as *The Centenary Edition of Wilhelm Westhofen's the Forth Bridge* (Moubray, Edinburgh, 1989).

Woods, May and Warren, Arete, *Glasshouses* (Aurum Press, London, 1988).

Endnotes

1. R.F. Tylecote, *A History of Metallurgy* (Institute of Materials, Minerals and Mining, London, 1992), p. 125.

2. The prime sources for the figures in Table 7.2 are: wrought iron 1870 – R.F. Tylecote, *A History of Metallurgy* (Institute of Materials, London, 1992), p. 166; wrought iron 1900 – J.C. Carr, W. Taplin and A.E.G. Wright, *History of the British Steel Industry* (Blackwell, London, 1962), p. 195; steel 1870 and 1900. T.K. Derry and T.I. Williams, *A Short History of Technology* (Clarendon Press, Oxford, 1960), p. 484.

3. M. Bussell, *Appraisal of Existing Iron and Steel Structures*, Publication 138 (Steel Construction Institute, Ascot, 1997).

4. J.E. Breakell, K. Foster, *et al.*, *Management of Accelerated Low Water Corrosion in Steel Maritime Structures*, Construction Industry Research and Information Association Report C634 (London, 2005).

5. E.G. Warland, *Modern Practical Masonry* (London 1929; 2nd edn 1953; reprinted Donhead, Shaftesbury, 2007).

6. P. Gibbs *Corrosion in Masonry Clad Early 20th Century Steel Framed Buildings*, Historic Scotland Technical Advice Note 20 (Historic Scotland, Edinburgh, 2000).

7. Helen Hughes (ed.), *Layers of Understanding: Setting standards for architectural paint research: proceedings of a seminar held on 28 April 2000* (Donhead, Shaftesbury, 2002).

8. See *Structures & construction in historic building conservation*, Chapter 2.

9. See *ibid.*, Chapter 7, and the English Heritage leaflet *Office Floor Loadings in Historic Buildings* (1994).

10. See also *Structures & construction in historic building conservation*, Chapter 10, and Bussell, *Appraisal of Existing Iron and Steel Structures*.

11. Statutory Instrument 2007 No. 320: *The Construction (Design and Management) Regulations 2007*, www.opsi.gov.uk/si/si2007/20070320.htm (accessed 9 April 2007).

12. J.M.C. Cadei, T.J. Stratford, *et al.*, *Strengthening Metallic Structures Using Externally Bonded Fibre-reinforced Polymers*, Construction Industry Research and Information Association Report C595 (London, 2004) and also S.S.J. Moy (ed.), *FRP Composites: Life extension and strengthening of metallic structures*, ICE Design and Practice Guide (Thomas Telford, London, 2001).

13. RAL is a system to describe paint colours. It was developed in 1927 by Reichsausschuß für Lieferbedingungen (und Gütesicherung), now the Deutsches Institut für Gütesicherung und Kennzeichnung e.V. Today RAL has over 1900 colours.

8 Understanding decay in building timbers

Brian Ridout

Most wood decays eventually if it is damp, and the rapidity of its decay depends upon its durability. Durability may be inherent or artificially provided by impregnation with chemicals.

These statements would generally be accepted and take the theory of timber conservation about as far as many professionals wish to take it. A good spray with something that says 'preservative' on the label is deemed to be a wise precaution and is particularly useful if accompanied by something called a guarantee. The meaning of the guarantee is probably a little hazy. It might mean that timber that hasn't been infested with 'woodworm' in two hundred years will not become infested with 'woodworm' in the next few decades; or it might mean that wood will not be decayed by fungi if kept dry, thus taking us back to where we were in the first place.

The problems with this cheerful acceptance of perceived wisdom and trade hype have been that vast amounts of biocides have been flung unnecessarily into buildings, and teams of 'specialists' have caused more damage to fine interiors in the pursuit of death-watch beetle or dry rot than the organisms they sought to destroy.

Slowly, very slowly, at the close of the twentieth century and the beginning of the twenty-first, people have begun to realise that biocides are not a panacea for all decay or infestation problems. If insects or fungi are destroying the timber within our buildings then biocides may be appropriate, but we must be cautious about relying on the man who makes his living by selling remedial treatments. Some make a serious attempt to advise, many make a serious attempt to maximise profits and few have any interest in conservation.

If we are to maximise the historical material we conserve in our buildings then biocides must just be one tool in our workbox. They must not be allowed to replace thought and knowledge. The amount of knowledge required to make an informed judgement is actually not that great. But it does require us to abandon the notions that wood is a homogeneous material, that decay is inevitable if wood moisture contents rise and that organisms such as dry rot have somehow adapted to a life in buildings.

There are questions that should be asked when damaged timber is found and remedial action is contemplated:

- Why is the problem there?
- How much damage has the decaying or infesting organism caused and why is that damage limited?
- Is the decay or infestation current or historical?
- Will a targeted biocide treatment serve any useful purpose?

Critics will note that the list is not headed with 'What is causing the damage?' This is deliberate because such a question leads us to a stereotyped response that typifies our problem with remedial treatments. Dry rot may be dead, or unable to cause much damage, while a 'wet rot' may be causing extensive decay. Contrary to perceived wisdom, strand-forming wet rots will travel through walls (though rarely to the extent that dry rot does), but because this is not supposed to happen the strands are either not noticed or the fungus is called dry rot. Calling the fungus dry rot will inevitably lead to a response that may be out of all proportion to the problem.

Let us examine each of the questions we should ask. First, why is the problem there? All of the fungi and insects that damage timbers in our buildings belong in the woodlands outside. They are all part of the carbon cycle that takes a dead branch to the forest floor, decays it into soil and recycles the nutrients released back into the trees. The breakdown of wood in this cycle creates environments for a progression of organisms to exploit, and if we allow our building timbers to replicate any one of those environments then the appropriate organism may cause damage. To a fungus, a poorly maintained roof is, after all, just a heap of dead wood.

None of the organisms that cause problems for timber conservation have adapted to a life in buildings, and we must not expect them to tolerate conditions in buildings that they could not cope with in their forest environment. Buildings may provide a sheltered environment that is ideal for some fungi (dry rot and the wet rots *Asterostroma* and *Donkioporia* are rarely found outside) but the same restrictions still apply. What are these restrictions?

Dead branches on standing trees provide an interesting habitat that may be damp or dry for extended periods of time. The organisms of interest to conservation from this environment are the anobiid beetles: furniture beetles and death-watch beetles (collectively and confusingly called powder-post beetles in the USA, whereas we use the term powder-post for the *Lyctus* beetles).

These beetles can tolerate rather dry conditions (some genera better than others) but not without consequences if dry conditions are extended throughout the year. Evidence suggests that drying the timber prolongs the larval growth period, which produces smaller adults that lay fewer eggs. The beetles are not likely to infest, and a population is likely to decline, if the wood moisture content stays permanently below 15%, which would be typical for a dry and well-maintained building (see Ridout, 2000). It is possible that particularly nutritional wood might offset this decline to some extent. If the wood moisture content drops below about 10% then the eggs and small larvae will desiccate.

These insects will only attack the sapwood of our commonly used construction timbers and sapwood damage may occur anywhere within the building. The heartwood of these timbers contains a variety of substances that formed part of the tree's natural defence system against pathogens so that the beetles cannot move from the sapwood into the heartwood unless these substances are denatured.

The dead parts of a standing tree will always contain fungus and the fungus both softens the wood and changes its chemistry. This combination makes durable heart wood available to beetles that would otherwise be restricted to sapwood. The same effect is observed in buildings around the world. A little fungus denatures wall plates or the ends of traditionally durable building timbers and makes them susceptible to beetles and termites. Our task is to recognise what has happened so that we do not treat a large amount of unmodified heartwood that the insects cannot attack. Remember that the decay may be historical but the heartwood will remain modified.

When the branch falls to the forest floor it becomes wetter and the next shift of insects and fungi takes over. The insects will probably include weevils and there are several species that we might find in a similar habitat within our buildings. A similar habitat in this case might be a damp wall plate under a suspended ground floor. The weevil/fungus combination will destroy the plate unless it dries, in which case the fungus will die and the weevils will fly away.

The fungi that will mostly decay our branch or log on the forest floor are saprophytes. Their niche in nature is the breakdown of dead organic materials, and it is these saprophytes that cause the majority of the damage to our building timbers (termites may be a far greater problem in dryer climates).

There are many different types of saprophytic fungi in a woodland, and if one cannot grow well on the log then there will always be another that can. Even the most durable of woods is slowly consumed by a progression of organisms in a damp environment, although this may take a very long time.

This variety and versatility of decay organisms has caused considerable difficulties for the producers of fungicides. Formulations that worked well under laboratory conditions have performed poorly when challenged by the mighty array of organisms in nature. Something – a mould perhaps – has been able to initiate the process of modification. The fungicide has just changed the habitat so that a different range of colonisers is involved.

One vital factor to remember about our forest floor environment is that the log becomes damp and remains damp. Many people now realise that the key to the decay process is water; most forget that the water has to remain if the fungus is to stay alive. Forget silly stories about dry rot producing sufficient water from the breakdown of wood to survive in a dry building – it doesn't happen.

The importance of this cannot be overstated and may be illustrated by a visit the author made to a house in Dublin. There had been roof repairs a few years previously when tarpaulins had become dislodged overnight allowing water down into the building. The occupants and their advisers now wished to strip the interiors and treat the walls in case dry rot had developed and was lurking behind the wall linings. This work was to be covered by an insurance claim. It was explained that the presence of dry rot caused by the water penetration was not just unlikely, it was impossible. If, by some remote chance, a dry rot spore had managed to germinate where water was trapped for a while then the fungus must die as the building dried. The architect, structural engineer and remedial man all looked on in total disbelief. Then the housekeeper became angry and accused me of being obstructive. All she wanted was the best for their beautiful house and that apparently was to strip away all of the interior finishes. I retired defeated and bemused.

This story demonstrates the damage that can result when we forget the origins and limitations of our decay organisms and how the problem can reach ridiculous proportions in our perception and treatment of dry rot.

The next question to ask is how much damage has been caused and why this is limited. It can only be answered by delving back into history and investigating how the decay problem and our reaction to it have developed.

Prior to the eighteenth century most of the structural timbers that were used in British buildings – at least those that have survived – and in ships were oak. But as the century progressed oak became expensive, and economics, together with other factors such as fires in major cities and fashion, accelerated a change away from timber-frame construction. Softwoods began to be used in large quantities.

We had been importing pine (usually called fir) from Norway for centuries but this was mostly as planks. Now softwoods were being used for structural timbers in situations previously reserved for oak, and during the middle years of the eighteenth century the great European pine forests that could supply the Baltic ports began to be exploited. These forests could supply timber of dimensions that Norway no longer found easy to provide. Timber had always been difficult to ship profitably because it was too bulky compared to its weight, and it tended to be imported as part of a cargo. Now the trade became sufficiently profitable and well organised to dedicate ships solely to timber importation.

There would not have been a serious decay problem if the properties of the timber had been better understood. Unfortunately it was frequently just seen as a lighter and cheaper alternative to oak and the connection between decay and moist environments was not made. Pine was used for the upper works of dank ships, or embedded in the damp floors of houses, and the consequence was an epidemic of dry rot. At least eight books and pamphlets were published on the subject during the first three decades of the nineteenth century.

The damage was called dry rot, not because the problem was uncon-
nected with water but because people did not accept that it was. The
damage that they were used to in oak they believed to be caused by wind
and rain and they called it wet or common rot, but this new form seemed
frequently to occur behind a sound skin of timber. Those who were familiar
with the flora of woodlands, like the botanist C.E. Sowerby, had no difficulty
in understanding what was going on, but they were not generally believed.
One popular theory was that the damage was caused by a flux of heat; its
true cause was not finally accepted until the 1860s.

We now know that dry rots are caused by brown rot fungi and wet rots
by white rot fungi, and that both require lots of water. But the term dry
rot still haunts us with confusion. Brown rots were not a new phenomenon;
they were just thrown into public awareness by the change in timber
usage.

These problems had been resolved by the end of the nineteenth century
and the causes of the decay were understood. If you found dry rot
then you repaired the damage and removed the source of water. Not
new concepts really, because a man called Johnson had written a book
on the subject in 1797. The term dry rot was also changing and had
become restricted to those fungi that produced plenty of surface
growth. The remainder of the brown rotting fungi were relegated to the
wet rots.

The timber decay problem was now about to become serious again, and
the primary cause was sapwood. The pine wood used during the eighteenth and nineteenth centuries was not as durable as oak perhaps, but it
resisted decay rather well. The reason was that the trees had grown for
centuries in natural woodland and were mostly mature heartwood. The
twenty or so years of sapwood growth formed an insignificant percentage
of most logs. Unfortunately, two- or three-hundred-year-old trees were not
a sustainable resource and by World War I the wood was coming increasingly from regenerated forests. This was the problem that Norway, our
traditional supplier of pine, had begun to experience in the eighteenth
century and it was happening again over a wider area.

Timber shortage during the war caused considerable problems, and
when the war ended the UK government were determined never to be
caught short of timber again. They made two initiatives; the first was to set
up the Forestry Commission in 1919 to establish and manage large plantations of mainly softwood trees, and this form of production has become
commonplace and necessary to sustain our growing demand for wood. The
shift from wild forest to regenerated forest and plantations is now being
replicated on a global scale. The consequences for biodiversity, carbon
dioxide absorption and a host of similar topics are hotly debated, but the
consequences for building conservation are not – even though we now
have a century of experience.

The problem with growing trees as a managed crop is that they are felled
as soon as they reach a marketable size. This is likely to be after about fifty
years' growth as far as Scots pine is concerned. Now the twenty or more
years of sapwood growth becomes significant, and the problem is com-

pounded by the sale of thinnings as the trees are given more space to grow. The result is that some sections of softwood used for construction and repair may contain more than 50% sapwood.

Much of the pine wood used in Britain since World War I will not give the same durability in service as its historical equivalent, even though it is cut from the same species of tree. This wood may be easily decayed by organisms like furniture beetle and dry rot.

The second government initiative after the war was to set up the Forest Products Research Laboratory. This organisation did not have a laboratory in its early years and the problem of dry rot was given to Professor Percy Groom at Imperial College in London. The late John Savory, who became head of Biodeterioration at the Princes Risborough Laboratory (the name of the FPRL was changed) informed me that Groom was chosen for the task because he could read German and most of the research on dry rot up to that time had been undertaken in Germany.

The result was the Forest Products Research Bulletin No. 1, *Dry rot in Wood*, which was published in 1928 and remained in print through six editions until 1960. It is important to remember that this document was a compilation and not based on Groom's research. Many of the strange notions that plague those of us concerned with dry rot originate, or were brought together, in Bulletin No. 1. Typical would be the ideas that buildings dry down through a zone of moisture content suitable for dry rot; that wet rot turns into dry rot as it dies; that the fungus produces sufficient moisture from the breakdown of wood to sustain itself even when the external source of moisture has been removed; and that the fungus carries water to wet-up dry timber.

The last idea is firmly believed, even by some academics, because the fungus produces strands that carry a watery solution of nutrients – but so do the strands of other fungi found in buildings. Long experience has shown that this ability has little or anything to do with a dry rot outbreak. Savory (1964) tried to overcome the conundrum by suggesting that the fungus might be able to humidify a static environment, but I know from discussions with him that he never considered this to be of much practical significance.

The term 'dry rot' and its attendant mythology eventually became restricted to one fungus (*Serpula lacrymans*) in a British Standard published in 1963. All the rest of the fungi found in buildings were lumped in with the wet rots.

Sifting the truth from the mythology becomes easier if we remember that dry rot is produced by a fungus that originated in logs on the forest floor – in the Himalayas, the Rocky Mountains, or perhaps central Europe. The fungus may thrive in buildings if conditions are suitable because they provide a stable environment, and probably because building materials provide a good source of calcium and iron. These two elements seem to be necessary for the fungus.

Dry rot's moisture requirements do not differ from those of other brown rotting fungi. It may grow at a wood moisture content as low as 22% but it will not cause much damage at moisture contents below about 25%. This is set into context by remembering that wood in a dry but unheated building would have a moisture content of around 15%.

The strands that have caused so much confusion spread out from the fungus on the forest floor, carrying nutrients liberated by decay, so that the fungus can find other damp logs to colonise. What the fungus does in a forest is what it does in a building and we must not expect new and dramatic abilities.

Some of the problem is that dry rot growth can look white and fluffy even when it's dead; and concealed damage can deform rapidly as it desiccates. Both phenomena lead to the conclusion that the dry rot is active, even though the source of moisture may be long gone.

Similar confusion results when we forget the natural habitat of the furniture beetle. A few faces of timber full of beetle holes in an otherwise intact Victorian roof indicate a little sapwood resulting from the way in which the wood was converted, and not roof timbers in danger of being comprehensively infested.

Death-watch beetle and furniture beetle may cause more damage where there has been prolonged water penetration and decay at some time because this also replicates the beetle's natural habitat. Water penetration is rarely comprehensive and a competent surveyor will know were to look for building faults. The presence of damage, or even active infestation, in these areas is no justification for treating the entire building with insecticides.

Our experience with modern timbers in modern buildings has coloured our approach to historic timbers. Dry rot and furniture beetle will cause damage at a rate and to an extent in twentieth-century plantation-grown wood that would be impossible in the wild-grown historical equivalents. Unfortunately our perception and response to the two situations is frequently the same, to the detriment of the building, its finishes and our living environment.

References

British Standard 565: 1963, *Glossary of Terms Relating to Timber and Woodwork* (British Standards Institution, London).

Ridout, Brian V., *Timber Decay in Buildings the Conservation Approach to Treatment* (E & FN Spon, London, 2000).

Savory, J.G., 'Dry rot: a reappraisal', in *Record of the 1964 Annual Convention of the British Wood Preserving Association* (London, 1964), pp. 69–76.

9 Timber

Charley Brentnall

There is an extraordinary diversity of timber buildings, structures and components throughout Britain and the world, from humble sheds and hovels, through houses, to cathedral roofs and spires – most of which, even when outwardly expressing masonry, hide a roof frame or floor of wood. Salisbury Cathedral spire, for example, under its 140 metres of stone relies on a tension structure of oak cut from small-diameter trees. Other structures that were never designed to be revealed may be clad perhaps in boarding or tile, or plastered over. Then there is the second fix of flooring, panelling and joinery. All are tasks for the conservator.

Roman and Saxon timber is only found in below-ground archaeology, with some of the best in urban waterlogged sites. The earliest extant carpentry dates from the eleventh century, and more examples survive in every successive period. They leave a heritage of building types – remarkable examples of ingenuity and design – and also a record and test bed of hundreds of years. The vast octagonal lantern at Ely cathedral, with a timber vault carried on eight immense posts, is humbling to take in and it is daunting to appreciate the achievements of its past framers. Those corner posts would probably now be impossible to source and the carpentry hard to match, but so much has been learnt from studying this architecture during the recent explosion of new green framing from around 1990.

Early medieval frames tend towards heavier member sizes and more open panels, roofs with coupled rafters and no purlins at first. Central and then side purlins were introduced, giving more stability. Close studding followed in the Perpendicular period. Hewett (1980) identifies the sixteenth century as the zenith of English carpentry – after that, it becomes 'decadent' in its reasoning until the eighteenth century brought in logical truss forms and uniform timbers set on edge. Naval war campaigns are blamed for the arrival of slighter timbering and short lengths, sometimes with short lengths of studs or rafters framed into purlins or cut onto raking wall braces. Imported softwoods from the Baltic or Dominions became the norm in Georgian and Victorian times.

Brunskill and others have demonstrated the geography of the vernacular styles, interestingly tending to follow the south-west–north-east sweep of the country's geology. At times these can be further localised too – a rich language which is at present sadly missed and untapped by contemporary framers.

Scotland has a heritage of timber more akin to that of the Continent with strains of the Netherlands, Germany and France – possibly through contact with craftsmen from these countries while at war with England (see, for example, the centred carpentry of Edinburgh and Stirling Castles, and the galleried styles of urban housing). The north of England links through to the south-west with heavier kingpost roofs and crucks, and trenched or butt purlins, while East Anglia and the south-east favour clasped purlins and generally a lighter proportion of timbers.

Timber as a material

The dominant **species** used in framing are European oak – *quercus robor* and *petraea* – and chestnut and elm. Softwoods (mainly Scots or Baltic pine) and imported timbers were common from early mediaeval times onwards (Figure 9.1). Timbers less commonly used (or more susceptible to decay) are ash, beech, poplar, hazel, birch and others.

In the **conversion** of timber, the use of saws came and went with the Romans, to return only in the twelfth century. Until saws were used, the practice was with axe and wedge, techniques which put the craftsman in touch with very different qualities of timber and its fibres. The jowl post and teasel tenon and tie dovetail – the 'English tying joint' – are synonymous with English carpentry from the mid-twelfth century to the start of the twentieth (Continental framers without exception use 'reversed assembly', which to this day is viewed with suspicion by English carpenters). The jowl formed from the vigour of the upturned rootstock of trees makes up

Figure 9.1 Eighteenth-century slow-growing Baltic pine (left) compared with modern fast-grown Douglas fir. The former will usually be far more durable.

Figure 9.2 Traditional hand-hewing conversion of small-diameter trees.

for the inherent shrinkage of the male dovetail across its width, allowing the teasel tenon to take the roof loading and avoid splitting down the jowl.

Most historic timber was first converted with an axe (Figure 9.2). A tree as close to the desired timber dimension as possible was hewn to a square and then re-sawn if necessary. Differing sawing techniques leave particular tool marks on the timber. See-sawing, used by the Romans and across the globe, leaves a distinctive break-off point where the two converging angles of cut meet. In Britain this fell out of use at the end of the fifteenth century but continued on the Continent until World War II.

As for **durability and defects**, the bark and paler sapwood of trees are non-durable and susceptible to insect and fungal attack, but even these if kept dry can last centuries. The use of breathable materials such as soft lime mortar allows wicking – which will counter the dangers of hard and impervious materials and finishes. Detailing that protects timber from damp should be favoured, for example good overhangs to roofs and gables (Figure 9.3). Keep damp-proof courses away from timber where water will pool or sweat against its underside or, if this is not possible, at least bed them on a soft mix above the dpc.

Timber **properties** are well documented in reference publications by the Building Research Establishment (BRE), the Timber Research and Development Association (TRADA) and British Standards. These provide information on durability, strength characteristics, weights, seasoning and shrinkage and other properties (Figure 9.4). For suitable framing specification, see Ross (2007). In most cases it is usual to specify repair timber to match the moisture content of the original material, and for this to be air dry (for

Figure 9.3 Detail of Paycocke's House, Coggeshall, Essex. Good roof overhangs, breathable limewash paint, and soft lime mortar keep the timber dry.

Figure 9.4 Differential shrinkage between tangential (7.5%) and radial (4.5%) timber in oak.

Figure 9.5 Selecting trees for crucks near Clovelly, Devon. Finding a particular shape can involve a countrywide search.

external or unheated spaces) or kiln dry (for heated interiors). Timber moisture content can be checked approximately with a moisture meter.

In terms of **procurement**, current supplies are available from UK timber merchants, although much stock presently comes from France and Eastern Europe, undermining the local forestry industry.

For each project it is usual to draw up a bespoke cutting list of **sizes** and **lengths**, to a specification dictated by the use in question. The hardwood trade still uses the imperial measure but most mills will quote in metric.

For more unusual sections, lengths or shapes, extra time should be allowed for procurement: there are progressively fewer mills with saws that can accommodate longer logs – beyond 7 metres – on their saw; a particular cruck bend may require finding a single tree to achieve a curve (Figure 9.5).

Timber is one of the most **sustainable** construction materials – renewable, low embodied energy, and locking up CO_2 – provided that the rate of use is matched by regrowth. UK home-grown timber is mostly controlled by felling licences which require replanting. Certification schemes such as the Accreditation Programme of the Forest Stewardship Council (FSC) will ensure standards and a chain of custody.

The timber survey

The information gathered from a survey of an existing timber structure should inform the overall conservation strategy, which in turn should drive a repair schedule. Sketching or making a measured drawing of a frame is a wonderful way to understand it fully. The survey should aim to

- establish the current content and condition
- consider the holistic context
- understand the structure
- identify any structural or material failures and their causes.

Non-destructive testing of suspect timbers can be carried out using a **micro-drill** that measures the density of a beam, highlighting voids or rotten material. **Dendro-dating** uses core samples which include intact sapwood. The variable annual growth rings are compared with computer records of dated historic samples, matching the climatic peculiarities of an era.

It is usually easy to reconstruct the past design of carpentry or joinery from a surprisingly few remaining members. Empty mortices, shadows of missing mouldings, pressure marks of long-removed members – all can lead seductively to the recreation of an 'original' building, but usually with the destruction of equally valid later periods of fabric. Likewise the natural desire to match timber details with 'traditional' carpentry timber-to-timber repairs may demand stripping out surrounding materials for access, and cutting back historic timber to create a successful joint. A 'restoration' can see the destruction of plasterwork, paint finishes and secondary joinery, and the loss of the patina of age. It is all too easy to end up with a beautifully repaired frame but a substantially new building. A wise carpenter will temper his love of his own trade with balance and respect for those of others.

Repair techniques

Timber-to-timber repairs in traditional carpentry are perhaps the most obvious choice when selecting a technique. However, as noted above, it is important to be aware that this decision can be one of the least conservative in nature. To scarf a new end onto a beam with a structurally sound result may require the original to be cut back not only to good timber but beyond a series of joints, with the subsequent loss of historic material.

Slip tenons, morticed or slotted into the end of a stud or beam, can replace the rotted original. A chased mortice is only possible if some of the members can move apart, or in diagonal members such as braces. Scarfs will at best achieve 75% of the strength of a full timber and if in a high stress zone are best if bolted or glued.

Metal reinforcement has been used for centuries in timber construction. Steel strap and threaded bar can be the most cost-effective and conservative repair – reversible apart from a few screw or bolt holes. Often the metalwork can be hidden from view, for example placed behind the weather board of a barn, or discreetly above a purlin. Alternatively, it may be possible to remove a veneer or plank of timber from a face, then to let in an appropriate section of steel before replacing the plank above it. Elderly joints can have strap repairs placed across them with very little additional work.

Generally, the differential expansion of the two materials is negligible over the distances concerned and will be tolerated. The well-documented exception to the rule is continuous steel straps placed across log-built walls where the accumulative movement of cross grain can become significant.

The number of bolts in a tension repair can be reduced by up to four with the use of split rings or sheer plates. If any of the timber is green or other building fabric in a repair is damp while bolts are being used, provision should be made for tightening as they dry out, and the bolts left open or the plugs removable.

The acidity of the timber should be checked as if high it can corrode modern iron fastenings regardless of galvanising, especially in damp or wet conditions. If this is the case, stainless steel is preferable – use austenitic 304 or 316 (which can be checked with a magnet, 300-series being non-magnetic).

Resin repairs are often considered by some as being non-reversible, and therefore unacceptable in conservation. However, this argument should be challenged by considering that there is nothing more non-reversible than a beam that has been replaced by new. Resins can allow a piece to be retained that otherwise would be discarded for ever.

Glues and resins are specialist materials which should only be used in the correct conditions and strictly to manufacturer's instructions. Typical site conditions seldom match those of a workshop and BS 8000-5:1990 states that '[s]ite gluing of any type should be undertaken only in exceptional circumstances'; it is as well to follow this wisdom. Generally, resins and glues are sensitive to moisture content, dust and contaminants. Failure to limit these will result in a lack of bond; for example, drilled holes for rod reinforcement that contain dust or that have glazed surfaces will provide a poor bond. There are **glues** that can cope with higher moisture contents – even working under water; however, no glue will cope with significant shrinkage of timber of larger-size section as this will rip the fibres from the bonded surfaces.

The Weald and Downland Open Air Museum, Chichester, West Sussex, has pioneered a series of successful **repairs** that leave the maximum amount of historic surface and avoid a patched appearance. Inserted tenons can replace rotten ones, glued into 'V' cuts and left open (Figure 9.6) or with a veneer taken from the original stud waste to hide the replacement slip tenon (Figure 9.7). In the case of an eroded beam face and rotted mortices, rather than applying multiple patch repairs a slot may be cut behind and a new timber introduced into the slot to reinstate structural integrity while leaving damaged peg holes to speak for themselves and retain the patina of age. Where timber has eroded, labour time can be kept to a minimum by using gap-filling resins to bed a new core (Figure 9.8).

Figure 9.6 A tenon has been repaired by resin-gluing a 'V' cut, air-dry insert into the base of a stud.

Figure 9.7 A variation on Figure 9.6 is to cut veneers from the original waste offcut and apply these to the sides of the new insert fish tenon.

Figure 9.8 Resin casting a new timber core and tenon to a jowl post which has been hollowed by death-watch beetle. The intact exterior skin has been temporarily coffered with ply and clay to prevent resin leaking through shakes.

Timber cleaning can be carried out *if* appropriate, and in a manner appropriate to the surface: soot-blackened or frassy timber (worm-eaten material, usually covered by a largely intact skin) requires the gentlest of bristles or vacuum pressure, while sound oak in a barn frame will take a stiff pale brush in the breeze. Pressure washing will bring the colour back but soaking can leave tannin stains on the surrounds. Sandblasting will remove any historic surface and leave the grain raised, turning frassy timber to driftwood. More sucessful is the patented JOS cleaning process, which uses a mixture of low air pressure, very little water and a fine inert abrasive powder, formed together into a rotating vortex.

Prior to the repair process, thought must be given to adequate **temporary support** for the structure and **access** for labour and material. Scaffold cradles are easy to construct and can be combined with access needs (Figure 9.9). Lifting points and forked 'U' heads with screw jacks for jacking can be incorporated. Temporary works should be engineered. It is usual to position the inside line of **scaffold standards** one board out from a wall and decks about 600 mm below ties or plates to leave work room around

Figure 9.9 Charlton Court Tithe Barn, Steyning, West Sussex, being repaired under a temporary steel building. The frame is supported by a scaffold cradle, and partial roof dismantling has allowed scarf repairs to be undertaken.

the timbers. Temporary **bracing** can be achieved with nailed softwood or guys in cable or rope. When fixing temporary bracing or protection direct to historic timber, be aware that the nails or screws will scar the recipient, and if the operations require their constant removal and replacement it is worth considering fixing a **sacrificial block** to receive the temporary fixings.

References and further reading

British Standard 4978: 1996, *Specification for Visual Strength Grading of Softwood*.
British Standard 5268-2: 2002, *Structural Use of Timber: Part 2: Code of practice for the permissible stress design, materials and workmanship*.
British Standard 5756: 1997, *Specification for Visual Strength Grading of Hardwoods*.
Building Research Establishment, *Handbook of Hardwoods* (HMSO, London, 1977).
Building Research Establishment, *Handbook of Softwoods* (HMSO, London, 1977).
Building Research Establishment, *Recognising Wood Rot and Insect Damage in Buildings* (BRE, Garston, 1987).
Charles, F.W. and Charles, Mary, *Conservation of Timber Buildings* (Donhead, Shaftesbury, 1995).

Edlin, Herbert L., *Woodland Crafts in Britain* (David & Charles, Newton Abbott, 1978).

Harris, Richard, *Discovering Timber Framed Buildings* (Shire Publications, Princes Risborough, 1993).

Hewett, Cecil A., *English Historic Carpentry* (Phillimore, Chichester, 1980).

Hewett, Cecil A., *English Cathedral and Monastic Carpentry* (Phillimore, Chichester, 1985).

International Wood Committee, *Principles for the Preservation of Historic Timber Structures* (ICOMOS, 1999).

Larsen, Knut Einar and Marstein, Nils, *Conservation of Historic Timber Structures* (Butterworth Heinemann, London, 2000).

Newman, Rupert, *Oak Framed Buildings* (Guild of Master Craftsman Publications Ltd Bristol, 2005).

Powys, A.R., *Repair of Ancient Buildings* (J.M. Dent & Sons, London, 1929).

Rose, Walter, *The Village Carpenter* (Stobart Davies, Hertford, 1937).

Ross, Peter, Mettem, Christopher, Andrew, Holloway, *Green Oak in Construction* (TRADA, High Wycombe, 2007).

TRADA Green Oak in Construction 2006.

TRADA Wood Information Sheets.

10 Wattle and daub

Tony Graham

Introduction

Wattle and daub epitomises vernacular construction. Its continuous use for at least 6000 years owes much to the cheapness and abundance of raw materials. It starts with primitive building and spans the history of England until the craft's demise during the eighteenth century (Figure 10.1).

The historic value of a building is often manifest not only by architectural style but also by the superimposed effects of patina and decay, giving 'age value'. In wattle and daub this may emanate through its cracked and undulating surfaces, its partial decay that exposes its underlying core of withies or its soft limewashed finish. This all lies in stark contrast to the lifelessness of a cement-rendered panel.

Despite the legislation protecting the 'special character' of historic buildings, damage is still done through insensitive repair. It is therefore important that government guidance is adhered to:

> Traditional fixing and repair methods should be perpetuated. Proper attention should be given to the in-filling panels which are an integral part of any timber-framed building.[1]

Panel types

The form of a wattle backing is chiefly determined by the shape and size of the spacing between the frame since it is necessary for the panel to be sufficiently rigid to withstand loading, such as from wind or being leant upon. Most were rectangular, like the majority in post and truss and box-frame constructions: non-rectangular panels required special consideration. The dauber would need to be able to fill a great variety of panel shapes, depending on their location within the frame, decoration, bracing and panel size. Narrow panels result either from close studding or where a stud, such as for a window or door jamb, breaks a larger panel; to fill narrow panels the construction could be rotated so that the staves were horizontal and withies vertical, or more frequently, and especially for close studding, lathing was used instead of wattle. The laths were either sprung into grooves made in the sides of both studs or nailed to fillets of oak which themselves were nailed to the stud sides. Where the latter technique was

Figure 10.1 A wattle and daub panel set within a timber frame.

used, the daub may be replaced with a haired plaster applied directly to the laths.[2]

Frame braces introduced tapering and curved panel edges that caused complexities in the wattling. Where laths were used, the nailed fillets could simply follow the line of the brace with varying length of lath applied between them. However, where staves and wattle were used, they needed to be short near the corners and consequently their insertion required much skill. Many other methods of providing a compact wattlework were used, such as running the withies diagonally, following the line of the brace.

Where the bracing was entirely ornamental, the non-structural decorative 'struts' were made thinner than the structural frame and the staves and wattling kept simple by being placed behind them.

Decoration

Although most daub work was left plain, it was also commonly painted or profiled. The simplest form of decoration was to colour the limewash using cow dung tint, ox blood or earth-based pigments. Internally, panels may also have been pigmented, but wealthy house owners sometimes had the completed panels decoratively painted. Examples of medieval work survive, including floral patterns, chequers and heraldic detailing. Repeating patterns could be extended over the timbers so that the whole wall was covered.

Panels may have been given interest by lightly combing the finished surface prior to limewashing. From the sixteenth century, external walls were frequently decorated with incised patterning, a rudimentary form of pargetting also known as 'stick work' or 'combed work'. The patterns would have been formed by crude wooden combs, a stick or a large nail.[3] Gypsum was used for plasterwork where available, such as in the Isle of Purbeck, around Knaresborough in Yorkshire and the Trent Valley. Since its properties were conducive to modelling ('raised' work), it is not surprising that ornamented pargetting developed. It became particularly fashionable in the sixteenth century and continued into the seventeenth, especially in East Anglia where the whole frame would be covered and intricately decorated.

Staves

The staves were usually oak, but hazel, holly, birch, alder and ash were also used.[4] Chestnut was quite durable but supply was generally restricted to the south-east. The staves were either selected as coppice in the round or riven from the heartwood of larger timbers.

The staves of wattle panels had to be of the correct thickness so that the withies or laths could be easily worked around them without splitting or creating a panel that was too thick, as this would protrude too closely to the surface of the frame. Riven oak staves were usually 15–25 mm deep by 60–90 mm wide whereas hazel staves were typically 20–30 mm diameter. Bark was often removed to reduce the risk of beetle attack. To assist weaving, the outside pair of staves was often thicker and shaped to a truncated wedge section, with intermediate staves shaped to a truncated diamond section. This allowed each withy or lath to lie more flatly against the side of the stave, rather than touching just the protruding corners of an unshaped rectangular-sectioned stave. If nailed laths were to be used, the staves needed to be thicker: typically 50 mm by 75 mm, and looking more like studs.[5]

The tops of all staves were prepared to fit the underside of the rail. For an augered hole, they were roughly pointed: chamfered on all four sides, or chamfered on just two sides to fit the width of a mortice. The bottoms were shaped to fit the groove in the lower rail: chamfered front and back to almost a point, with the sides just slightly chamfered to allow the stave to be more easily swung into position.

Withies and laths

The malleable twig withies were used in the round or split into halves or slats and woven around the staves in the same manner as a hurdle or a basket weave, their direction of entry alternating with each course. The elasticity of the green withies provided stiffness to the panel. Green cleft oak or beech lath could be woven in a similar manner, as could thin bark strips.[6] Evidence suggests that laths may not have been used until the fourteenth or fifteenth century, and such early use may have been a Wessex practice, although withies also continued to be used wherever the craft prevailed.

In buildings that survive today, the predominant withy material found is hazel, but the use of willow (sallow/osiers) was also common. However, slender rods of almost any other flexible green wood were used, such as ash, birch and lime, if close to hand. Reed was also employed as a backing and was particularly suited to close studding.

Daub

The selection of materials for daub is not as critical as for solid earth walling since wattle and daub is not structural. However, an appreciation of the materials and their characteristics provides many benefits as it is the basis for an understanding of historical methods in archaeological and conservation work and helps to maximise the reliability and repeatability of repairs and new work.

Soils

The physical characteristics of a daub are primarily dictated by its main constituent, soils, the properties of which are key to its performance. These properties may be measured on site or in a laboratory and can be used to understand the historic selection and mixing of soils or in the specification and selection of materials for new daub:

- constituents and particle sizes
- plasticity, as a modulator of linear stability
- strength

Dung

Cow dung was also used in daub, and so one may suppose there were particular benefits in its inclusion. Unfortunately, there appears to be no historic reference to the supposed properties of dung that would have encouraged its use. It has been proposed that mucus in cow dung reacts with lime to form a gel, increasing strength prior to carbonation of lime and stabilising clay. However, research by the author suggests that the small proportion of lignin present in cow dung may help make a dry daub mix more workable without the addition of water.[7] It may be increasingly difficult to reproduce these benefits today since modern strains of ryegrass and cattle feeds have reduced the amount of lignin present in dung.

Knowledge has also been lost as to whether fresh, old or weathered dung was used. Since there is no historic reference to the dung being old or weathered, it is conceivable that this is a recent invention resulting from modern attitudes toward odour and hygiene. In any case, dried and fresh dung differ mainly in the water content and so are likely to affect only the amount of water, if any, added during mixing of the daub.

Until the interaction of cow dung and soil is scientifically characterised, it would be prudent to include dung in conservation work because of the evident durability of historic daubs that incorporate it.

Fibre

Straw fibres reinforce a daub, which is otherwise weak owing to the volumetric instability of the clay; cracks that are able to form across the total thickness of the daub would jeopardise the structural stability of the panel if not compensated for by the inclusion of such fibre. Straw is most commonly used, although hay, flax stick reed and animal hair are a few examples of other appropriate fibres.

Fibre may also help dissipate the shrinkage of daub during drying. This may be likened to 'bed joint reinforcement' of masonry walls and functions by embedding a ductile material within the fabric. This results in microcracking of the surrounding fabric along the length of the reinforcement, rather than a visible crack at a single location. Straw may decrease linear shrinkage by approximately 25% per 1% of added fibre.[8] However, it has also been demonstrated that the addition of fibre in large proportions (6–8%) may cause a decrease in compressive and tensile strengths. There is therefore an optimum proportion of added fibre of approximately 2–4%.

Defects and decay

Wattle and daub has a reputation for being friable and unable to endure the damp British climate, yet this is something of a myth; decay is generally due to lack of respect for the fabric, neglect and lack of maintenance. Where sheltered, wattle and daub may last almost indefinitely, as demonstrated by intact fourteenth-century panels. Even in exposed locations, a daub panel will survive if appropriately maintained.

The most significant cause of daub decay is water absorption and erosion. Unprotected daub is essentially exposed soil, and direct contact with rain may cause the clay matrix to be dissolved, which can be worsened by water run-off. Additionally, cracking and failure are often caused by frost action upon absorbed moisture or by cyclical expansion and contraction of the clay. The resulting cracks either appear at the surface or are parallel with the surface as 'delamination' (separation into detached layers). Such problems are most easily prevented through the shedding and binding characteristics of a limewash protection.

Moisture is also a catalyst for decay in the wattle or laths, increasing the susceptibility to fungal rot and beetle attack. In all cases, removal of the water source is the key remedial action and should never necessitate the stripping out of panels.

Mechanical damage is increasingly common, caused by contractors or window cleaners leaning ladders on a panel. Instructing them to use only the timber frame for support is the simplest means of prevention.

Vibrations caused by nailing, such as during the repair of laths, but also by traffic and nearby works also represent significant risks to historic daub, and since the effects are cumulative exposure should be minimised.

Maintenance

The conservation of wattle and daub relies on maintaining the way buildings traditionally behave, primarily allowing buildings to 'breathe' and enabling materials to flex and swell. Most problems can be identified visually (Table 10.1) and minor defects should be quickly remedied as part of an ongoing inspection and maintenance programme to ensure minimal loss of historic fabric and to reduce the long-term maintenance costs.

Table 10.1 The visual inspection of wattle and daub.

Observation	Defect
Flaking, thin or missing limewash	Lack of regular limewashing
Cracked panel surfaces	<ul><li>Localised or general failure of render or daub</li><li>Damp</li><li>Poor workmanship of new work</li><li>Structural movement of the timber frame</li></ul>
Missing render and/or daub	<ul><li>Local failure of daub</li><li>Damp, frost damage or erosion</li><li>Delamination or physical damage</li></ul>
Daub projecting beyond the surface of the frame	<ul><li>Delamination, i.e. debonding from wattle or lath</li><li>Failure of wattle or lath</li><li>Poor workmanship</li><li>Physical damage</li><li>A later plaster top coat added to original surface</li></ul>
Cement render or patches	Inappropriate materials
Modern impervious paints or coatings	Inappropriate materials
Use of impervious gap fillers such as expanding foam or mastic sealants	Inappropriate materials
Dampness	<ul><li>Water or moisture due to other building defects.</li></ul>
Organic growth	<ul><li>Loss of 'traditional performance'</li><li>Inappropriate planting or lack of weeding around footings</li><li>Damp</li></ul>

Repairs

The degree to which intact daub and wattlework can decay is often an unnecessary cause of alarm: if the panel is still doing its job of closing the gap in the frame then, by definition, it is functioning correctly. In this case stripping the daub is unwarranted and must be avoided since, once started, it is often impossible to replace the daub without first renewing much of the wattlework.

When considering structural repairs to a timber frame, these must take precedence over conservation of wattle and daub, but attempts to preserve the infill can be made using temporary bracing. Some cracking may be expected by the disturbance, but this can usually be repaired using the methods discussed below.

Daubs

If an external daub has cracked, eroded or delaminated from its backing, attempts to secure it should be tried before considering replacement. Where decay only affects part of a panel, replacement can be limited to the unsound area.

Cracked daub, which is otherwise sound, can be consolidated using a lime mortar. Hairline cracks are most economically addressed through a regular programme of limewashing during which the cracks will be filled over time. Where large pieces of daub have become detached, they should be replaced like for like using daub rather than the void filled with lime mortar. Detached daub can be salvaged and reused to avoid unnecessary labour: the daub is re-wetted in a bucket of water and the scum of old organic matter removed from the surface; it is then dried and new fibre is added. When placing daub onto historic wattles, it may be wise to prepare the mix a little wetter than for new work so as to prevent damage to friable withies.

Small areas of delamination should not cause concern, but larger areas may be at risk from falling away. These defects can either be left to run their course, tied back using a mechanical restraint, removed and replaced, or grouted. The selection of the method may be guided by the type of backing and whether access is available from both sides.

Edge gaps at the interface between daub and timber frame are the result of the shrinkage intrinsic to all clays combined with the natural movement in a timber frame. This has always been stated as a weakness of wattle and daub. However, where a panel is correctly finished flush or recessed within the frame, the probability of rain penetration is minimal. These gaps can be routinely filled with an appropriate material – either daub or a non-hydraulic lime mortar. The use of mastics or expanding foams is not recommended as they exacerbate decay by trapping moisture against the frame.

The base of an infill panel can be particularly vulnerable to trapped water, especially where a panel is recessed behind the surface of a frame. A system of using a timber fillet and lead flashing has been proposed, but any moisture that does find its way under the lead may actually increase the rate of timber decay. An alternative is to use a sacrificial fillet of lime mortar to dress the edge of the panel so that it forms a run-off to the vertical face of the timber rail. During rainfall the mortar is likely to allow more water ingress than a lead flashing, but it will quickly reabsorb moisture via capillary action and then expel it into the atmosphere during drying.

Wattlework

Withies and woven lath are often friable owing to decay. The principles for their repair are as follows:

- Limit disturbance to situations where wattle decay is the underlying cause of daub failure or where it is unable to withstand the applied forces during subsequent redaubing.
- Repair like for like: hazel withies should be repaired with green hazel; cleft oak should be replaced with similar.
- Limit the use of modern materials to those situations where traditional methods would cause greater loss of historic fabric.

Where decay is localised, new sections of withy or lath should be 'slipped in' to the existing wattle to avoid unnecessary stripping of sound daub. Often lateral access is limited by sound daub, in which case short repair lengths may be used, being supported by the staves and passing through the hollow daub 'tube' remaining after removal of the decayed wood. If the withy is too short to support itself by tension using the staves, it should be tied using twine or copper wire.

Lath

The approach to lath repair is similar to that for wattlework in that replacement is limited to the forming of a sound backing to failed daub or render. Repairs should use similar material to existing. Sound laths that have loosened because of corroded nails can be reattached. It is essential that the laths are not re-nailed since the vibration may cause daub or friable plasters to crack. Instead, they should be secured using brass or stainless steel screws.

After considering all repair options, it may occasionally be decided that a panel cannot be saved owing to the poor condition of its wattlework. In this case, a panel may require complete renewal.

Removal of impermeable paints and coatings

Wattle and daub panels have often been covered with an impervious coating such as acrylic emulsion, alkyd masonry paint or high-build 'construction paint'. This may cause rapid decay of wattle and daub and should preferably be removed and replaced with limewash.

Masonry paints will often delaminate within approximately five to ten years after application. They may then be removed by carefully lifting off with a small trowel or scraper. Where a modern paint remains firmly bonded to the plaster or daub, the choices are either to leave the paint or to use a more aggressive method of removal. Unfortunately, there is little experience in paint removal from earth materials such as daub and cob. Trials by the author have suggested that the most effective means may be either an alkali-based chemical 'poultice' stripper or a combination of chemical softener and super-heated steam. Proprietary steam systems that soften most paints without transferring excessive quantities of moisture to the plaster and daub are now available to conservators. In either case, careful selection of chemicals is important so as to avoid introducing new problems such as salt residues.

Replacement

The basis of renewal should be like for like replacement using traditional materials and methods: wattle and daub should not be replaced by materials that are more commonly understood by modern contractors, such as lath and plaster. Various schemes involving the introduction of modern materials have been suggested elsewhere, but the justification for these is usually unfounded. The only scenario under which upgrading wattle and daub is warranted is a change of use of an unlisted building.

Analysis of daub

The analysis of a daub creates an archival record and helps in specifying new work. However, analysis can prove expensive so the level of detail sought may be guided by the importance of the building. A thorough analysis is performed using a combination of field tests for soils, microscopy, sedimentation, particle size analysis and chemistry.

The quantitative results can be displayed diagrammatically either by plotting as a cumulative distribution chart as per BS 1377-2:1990 or using a stacked bar graph, accompanied by a description of the daub.

After the appraisal process is complete, including a structural evaluation and recording, the panel may be stripped in preparation for renewal.

The wattle

A backing of wattle is formed by the following process:

- Prepare staves by splitting heartwood of oak using a froe.
- Sharpen tops to fit stave holes.
- Bevel bases to fit groove.

- Insert staves by sliding base sideways.
- To provide the withies, coppice and split sufficient hazel rods, preferably during winter when there is less sap.
- Ensure correct length by weaving a reference withy. Prepare remaining withies by cutting to same length as the reference.
- Narrow the ends if fitting into stud grooves.
- Weave withies, alternating the side of the staves with each row.
- Tamp down withies to base of panel to make compact.
- Complete insertion of withies up to the top of the panel.
- Leave the panel to season. Tamp down and add additional withies to fill any resulting gap at the top.

Preparation of daub

The earth should ideally be cut from the grounds of the building to avoid unnecessary transport. Prior to removing the required quantity of earth for the daub, a sample should be taken. This should be compared with any analysis performed on the historic daub using the tests already described. Where a match is not required, the objectives of the sample tests are to ensure the daub will have properties conducive to easy application and durability, keeping the clay content as low as possible so as to avoid cracking but producing a mix that binds. For new work, an approximate guide to a suitable earth is:

clay   5–15%
silt   20–55%
sand   20–55%
gravel   0–20%

Excavated soils that are overall suitably graded may contain a small number of coarse gravel particles and the occasional cobble. The maximum aggregate size is defined by the need to form balls or 'cats' of workable size, the ability to drive a daub through the gaps in the withies or lath, and the need to ensure aggregate particles do not project beyond the surface of the daub. The constituents of a daub should complement the soil and will depend on locally available materials. Some example mixes are shown in Table 10.2.

A suitable method of mixing involves picking out any coarse gravel, adding additional aggregate or clay as necessary, then mixing thoroughly by 'treading' with the heel of the boot. When compacted, the daub should be lifted and turned using a shovel – a 'cob-pick'. Working on tarpaulin also helps to turn daub. The result should be well-mixed 'sandy clay'. A little water may be required to permit the clay to coat the aggregate and to make the daub workable, but the daub must be kept as dry as possible. Cow dung is also mixed by treading, but only sufficient dung should be added to make the daub feel plastic. Fibre, such as hair, chopped straw or hay, is scattered evenly onto the earth, with further treading to complete the mix.

Table 10.2 Example daub mixes shown as ratios of constituents.

Constituents/parts						Source
Soil	Cow dung	Straw (dense)	Hair	Lime	Chalk	
12	1	1	–	–	–	Ashurst and Ashurst (1988), p. 120
8[a]	1	1	–	–	–	Reid (1989), p. 12
4	1	–	yes	1	–	
12[b]	1	2	–	–	–	
2[c]	1	1	–	2	3	
12[d]	1	2	–	–	–	Wright (1991), p. 100
7–9	1[e]	yes	–	–	–	Thompson (2003), p. 2*
1[f]	1	yes		1		Lander (1986), p. 210

a. Stiff sandy clay soil.
b. 6 parts clayey soil plus 6 parts sharp sand; dung specified as fresh.
c. 1 part clay soil plus 1 part sand.
d. 6 parts clayey earth (<15% clay) plus 6 parts sharp sand.
e. Cow or horse dung.
f. Stated as being a 'repair mix'.
* 'Notes on wattle and daub' (unpublished course notes, Singleton, Weald and Downland Open Air Museum).

Application of daub

Prior to daubing a historic building, it is advisable to form test panels to verify the performance of a daub. Application was either by throwing or by pressing the balls, or 'cats' of daub onto the wattle backing. From the evidence of large cracks in historic daub, throwing of a wetter mix may indeed have been a common technique but, for conservation work, it would be judicious to choose the dryer mix placed as cats, so as to minimise cracking and maximise strength.

The method by which daub cats are applied to a wattle or lath backing is as follows:[9]

1. Thoroughly dampen the withies or lath with a sprayer. They should not be dripping with excess water.
2. Form a cat of daub in the hand and kneed it to 'knock it up'.
3. Working from the base of the panel, press the cat *in* and *down* into the wattle so as to ensure that the daub is well keyed into the backing.
4. Work along the panel, then upwards, merging each cat with adjacent ones so as to form a homogeneous mass.
5. Build up additional layers of cats to the thickness of the timber frame.
6. Roughly flatten the surface using a damp (but not wet) sponge wrapped in chamois leather.
7. Using the end of a piece of lath or a suitable small tool, compress the outer 20 mm of the panel against the timber frame.
8. Finish the panel to the local tradition before drying commences:

a. If panels are not to be plastered, add detail or decoration.

b. To accept a plaster, key the daub surface using a comb scratcher.

Cracking of new daub is not a sign of poor workmanship but is caused by the clay drying. Large cracks may be the result of a highly shrinkable clay, excessive fines in the soil or too much added water. Even so, lateral cracking does not necessarily mean poor bonding to the wattle: cracks are likely to be reinforced by the fibre and may therefore be considered as cosmetic. They may subsequently be filled either by reworking the re-dampened surface of the daub or by filling with fresh daub after rewetting of the cracked edges. Where panels are to be plastered, cracks in the daub will subsequently be filled and may be considered positively in that they provide an additional key.

Building Regulations

The Building Regulations are relevant to wattle and daub particularly in the requirements relating to Part B (fire safety), Part C (resistance to moisture), Part E (resistance to the passage of sound) and Part L (conservation of fuel and power). Fortunately, Parts B, E and L have specific provision for 'historic buildings', and amendments to Approved Documents for Parts E and M (access) have extended definitions to include 'vernacular buildings of traditional form and construction'. This therefore embraces all construction in which wattle and daub is likely to be found or specified. (See *Structures & construction in historic building conservation*, Chapter 3.)

For repairs of wattle and daub, the provisions for 'historic buildings' avoid damaging a building's character or its long-term durability by enabling solely traditional craft methods to be used.

Reinstatement

For the limited cases of new build and change of use of unlisted buildings, Part L presents the most troublesome issues. This is because the thermal conductivity of wattle and daub is certainly quite high and so has a poor U-value. It may be possible to compensate for the thermal performance in other aspects of the building design so that the requirement can be met. However, if this is not feasible then the panel design may need to be 'upgraded'. It is only under these circumstances that the use of modern materials can be justified. Several methods are described by Reid (1989). If all else fails, the principles of conservation may lead to a more radical solution: it may be preferable for the long-term survival of the historic wall fabric to dry-line and insulate the walls internally, leaving the wattle and daub 'as is'. The dry-lining is then a reversible measure to meet present regulations, with the hope that building technology improves to ultimately allow the wattle and daub to be once more exposed.

It must be added, however, that to help achieve an appropriate balance between historic building conservation and energy efficiency, English Heritage are producing guidance notes entitled *Energy Efficiency in Traditional Buildings*. The approach of the guidance is to ensure that due respect is paid to the fabric of all traditional buildings of historic or architectural interest (not necessarily listed).

Conclusion

A wide range of techniques that can be used to conserve historic wattle and daub are available. To safeguard the increasingly scarce examples of the craft, it is imperative that the current custodians take advantage of the methods presented rather than replace decayed panels with modern materials.

References and further reading

Ashurst, J. and Ashurst, N. *Practical Building Conservation: Volume 2: Brick, Terracotta and Earth* (Gower Technical Press, Aldershot, 1988).

Bowyer, Jack, *History of Building* (Crosby Lockwood Staples, London, 1973).

Clifton-Taylor, Alec, *The Pattern of English Building* (Faber and Faber, London, 1962).

Lander, Hugh, *The House Restorer's Guide* (David & Charles, Newton Abbot, 1986).

Minke, Gernot, *Earth Construction Handbook: The building material earth in modern architecture* (WIT Press, Southampton, 2000).

Oxley, Richard, *Survey and Repair of Traditional Buildings* (Donhead, Shaftesbury, 2003).

Planning Policy Guidance 15: *Planning and the Historic Environment*, Department of the Environment (The Stationery Office, London, 1994).

Reid, Kenneth, *Panel Infillings to Timber-framed Buildings* (Society for the Protection of Ancient Buildings, London, 1989).

Wright, Adela, *Craft Techniques for Traditional Buildings* (Batsford, London, 1991).

Endnotes

1. Planning Policy Guidance 15, para. C.16.
2. Kenneth Reid, *Panel Infillings to Timber-framed Buildings* (Society for the Protection of Ancient Buildings, London, 1989), p. 3.
3. Alec Clifton-Taylor, *The Pattern of English Building* (Faber and Faber, London, 1962), p. 358.
4. Adela Wright, *Craft Techniques for Traditional Buildings* (Batsford, London, 1991), p. 97.
5. J. Thompson, 'Notes on wattle and daub' (unpublished course notes, Singleton, Weald and Downland Open Air Museum, 2003), p. 1.
6. Reid, *Panel Infillings*, p. 3.
7. Lignins are increasingly being used in modern manufacturing as binders and dispersants. As a binder lignin can stabilise soils and as a dispersant it improves cements.
8. Gernot Minke, *Earth Construction Handbook: The building material earth in modern architecture* (WIT Press, Southampton, 2000).
9. Thompson, 'Notes on wattle and daub', p. 3.

11 Sash windows

Gus Astley

The sash window is one of the major elements of most Classical buildings and provides, in every Georgian city, a major contribution to the small-scale detail on the facades of buildings. One of the main reasons for the sash window becoming the preferred window for houses during the eighteenth century was its basic symmetry and elegance. Sash windows were also popular (and still are) for the far more practical reason that as a window they provide the most controllable means of ventilation within a room. The balanced nature of the sash mechanism is such that the window can be opened as much or as little as necessary either at the top or the bottom – or both.

Sash windows were first recorded in the late seventeenth century; the first reference is at the Royal Palace of Whitehall in 1670, and they were introduced at Dyrham Park, Gloucestershire, in 1692. An interesting fact about sash windows is that the craftsmen, rather than the architect, seem to have had a great deal to do with the design of the window unit. In early drawings, as in one by John Wood (Figure 11.1), it is noticeable that the position and proportion of the windows were drawn, but the details are not (despite John Wood's trade being that of carpenter!).

This chapter will discuss the basic rules and development of different details with respect to sash windows. Particular reference is made to Bath, though the chief characteristics apply elsewhere. One important exception is that all traditional sash windows in Bath, of whatever date, do not have a timber sub-sill. The bottom sash closes straight down onto the stone sill to the window opening. There are some notable cases where major early 'conservation' schemes got the detail of replacement windows entirely wrong. The buildings on the south side of Kingsmead Square are a particular example of the mistaken provision of timber sub-sills.

Many of the Georgian craftsmen and designers were well versed in the rules and examples contained in the pattern books of the period. Armed with this knowledge, however, they were confident enough to design and work intuitively rather than adhere rigidly to the rules and patterns. This added a human touch, which results in the wealth of subtly different details not only across regions but within, at first glance, highly uniform cities like Bath. In trying to carry out sensitive conservation work, one should therefore not only be aware of the basic rules but also be very careful to respect the intrinsic differences in detail in each individual building.

The proportion of windows in Georgian buildings is usually such that the size and degree of detail of windows gradually reduces from the grandest

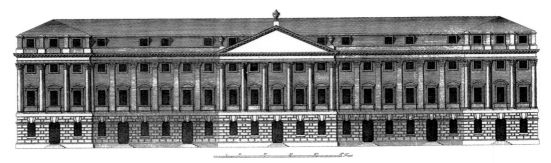

The ELEVATION, to the South, of the principal Pile of BUILDING of QUEEN-SQUARE in BATH, as defigned by John Wood, Architect, A.D. 1728.
F.Foudrinier Sculp.

Figure 11.1 Elevation of the north side of Queen Square, facing south, from John Wood's *A Description of Bath* (1742–43; 2nd edn 1749; reprinted 1765 and 1969).

at first floor (the *piano nobile*), to the next grandest on the ground floor, and to the lesser scale at second floor; this often meant that the details of the window joinery differed from that of the main floors. Basement windows are normally about the same size as ground floor windows; they normally line through vertically with the ground floor windows above and retain the normal height-to-width relationship similar to the principal windows. Attic windows were diminutive dormer windows (many have been enlarged), which were kept as small as possible and were not seen as an important part of the design of the facade. From Figure 11.1 it can again be seen that the tendency was to align dormer windows with the windows below. As both basement and attic windows were for providing light into the service areas of the house, they were not considered as important as those on other floors.

The relationship of window width to height varied, but it was normal, after the middle of the eighteenth century, for the principal windows to be roughly twice as high as they were wide. A simple, consciously designed proportional system can sometimes be demonstrated in the elevations of eighteenth-century houses; for instance, the first and second floor windows of a three-bay house may be spaced to form a square. However, there was no generally accepted set of rules. Almost universal with windows in Classical buildings, however, is that the horizontal spacing between windows on a facade is not the same as the spacing between the outside edge of the windows at either side and the corners of the building. This is a detail often missed in 'Georgian-style' modern buildings, with the result looking rather odd.

The subdivision of sash windows into panes changed during the eighteenth century. At the start of the century, windows were normally divided into two sashes, each three panes wide and three panes high. This gave what is known as a 'nine-over-nine' glazing proportion and is typified by almost square window panes. These early nine-over-nine sashes had very thick glazing bars and meeting-rail sections and the thickness of glazing bars and meeting rails was the same. The early intention, therefore, appears to have been to subdivide the window openings into eighteen panes with a grillage of glazing bars of the same thickness.

Very soon after the beginning of the Georgian period, however, the more normal proportion of two sashes, each three panes wide and two panes high (six-over-six sashes) became the accepted proportion. This visually has a distinctly greater vertical emphasis which, together with the thinner joinery section and larger glass panes, helps to lend a greater sense of elegance to the buildings. This 'striving for visual elegance' may, of course, be a manifestation of the normal speculative builder's desire to cut costs and reduce the amount of timber being used in the window joinery. This is unlikely to be the case, however, because the narrowing down of the sections coincided with a general tendency to provide larger and deeper windows which would allow the occupants of the house to gain more of a view out (a desire which steadily grew during the eighteenth century).

What effect available glass sizes had on the subdivision of windows it is difficult to say. It can be categorically stated, however, that the technology at the time could not economically produce single sheets of glass the size of a window sash. Some division therefore had to take place (see Chapter 12).

As stated above, the size of the joinery section in windows steadily changed through the eighteenth century. At the beginning of the great boom in building in the 1730s, the standard glazing bar sections were very thick – normally about $1^1/_2$ inches (38 mm) – and meeting rails were of the same dimensions as glazing bars. The sections were then progressively reduced until, at the end of the eighteenth century standard dimensions were $^5/_8$ inch (16 mm) for glazing bars and $^3/_4$ inch (19 mm) for meeting rails. These standard dimensions appear to have been used throughout the nineteenth century and the early years of the twentieth century. It is only recently, when craft tradition has been lost in much of the building industry, that the 'mock Georgian' approach of putting rather thick glazing bars into otherwise poorly portioned standard (normally casement) window units has reintroduced thicker glazing bars and destroyed the traditional elegance and visual balance of windows.

By way of a case study, the moulding profiles of the majority of Bath's glazing bars will now be discussed, although, with some regional variation, these also apply elsewhere. They fall into four distinct patterns. In chronological order, these are ovolo; astragal and hollow; keel mould; and lamb's tongue (Figure 11.2).

Ovolo glazing bars are the earliest pattern used and are still the most popular, having continued to be used throughout the Georgian and Victorian periods and up to the present day. The only change has been in the dimensions.

In early windows such as those found in Queen Square, Bath, the bar thickness and meeting rail were about $1^1/_2$ in (38 mm). (Many early houses were 'modernised' in the later eighteenth century with window joinery of that period, although often only on the front elevation.) In these early

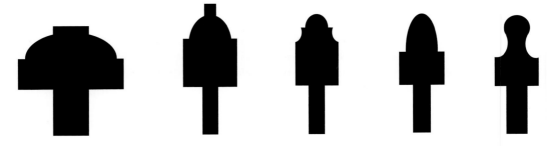

Figure 11.2 Glazing bar sections (left to right): thick ovolo (Queen Square); narrow ovolo (Royal Crescent); astragal and hollow (Sydney Place); keel mould; lamb's tongue.

windows, it is interesting to note that the meeting rail to the top sash continues the moulding profiles from the sash stiles. This can be illustrated by imagining you start with a standard glazing bar. You then lengthen it outwards to the thickness of both sashes, then by cutting this lengthened bar in half you form the two meeting rails. Finally, imagine that you can divorce the upper part of the glazing bar moulding from the bar and push it outwards to the line of the glazing in the upper sash. After all this, you end up with the standard early meeting rail detail. One interesting difficulty encountered with this early moulding detail is that you have no suitable flat horizontal surface on the inner face of the upper sash to enable you to fix the sash fastener. You are forced to cut a rebate out of the moulding on the meeting rail to facilitate fixing it.

An early detail which it is worth looking for carefully is the two-part glazing bar. This is thought to be among the earliest details used. An example of this detail came to light in one of the chapel windows at Prior Park, Bath, after the disastrous fire of 1991. This detail is difficult to spot because the jointing between the pieces has usually been obscured by paint layers.

By the time most of Bath's Gay Street properties were built (leases signed in 1755), glazing bars were still of ovolo section but had been narrowed down to $1^1/_8$ in (29 mm) and only some of the windows appear to have the moulding on the bottom rail of the upper sash.

By the time development reached Brock Street, Royal Crescent and streets such as Rivers Street (1760s and 1770s), the glazing bars had narrowed down to 19 mm ($^3/_4$ in) and definitely had no mouldings on the bottom rail of the upper sash.

Finally, towards the end of the eighteenth century, polite houses started to use the **astragal and hollow** section to the later bar thickness of 16 mm ($^5/_8$ in). This dimension was too slender, however, for meeting rails to copy. Meeting rails were therefore normally 19 mm ($^3/_4$ in) deep to provide adequate strength. Astragal and hollow glazing bars were the most elegant bars created during the eighteenth century and grace many of Bath's finest terraces, squares and crescents built during the 1790s and the early part of the nineteenth century. These bars consist of a convex semicircular 'astragal' facing inwards with a concave 'hollow' mould on either side. The resulting play of reflected light on the curves of these moulds, seen together with the straight edges at the junctions between the curves and with the rest of the bar, gives a particularly elegant appearance.

A variation of the astragal and hollow section is that in which the astragal is not just a half circle but actually becomes quirked or undercut. This may just be a later misunderstanding of the original section or even the result of overenthusiastic paint-stripping during decoration. There are, however, several example of the variant.

Keel mould bars, which are named here after the keel mould found on medieval masonry columns, are typical (on the exterior) of shop fronts in Bath. (They are also typical of the later development of the Bathwick Estate properties and give a particular character to the properties.)

Lamb's tongue mouldings are typical of the middle to late nineteenth century. The moulding is supposed to be similar to the cross section through a lamb's tongue. The start of the use of lamb's tongue mouldings coincides quite closely to the first use of 'horns'. These are the continuation downwards below the meeting rail of the stiles of the upper sash. Horns have various profiles, from simple to ornate. The existence of horns on upper sashes (as long as they are original) is a useful dating tool. Horns did not appear until the latter half of the nineteenth century. Care should be taken, therefore, to make sure that new or replacement windows respect the correct detail for the date of the building.

It should be noted that, of the standard sections mentioned above, the ovolo profile is the only one where the glazing bar profile is the same as the profile on the sash style. In all the other profiles, the glazing bar offers some form of curved profile towards the interior. Trying to bring a curved profile in at right angles to an adjacent face orientated at about 90° from the profile will very easily result in an unsightly wavy edge. This was not something that joiners would have accepted. The sash styles of astragal and hollow, keel and lamb's tongue glazing bars therefore have an extra square fillet provided on the inner face of *sash stiles only*. This results in the inner face of glazing bars being set marginally behind the inner face of the sash stiles. A lack of knowledge of the correct details often results in serious errors being made by people trying to replace glazing bars in windows which only retain the fuller moulding on the stiles. One finds that this results in attempts to match the stile mouldings on the glazing bars with the result that an extra fillet is added to the centre of the curved inner face of the bar. This reduces the elegance of the bars and tends to increase the dimension of the bar section.

12 Window glass

Michael Forsyth

The history of glass and glass-making is closely interrelated with the development of the window and window joinery, and this short introduction to glass should be read in conjunction with Chapter 11.

Glass for windows is a fusion of sand (silica) and lime (calcium oxide) produced by heating the materials to a high temperature in a furnace together with wood ash or soda to reduce the temperature at which the particles fuse. Metal oxides in the sand and other impurities gave early glass a green or yellow tint, and before the Industrial Revolution charcoal furnaces produced inconsistent results.

Early houses were dark and smoky with only doors and small open apertures for natural lighting.[1] Glass did not become common in lesser houses until the seventeenth century when small panes were leaded into iron casements fitted within stone mullions, which in finer houses were often formed into large bay windows.

Broad sheet or muff glass

Mullioned windows were glazed with poor-quality broad sheet or 'muff glass', which was first produced in England in Sussex in the thirteenth century. It was manufactured by extracting a lump of treacly molten glass from a furnace on the end of a long blow pipe. The glass was then worked by being blown and swung by the glass blower into an elongated balloon shape. The ends were then cut off to form a rough cylinder, which was cut along its length with shears and laid flat on a metal plate. The contact of the material with the hot surface made the glass obscure, distorted and with trapped air bubbles, and the size was quite small. Broad sheet continued to be manufactured well into the eighteenth century as a cheap alternative to crown glass. From the early seventeenth century it was also painstakingly hand ground and polished to produce higher-quality mirror glass.

Crown glass

A superior manufacturing method was developed by French glass makers in Rouen in the 1330s and the technique was imported to England in 1678 when a manufactory was established in Southwark – the Bear Garden Glasshouse adjacent to the Bear Garden owned by the Duke of Buckingham, with tables displaying his ducal coronet: hence the product became known as crown glass.

Much as with broad sheet, the glass blower formed a sphere of molten glass, but the blowpipe was then replaced by an iron rod, or 'punty', which was rotated rapidly. The centrifugal force caused the glass to form into a very thin, large-diameter disc, which was laid onto a table to harden. The glass could then be cut into window panes of various sizes. The centre of the disc containing a knob – the 'bull's eye' or bullion – where the rod was attached was used in lesser locations such as servants' garrets and basements.

By the eighteenth century crown glass was of good, unblemished quality and remained the preferred glass. It is easily recognisable in historic buildings because when seen against reflected light it has curved ripples formed by the spinning of the glass when hot. Crown glass gives considerable character and liveliness to old buildings compared with the lifeless appearance of modern, flawless glass.

Cylinder sheet

This process was imported from the continent in 1832 by Robert Lucas Chance and first produced at his works in Birmingham. Chance Bros won the contract to supply Paxton's Crystal Palace with 956 000 square feet of glass in 49 inch (1247 mm) lengths for the Great Exhibition of 1851.

It is an improved form of broad sheet where the molten glass is elongated by being swung in a deep trench to form a much longer cylinder. This is left to cool and harden before being reheated and cut open and allowed to flatten under its own weight. Larger, good-quality panes resulted and the process quickly superseded crown glass production. With the introduction of this glass the glazing bars to Georgian sash windows were commonly removed and the windows re-glazed with either one or two sheets per sash; such 'modernisation' was often a condition of renewal of the lease on the house. Cylinder glass was produced extensively until the early twentieth century when machines were developed to manufacture window glass.

Cylinder glass, like crown glass, is easily recognisable, having some random distortion.

Plate

Louis XIV's 'Manufacture Royale des grandes glaces' first used the process whereby molten glass was cast on a table, quickly rolled to an even thickness and then ground and polished before being mirrored. Soon afterwards Sir Christopher Wren installed glass made by this French method at Hampton Court. Very large sheets could be made but it was extremely expensive.

Figure 12.1 The Belvedere, by Willes Maddox, from *Views of Lansdown Tower* (Edmund English, 1844). An early use of plate glass at William Beckford's tower on Lansdown, Bath, 1825–26, giving an uninterrupted prospect (Beckford Tower Trust).

English polished plate glass was first produced in significant quantities at a manufactory at Ravenshead, St Helens, Lancashire, from 1773 (St Helen's became a world leader in glass production – see below), and by 1800 the glass was being ground and polished with the help of a steam engine. As it was thick, to bear its potentially large size, plate glass was heavy and it was not until 1845, when the government removed the weight levy on glass, that it became more affordable.[2] It was used especially for shop fronts to enhance the display of goods and, like cylinder glass, it also replaced six-over-six panes in domestic Georgian sashes, though cheaper cylinder glass remained more common. Figure 12.1 shows an early use of plate glass.

Plate glass is perfectly flat and undistorted and can be replaced by modern float glass.

Machine-made glass

In 1888 Chance Bros introduced machine-rolled patterned glass and in the early twentieth century hand-blown glass was largely replaced by various mechanical methods. In 1910 Pilkington introduced into the United Kingdom (from the United States) **machine-drawn cylinder sheet**, which was manufactured until the 1930s. Cylinders 40 feet (12 metres) high were drawn vertically from a tank and cut into four or five lengths, then treated in a similar way to traditional cylinder glass. **Flat drawn sheet**, a technique developed in Belgium in 1913 and imported into the United Kingdom in 1919, also drew glass vertically but in a flat sheet. A similar method is used to produce horticultural glass which is rippled in one direction. **Single and twin ground polished plate** (introduced in 1923 and 1938 respectively) used the casting process, but the grinding and polishing was carried out mechanically on a conveyor belt.

The standard glass produced today is **float glass**, invented in 1959 by Pilkington of St Helen's; molten glass is 'floated' over a bed of molten tin to produce a flawless, perfectly formed flat surface. It is manufactured from silica, lime and soda in varying proportions. Pilkington ceased production of plate glass in 1967 and other manufacturers quickly followed.

Retention and replacement of historic glass

Crown and cylinder glass exudes a wonderfully warm, soft and worn character to historic buildings, both to the external facade and to the light penetrating the interior and view from the interior. Broken panes previously replaced with plate or float glass should ideally be restored with crown glass, which is now manufactured once again in the United Kingdom.

During general renovation work to an old building, historic glass must be first recorded and then properly protected. It is extremely difficult to source old window glass, and of course, once broken, the material is irreplaceable. Occasionally a large broken pane can be cut down to fit a smaller window. Particular care must be exercised with scaffolding, and there may be a case for removing the sashes for safe storage. Glass should not normally be removed from a sash undergoing repair because hard, old putty poses a danger of breakage. Historic glass in a sash that is so rotted that renewal rather than repair is inevitable can be carefully cut out and reglazed in the new sash. There is a myth that horticultural glass can successfully simulate crown or cylinder glass, but the considerable one-directional distortion actually renders it totally unsuitable.

Endnotes

1. Reconstructed dwellings at open-air museums such as the Museum of Welsh Life, Cardiff, and the Weald and Downland Museum, West Sussex, provide a vivid impression of original living conditions.
2. The window tax – on the number of windows in a house – was still more iniquitous as many householders blocked up windows to reduce their tax liability; scratched on a pane to the rear of no. 16 Beauford Square, Bath, is the couplet 'God gave us light, and it was good, Pitt came and taxed it, damn his blood' (the tax was actually introduced in the reign of William III in 1696).

13 Exterior colour on the smaller town house

Patrick Baty

> The sashes are to be finished dark purple brown; the front door is to be painted green and to be twice varnished with the best copal . . .[1]

So reads a typical specification of the 1840s for a small terraced house of the type that can still be found in many English cities and towns (Figure 13.1).

> . . . all the other painting is to be finished with such teints of stone colour or drab or other plain colours as the surveyor may direct.[2]

Such a view of a sombre facade punctuated by dark voids can still be seen up to sixty years later in photographs of late Victorian and Edwardian street scenes.[3] Further study of these black-and-white images reveals that, as the twentieth century progressed, more of the facade succumbed to paint and an increasingly lighter palette was adopted. Initially this was not so much fashion as an attempt to combat the effects of soot and grime. Ironically, even after the Clean Air Act of 1956 the general tone continued to lighten and most cities are now awash with brilliant white paint.

Perceptions that had remained little changed for upwards of two hundred years had gone. Almost no examples of the earlier conventions survive, and when one does encounter an attempt to reintroduce the original subdued tonality it often looks contrived and out of place, surrounded as it is by its brutish successor.

This chapter sets out to show how the general appearance of our towns and cities has changed over the years and how, if carefully and responsibly carried out, the relentless tide can be turned.[4]

The introductory quotation shows how an impression of the past can be gained by studying the written word. However, more specific information is obtained by studying the buildings themselves. A number of tiny samples removed from representative elements of the facade and examined under the microscope can often yield a considerable amount of information. This includes the colour and type of paint first used, the changes that have taken place over the years, the frequency of decoration, and thus the overall appearance of the building during each decade. One can often pick up hints about the occupants' wealth and aspirations, and when combined with a study of surviving documentation a remarkably full story may be told. This technique is far removed from the scratch and match methods adopted by house owners and their architects in the past, characterised by that spurious pseudo-science, the 'paint scrape'.[5]

Bath Stone Colour

Portland Stone Colour

Bronze Green

Brunswick Green

Purple Brown

Pale Stone Colour

Figure 13.1 Some exterior paint colours.

In order to provide a focus, this chapter will concentrate on the middle-class town house built from the end of the eighteenth century and including such large-scale developments as those in London's Belgravia, Hove's Brunswick Town and Edinburgh's New Town, for example.

Brickwork

The main colour of many of these smaller buildings was provided by the bricks, which came in a variety of hues, red and reddy-brown giving way to the more fashionable white, grey or yellow stock bricks as the century progressed. Frequently, because of repair work or the use of mixed-quality bricks, the colour varied. However, any unevenness could be corrected by the application of a translucent wash – usually composed of limewater and iron oxide pigments. In later years soot was frequently used to help blend new with old. The effect was a subtle one, and in spite of an added binder would have been worn away by the rain over time. This was quite distinct from an opaque limewash.

At the beginning of the twentieth century, the use of limewash on some smaller buildings can be seen in photographs.[6] The purpose seems rarely to have been attention-seeking, but merely to combat the effects of seventy years or so of soot and grime. The use of limewash for purely aesthetic reasons was sufficiently unusual to have been recorded by A.R. Powys, who describes the 'excellent brickwork' of two 'new buildings of the lesser sort' in Flood Street, Chelsea, being successfully coated with it in the 1930s.[7]

Both types of washes (opaque and translucent) had the advantage of allowing moisture to be taken in and released later as vapour without disrupting the coating unduly. However, once an impermeable paint was applied, whether an oil paint or a modern emulsion-type paint, it acted as a barrier that was seldom effective, often trapping water and flaking off. The application of paint to brickwork is almost impossible to reverse successfully: once painted, always painted. This fact seems little understood, and year by year, in the relentless quest to be as bright as the neighbours, more brick facades fall to the paint pot. As well as creating another maintenance problem, many terraces now have a gap-toothed appearance instead of presenting a uniform aspect.

Although not as maintenance-heavy as the application of a masonry paint, one occasionally sees the results of historical misunderstanding in the form of the inappropriate use of limewash on town house exteriors. A deep red ochre, which goes tomato red when rained on, has made its appearance in recent years (Figure 13.2). Elsewhere there is the aftermath of a successful holiday in the Mediterranean in the shape of a colour-washed facade in hot colours on an 1840s terraced house.

The rot began in the early 1920s; however, at this time most house owners restricted their use of paint to the rendered ground floor area. Although many of the earlier buildings escaped attention from what Pugin called the 'restless torrent of Roman-cement men',[8] the ground floor elevation of terraced houses was often rendered and frequently lined out in imitation of ashlar. This may well have been in response to John Gwynn's

Figure 13.2 The result of using limewash rather than a translucent brick wash!

encouragement to use natural stone or stone-like renders, especially on public buildings, in his book *London and Westminster Improved* of 1766.[9]

Render

In London, the use of stone in a domestic context is uncommon; however, a number of early renders coloured and lined out to resemble stone were developed during the second half of the eighteenth century. Some of these were more successful than others; the original oil mastics of Liardet as used by the Adam brothers, for example, had a very poor reputation. Later proprietary products such as Roman cement, Parker's cement and Dihl's mastic were also used with varying degrees of success. These renders varied in tone and could be produced in a range of colours by employing different sands. On larger houses in the West End it was not uncommon to see the front of the house being rendered in a Bath stone colour while on the rear Portland stone might be imitated.[10]

A number of the London estates specified the colours to be used and the frequency of decoration. A building agreement of 1815 relating to newly built villas near Regent's Park includes the following clause:

> The walls to be of brick or stone – the fronts of all the buildings towards the Street to be of Bath Stone or Portland Stone or (if of Brick) to be cover'd with Parkers Cement coloured and Jointed in imitation of Bath Stone – the whole of the fronts towards the Streets to be of one and the same stone or to be coloured or painted to represent one and the same stone – the Cornices Architraves

203

Columns Bases Capitals Window Sills Ballustrades Copings Rusticks [rusticated ground floor] plinths and fascias to be all of Bath or Portland Stone or painted or Coloured to represent Bath or Portland Stone.[11]

For the most part these were self-coloured materials, but Roman cement was rather dark and was frequently disguised using a wash. This could either be applied in a single colour 'performed in a neat uniform manner' or could be given a naturalistic effect or 'frescoed' in order to imitate stone. Both of these were charged as extras, the former being 9*d*. more per square yard and the latter one shilling. It is assumed that few of the smaller houses would have been subject to these more expensive processes.[12] The introduction of Portland cement in the first half of the nineteenth century, however, meant that corrective washes were not always necessary and facades were sometimes left unpainted initially.[13] When Portland or Roman cements were painted, it might have been with something like Mr Cox's 'Adamant Colour' or 'Adamant Wash', a range of colours being obtained by the addition of different pigments.[14]

The render would have had a very realistic appearance when 'executed with judgement, and finished with taste . . . and jointed to imitate well-bonded masonry' with 'the divisions promiscuously touched with rich tints of umber and occasionally with vitriol'.[15] Until very recent years, a lone example of the mid-nineteenth-century treatment of a facade survived in Battersea, south London. The house retained its original render and vitriol wash, and when illustrated in *Country Life* in the 1990s[16] still displayed its purple-brown windows and ironwork (Figure 13.3). However, seven years later the windows had been replaced and brilliant white paint applied.

Figure 13.3 A copperas wash on render (note also purple brown windows).

While they were no doubt convincing, the problem with these renders was that even if they survived they would, being matt and rough-textured, have acted as a magnet to airborne dust. Indeed, there is a reference to one being in good physical condition after forty-five years but black with dirt.[17] Furthermore, the rusticated detail on the ground floor prevented the rain washing the surface evenly, leading to staining on the facade. Further problems became clear with these self-coloured materials and translucent finishes – patch repairs were very difficult to disguise, and uniformity increasingly difficult to maintain.

Many Victorians had strong feelings about the use of 'honest' materials. Pugin railed against 'all the mechanical contrivances and inventions of the day, such as plastering, composition, papier mâché, and a host of other deceptions' which 'only serve to degrade design'.[18] Even the author of a book on masonry, brickwork and plastering had this to say:

> When cement is used to cover the defects of a building, or to give the impression that it is some material other than what it is, its use is by no means legitimate.[19]

Perhaps it was the combination of this feeling and the increased blackening caused by the atmospheric pollution of a smoky city that led to oil paint gradually replacing the ferruginous washes.

Although it was initially applied in stone colours of various sorts, once white paint had taken hold the inexorable drive to brilliant white continued – so much so that many painters today seem not to know that the less harsh option still exists. Certainly their clients are rarely given the choice.

Windows

In terms of our representative town house, the windows were, almost without exception, made of painted softwood. Their treatment has changed over time, but the permutations have been few. In the eighteenth century an oil paint consisting of white lead pigment ground into linseed oil was the normal coating applied. The colour that resulted from this combination was a creamy off-white. Indeed, as an acknowledgement that a true white was unobtainable, such a mix tended to be referred to as 'stone' colour in contemporary texts.[20]

Surviving coloured designs from the end of the eighteenth century suggest that darker colours were occasionally employed, but they are seldom encountered at this period during paint analysis. From the 1820s, however, painted imitations of wood, particularly oak, were used on external joinery and these were invariably given a protective coating of gloss varnish.[21] Although graining was a more expensive treatment than plain paint, the varnish ensured a longer life.

Graining was but one of a number of different options to be employed during the nineteenth and early twentieth centuries. Unlike the painting of front doors, the treatment of windows seems to have been less prescriptive. Sample specifications towards the end of the century were suggesting that they be finished 'to choice', meaning either light, dark or grained. Stone colours of various shades were still in frequent use, but darker colours such as purple brown, chocolate, oak colour (brown having the tonality of that wood), drab and greens of various sorts could also have been used. Once again, early photographs show a range of different shades.

Doors

> The front door is to be finished green, and is to be twice varnished with the best copal varnish, and is also to have the number of the house painted thereon.[22]

In spite of having been taken from the same early Victorian specification quoted before, this could have been written at any time during the following eighty years. Even by the 1930s such a colour was still deemed suitable for older property in some parts of London:

> Some of the old Queen Anne houses of Chelsea or Westminster are quite suitable for a green or quietly coloured door, but woe betide the Bayswater or Earl's Court house that tries it.[23]

During this long period the type of green would vary. In the early years a rather murky colour would have been produced by adding a black pigment to yellow ochre. However, from the second quarter of the nineteenth century bronze greens and Brunswick greens became popular. The first group of colours were designed to suggest the green-brown of patinated bronze, while the second were brighter greens made possible by the recent introduction of the pigment chrome yellow.[24]

If not painted green, front doors were often grained in imitation of oak. It seems that there was seldom an attempt to achieve a uniform appearance, one house with another, and that one might be grained while its neighbour was green (Figure 13.4). A watercolour of a group of houses in Woburn Place, London, c. 1815, shows such a sequence of grained and green front doors.[25] A number of brownish colours were also employed. These ranged from reddy-brown, through browns of the tonality of oak, to much darker chocolate browns. Neither the doorcase, if there was one, nor the door surround would have been painted in the same colour as the front door – they would have matched the other external joinery or the window sashes.

As seen already, doors would often have had a glossy finish, which was achieved by applying two coats of copal varnish over the (already shiny) oil paint. The notion that a matt finish was desirable on external surfaces during the period is false, and based on the tendency of lead paint to 'chalk' after only a few years.[26] From an early date it was well understood that a paint with a degree of sheen was necessary to cope with everyday wear and tear, and the rigours of the weather.

Railings

Two colours predominated on external ironwork in the early days – a grey known as **lead colour** (Figure 13.5) and, rather curiously perhaps, **stone colour**.[27]

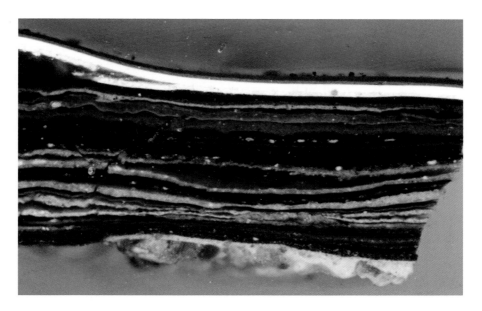

Figure 13.4 Cross section of paint layers on early nineteenth-century Bath front door (largely dark greens and oak graining).

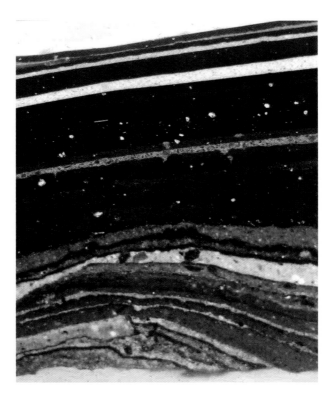

Figure 13.5 Cross section of paint layers on early nineteenth-century London railings (initial lead colour, then dark green followed by black).

. . . the front area railing is to be finished green . . .[28]

The first appearance of green, when examining the stratigraphy of domestic railings in cross section, usually indicates that the beginning of the nineteenth century has been reached in the sequence of layers.[29] The greens employed were the same as those listed above. This change to green seems partly to have been influenced by the writings of Humphrey Repton, who felt that certain colours were more appropriate than others for the painting of iron. He describes this clearly, decrying the use of lead colour for its resemblance to an inferior metal, adding

> but if we wish it to resemble metal, and not appear of an inferior kind, a powdering of copper or gold dust on a green ground, makes a bronze, and perhaps it is the best colour of all for ornamental rails of iron.[30]

Invisible green was a favourite of Repton's, and was so named because it 'harmonizes with every object, and is a back-ground and foil to the foliage of fields, trees, and plants, as also to flowers'.[31] It was never just one colour, but any dull green that worked well against a leafy background. In recent years it has been successfully reintroduced on the railings in many parts of London.[32]

The universal present-day use of **black** is a twentieth-century innovation and it is a myth that it was introduced as a sign of mourning on the death of Prince Albert in 1861. Its appearance in paint cross sections taken from exterior ironwork usually marks the second half of the twentieth century. With the introduction of alkyd resins, a black oil paint was no longer slow in drying.

Paint

The main constituent of the oil paints used until the 1960s was white lead, a pigment manufactured by corroding metallic lead. This was ground with linseed oil to form a paste which, in turn, was made into a paint by the addition of more oil, turpentine and tinting pigments.

Zinc oxide and latterly titanium dioxide replaced their more toxic predecessor, which is seldom used nowadays, its use being limited to Grade I and II* listed buildings in England and Category A buildings in Scotland.

Postscript

As can be seen, once solid colour in paint replaced the earlier translucent washes on render the original intention of the architect had been lost. It became impossible to turn the clock back to the beginning even if such a move were considered desirable. An appeal for the recreation of the past has not been the aim of this chapter; rather it has been to describe what has been done at various times and to point out that there are alternatives to brilliant white and black. These might involve the use of off-white on window joinery and door surrounds, a green or brownish colour on doors, a stone colour on render and dark green railings. Hardly dramatic, merely quieter.

However, unless dealing with a detached house, any change to the present overall approach to colour would have to be coordinated with neighbours, and even discussed with the local conservation officer. It is all very well employing a more low-key colour scheme that reflects the traditional approach, but if one house 'marches in step' alone, the unity of the terrace may well be spoilt.

Perhaps the last word can be left to Humphrey Repton:

> . . . here can hardly be produced a more striking example of the truth 'that whatever is cheap, is improper for decorations,' than the garish ostentation of white paint.[33]

Acknowledgements

Ian Bristow

Endnotes

1. Alfred Bartholomew, *Specifications for Practical Architecture,* 2nd edn (1846), para. 1086. Copal is a resin that was used in oil varnishes until the mid-twentieth century.
2. *Ibid.*
3. See, for example, The Archive Photographs series published by Tempus Publishing Ltd and The Francis Frith Collection published by Waterton Press Ltd.
4. This chapter is heavily based on an earlier article with a more focused theme, which appeared as 'The colours of Chelsea' in *The Chelsea Society Report 2003*, pp. 61–7.
5. Patrick Baty, 'The role of paint analysis in the historic interior', *Journal of Architectural Conservation,* March 1995. For examples of the mistakes made as a result of carrying out scrapes, see Patrick Baty, 'To scrape or not', *Traditional Paint News,* **1**, 2 (October 1996). The author has carried out analysis on numerous town houses in such places as London, Edinburgh, Bath, Hove and Bristol.
6. See, for example, Patrick Loobey (comp.), *Images of England: Chelsea* (Stroud, 1999), p. 58, bottom picture.
7. A.R. Powys, *From the Ground Up: Collected papers of A.R. Powys 1882–1936* (J. M. Dent & Sons, London, 1937), pp. 139–40. Powys was Secretary of the Society for the Protection of Ancient Buildings and the author of a number of books on architectural subjects.
8. Augustus Welby Northmore Pugin, *The True Principles of Pointed or Christian Architecture Set Forth in Two Lectures Delivered at St Marie's, Oscott* (London, 1841), pp. 56–7.
9. Ian C. Bristow, 'Exterior renders designed to imitate stone', in *ASCHB Transactions,* 22, 1997 (1998), p. 17 – an excellent paper on these early renders.
10. Bryan Higgins, *Experiments and Observations made with a View to Improving the art of Composing and Applying Calcareous Cements* (1780), pp. 213–16; cited in Bristow (1998), p. 19.

11. PRO CRES 26/176.

12. Peter Nicholson, *The Practical Builder's Perpetual Price-Book*. Appended to *The New Practical Builder, and Workman's Companion* (London, 1823), p. 141. The basic cost of applying the 'neatly jointed' render ranged from 1s. 9d. to 2s per yard. Frescoing was therefore half as much again.

13. William Aspdin, the son of the patentee, was manufacturing Portland cement at Rotherhithe by 1842.

14. W. Millar, *Plastering Plain and Decorative* (1897), p. 570.

15. Peter Nicholson, *The New Practical Builder, and Workman's Companion* (London, 1823), pp. 378–9. Raw umber is a green-grey earth pigment that is also available in a darker, redder form when heated (burnt umber). Ferrous sulphate was often known as vitriol or copperas. Although of a greenish colour, when mixed with limewater, and applied to a render it developed a strong Bath stone colour. The exterior of Apsley House, at Hyde Park Corner, appears to display a copperas wash to this day.

16. See Patrick Baty, 'Palette of the past', *Country Life*, 3 September 1992, p. 46, pl. 8.

17. James Elmes, *Metropolitan Improvements* (1828), p. 95. Cited in Bristow (1998), p. 18.

18. Augustus Welby Northmore Pugin, *Contrasts, or a Parallel Between the Noble Edifices of the Fourteenth and Fifteenth Centuries and similar buildings of the Present Day; Shewing the Present Decay of Taste* (London, 1836), p. 35.

19. Robert Scott Burn, *The New Guide to Masonry, Bricklaying and Plastering* (London, 1871), p. 241.

20. John Smith, *The Art of Painting in Oyl*, 9th edn (London, 1788), p. 46.

21. Mahogany was sometimes imitated, although usually this technique seems to have been reserved for larger or public buildings. A Specification of External Repairs for the Athenaeum Club in Pall Mall, dated c. 1865, stipulated: 'The sashes and frames of the two principal floors are to be best grained, in imitation of mahogany . . . and twice varnished with the best varnish.'

22. Bartholomew (1846), para. 1934.

23. Basil Ionides, 'Colour in everyday rooms', *Country Life*, 1934, p. 14. Ionides was an architect, designer and author on design matters. He restored Buxted Park in Sussex.

24. Pierre François Tingry, *Painter's and Colourman's Complete Guide* (London, 1830), p. 108, reported: 'A Dr. Bollman some years since prepared chrome yellow at Battersea of a very superior kind . . .'

25. The watercolour, *Woburn Place, built in ca.1800 to the design of James Burton and drawn in ca.1815 by a pupil of Sir John Soane*, is in the Sir John Soane Museum, London; reproduced in Dan Cruickshank and Neil Burton, *Life in the Georgian City* (London, 1990), pp. 160–1.

26. An account of 1774 reveals: 'The third year the gloss is gone – in the fourth if you rub the painting with your finger, it will come off like so much dust' (Francis Armstrong, *An Account of a Newly Invented Beautiful Green Paint*, 1773).

27. Lead colour has been reintroduced to the railings of the six buildings that form the south side of Charlotte Square, Edinburgh.

28. Bartholomew (1846), para. 1934.

29. Once sampled, the fragments of paint are embedded in a clear polyester resin prior to examination under the microscope. These are referred to as 'cross-sections'. See Baty (1995) for more on this.

30. Humphrey Repton, *Observations on the Theory and Practice of Landscape Gardening* (1840 edn), p. 264. Although occasionally found on internal ironwork, it is not thought that bronze powder was employed much on external railings.

Exterior colour on the smaller town house

31. T.H. Vanherman, *The Painter's Cabinet, and Colourman's Repository* (London, 1828), p. 8.

32. See, for example, the railings in Kensington Gardens and Regent's Park. One suspects that most passers-by have not noticed the transition from black to dark green.

33. Repton (1840), p. 264.

Index